10/02

Schmitt

THE
BICYCLE
THE MYTH AND THE PASSION

WHITE STAR PUBLISHERS

FOREWORD
BY FELICE GIMONDI

Of all sports, cycling is unquestionably the one that has remained closest to its origins over the decades – indeed, the rules of the late 19th Century essentially still apply today. And its basic concept is also unchanged: in cycling – at least since the evolution of the first models following the revolutionary invention of the chain drive – the winner is the cyclist whose feet pedal fastest. In short, man always prevails over machine, and to be transported by it he must propel it. Perhaps this is why the world's greatest cycling champions – from Binda to Bartali, Coppi, Magni, Merckx, Anquetil, Van Looy, Armstrong, Pantani and Cipollini – are linked by a common thread: that of their individual prowess on a level playing field.

Nevertheless, we cannot overlook the enormous changes the bicycle itself has undergone (alone in structural terms) over two centuries, above all as a result of research into materials to make it lighter and to enhance its aerodynamic and ergonomic properties. True, it's essence remains unchanged. It still consists of a simple frame with a seat and two-wheels. But from the *célérifère* to modern road-racing bikes, not to mention mountain bikes and BMX bikes, the difference in profile, style, and use are striking. Historically, it was always Italy that stood at the forefront of the cycling world, at least in terms of production (starting with Bianchi, which is more than a century old) and artisans, such as Colnago, De Rosa and Pinarello. I remember how, while stopping at a traffic light or pausing for a drink during my training at the 1964 Olympics in Tokyo, bystanders with cameras would appear out of nowhere and take pictures of my Bianchi from every angle. The components of my bike, too, were the source of enormous curiosity: people were fascinated by our nation's four famous C's: Campagnolo, Cinelli, Columbus, Clement.

Outside the world of road racing, until quite recently, bicycles were used primarily as a means of transportation, above all by the lower classes: workmen to get to the factory, students to go to school, and housewives to load groceries in the front basket. Today, the increasing cultural reference to bicycles as status symbols may be somewhat of an exaggeration, but in an age when cars and mass transit have robbed them of their supremacy and turned them into an "alternative" mode of transportation, they have undoubtedly become a sign of distinction and even prestige, especially in the United States – and one need look no further than the price tags of many bicycles on the market to see the truth of this assertion.

As the standardization of bicycle production creates new markets for manufacturers around the world, new customers are being sought – and found – on every continent, including Africa and Oceania. But even more encouraging than its global reach as a commodity is evidence that the growing popularity of the bicycle reflects not only the efforts of salesmen, but the innate desire of people around the planet to re-establish a direct, personal connection with nature. To some, this may seem like a backwards step, but it is actually a great leap forward, opening as it has, the eyes of millions who are determined to see beyond the confines of the overcrowded streets in which so many of us live.

THE BICYCLE
THE MYTH AND THE PASSION

Text
FRANCESCO BARONI

Editorial Director
VALERIA MANFERTO DE FABIANIS

Editorial Coordination
LAURA ACCOMAZZO

Graphic Design
MARINELLA DEBERNARDI

© 2008 White Star S.p.A.
Via Candido Sassone, 22/24
13100 Vercelli, Italy
www.whitestar.it

ISBN 978-88-544-0336-9

Reprints:
1 2 3 4 5 6   12 11 10 09 08

Color separation: Chiaroscuro, Turin

Printed in China

INTRODUCTION

The bicycle has forged more links between literature and science, sport, society and even political activism than any other invention. It allows us to take things slowly in an ever-accelerating world. In his relationship with the bicycle, man has remained more important than the means, even though the relationship is reciprocal: one gives life to the other and vice versa. For children, a bicycle is the first sign of freedom, enabling them to begin exploring the world, to learn the principles of safety and balance, and maybe even to achieve one of life's first victories: conquering fear when the stabilizers are removed. Cycling champions have given us cause to rejoice and celebrate with their successes – and reason to lament with their misfortunes. Unlike its more brazen rivals the car and motorbike, the bicycle has not been the subject of many films. Nevertheless, great writers have lavished praised on it, telling the story of the world as seen from a saddle with a handlebar between their hands.

The bicycle has been around for two and a half centuries and was first used by aristocrats as a pastime and a circus instrument. At times frowned on and even forbidden, it has become increasingly important in people's lives as a method of transport. Only with the emergence birth of today's celebrated cycling competitions did it become a piece of sporting equipment and a means of liberating people from ignorance and poverty. Competitions enabled Europe to accelerate its reconstruction efforts following the two world wars, and in the 1980s the bicycle was promoted as a way to keep fit, answering the search for healthy lifestyles and allowing for the rediscovery of the body's potential in relation to the environment.

In the twenty-first century, the bicycle has transcended the laws of physics and mechanical manufacturing processes and become a cult symbol, indeed a way of life, with its own set of rules and conventions. In our increasingly congested cities which prove hard to get around, the bicycle as a means of transport has come back into fashion following years of mass-motoring. It has also become a protest vehicle and a way of boasting a carbon-free lifestyle (take, for example, the critical mass movement which uses the bicycle as a symbol of standing out – and standing for something – in a polluted urban environment).

The story of this simple, essential means of transport has been little documented due to revolutions, nationalist periods and wars. Nevertheless, thanks to the insights of their enlightened thinkers, the countries of Europe – with France, Germany, the United Kingdom and Italy in the lead – have fed the technical development of the bicycle since its beginnings. In the 1930s, the United States started to play a key role, making up for the lack of influence it had exerted during the nineteenth century. Yet improvements and innovation were not always the fruits of intelligent ideas and know-how that materialized with the passage of time. Many were brought about by competition, and those countries with strong traditions in this field benefited the most by carving out the position of market-leader for themselves. Some of the most successful innovations came about for economic reasons, where the iron rules of the market and competition dictated how the game should be played. They brought reason to the production process and new innovations which were not only beneficial from a financial point of view but also at the technical level.

From its origins as a simple vehicle, driven by the feet in a simultaneous and alternating fashion, the bicycle has evolved to incorporate all those essential parts that we take for granted today: pedals, handle bar, tires, etc. The bicycle frame changed beyond all recognition during the first century of its development, when the original wooden (or heavy iron) structure was replaced with increasingly resistant, lightweight metals. The three-pointed shape of the bicycle has not changed since the late nineteenth century, although today's innovative materials and new welding techniques have given substantial freedom to its form and corners. The US made a great contribution in this respect, when in the mid-1960s, it unveiled several unchanging phenomena, which became known as the BMX and mountain bike.

If the 1970s saw the introduction of aluminum (and later titanium) on an almost industrial scale, the 1980s and 1990s were a period of great turmoil as the mountain bike was sold on a much larger scale and the first experiments with carbon fiber, which shook the entire market and sparked a new revolution in an industry that appeared to have been stuck for more than a century, took place.

This book tells an accurate history of the bicycle, but it is not intended to be a piece of exhaustive research. Many ideas, inventions and models have been lost along the way due to the events that have shaken the world, from carelessness or a failure to register patents. In the pages that follow, however, we will examine the most important models – as also the most significant fruits of the technical ingenuity, invention, and championship expertise to have left their mark on the evolution of this simple yet fascinating piece of equipment – along with several concept bikes, showing that even two simple triangles placed over each other can become a subject for study and the fruit for research into advanced design.

2-3 SOME OBSTACLES ARE INSURMOUNTABLE, EVEN FOR A MOUNTAIN BIKE.

4-5 DANILO DI LUCA CELEBRATES AFTER THE TRICKY BARDOLINO-VERONA TIMED LEG. THE FACE OF THE CYCLIST NICKNAMED "THE KILLER" CONVEYS THE GREAT DETERMINATION THAT AN ATHLETE MUST POSSESS TO WIN A RACE SUCH AS THE GIRO D'ITALIA.

6-7 FELICE GIMONDI IS ONE OF THE SYMBOLS OF INTERNATIONAL CYCLING. AS A PROFESSIONAL CYCLIST BETWEEN 1965 AND 1979, HE WON THE GIRO D'ITALIA THREE TIMES (1967, 1969 AND 1976), THE TOUR DE FRANCE ONCE (1965), THE VUELTA A ESPAÑA ONCE (1968), THE GRAND PRIX DES NATIONS TWICE (1967 AND 1968) AND THE PARIS-BRUSSELS TWICE (1966 AND 1976). HE ALSO WON THE PARIS-ROUBAIX (1966) AND THE MILANO-SANREMO (1974) ONCE, THE GIRO DI LOMBARDIA TWICE (1966 AND 1973), AND THE WORLD CYCLING CHAMPIONSHIPS IN 1973.

9 THERE WAS SPORTING RIVALRY BUT ALSO RESPECT BETWEEN COPPI AND BARTALI, SHOWN HERE DURING THE 1952 TOUR DE FRANCE.

11 A CYCLIST DURING THE INDIVIDUAL TIME TRIAL AT SAINT-ETIENNE DURING THE 1997 TOUR DE FRANCE. HE IS GIVING HIS UTMOST, BECAUSE IT IS NECESSARY TO PEDAL CONTINUOUSLY FROM START TO FINISH IN ORDER TO WIN.

12-13 DURING THE TEAM RACE THE FOUR ATHLETES MUST RIDE TOGETHER.

BEGINNINGS AND EARLY DEVELOPMENT

FROM THE VINCIAN GENIUS TO THE DRAISINE

The history of the bicycle is long and complex. With highs and lows, it is a challenging journey which, over the course of several technical improvements, has led to the point where this method of transport has become an integral part of daily life and an increasingly faithful companion as well as a witness to important historical events.

The early history of the bicycle can be traced to China, where it appears that in 2300 BC, a two-wheeled vehicle made of bamboo known as the "happy dragon" was used. Traces of the bicycle's forerunner have also been uncovered at the temple of Luxor in Egypt, where archaeologists have discovered a graffito dating back to 4000 BC showing a man seated on a bar suspended above two wheels. However, these images were often connected with the bicycle more imaginatively than scientifically, with the apparent purpose giving the bicycle a distant date of birth and to attributing its invention to a particular country.

Such flights of fancy reached a climax in 1974, when Leonardo da Vinci entered the public arena as the newest supposed "father of the bicycle." Attempts to persuade people that this was the case were extensive and led many to believe that da Vinci was the first person to envisage a two-wheeled vehicle powered by a chain. The design blueprint for this means of transport, found in the Atlantic Codex, was indeed extraordinarily similar to a bicycle. Its structure consisted of a frame, two equidistant wheels, and a chain transmission powered by a pedal mechanism. But the story behind this design – it was discovered while the Codex was being restored between 1961 and the mid-1970s – gave rise to contradictory theories surrounding the historical authenticity and reliability of the work. The first version of events, which appears in many sporting encyclopedias, is the one supported by those who embrace the idea that Leonardo da Vinci invented the bicycle more than three centuries before the celeripede, which is recognized by many as the first real velocipede, appeared. According to another theory, supported by Professor Augusto Marinoni

albeit with some reservations, the design does not necessarily belong to Da Vinci, but is more likely attributable to one of his students. Finally, there is the theory, now accepted as the most plausible, that the bicycle and the other designs that appeared in Da Vinci's works, on a page that was left wiped clean following restoration works, only appeared in 1961 in circumstances that have never been fully clarified.

These disputes aside, the first real ancestor of the bicycle only came to light at the time of the French Revolution, in 1791, when a new vehicle appeared in Paris. First known as a *cheval de bois* ("wooden horse"), and soon after renamed the "celeripede," in reference to the time-old dream of speed, it was built by the eccentric French nobleman Mede de Sivrac. The celeripede consisted of a sturdy wooden structure consisting of a supporting axle and two forks onto which the wheels, which were also made of wood, were attached by means of two round pins. Its design was straightforward and intuitive: the cyclist mounted it and propelled it by pushing his feet along the ground. Exhibited at the Port Royal gardens, it soon became a luxury item for adults, appearing in all kinds of fantastic and bizarre guises, from horses to snakes and lions. In its own way, the celeripede was beautiful, but it was also hard to push, given its heavy weight and its lack of a steering mechanism. It must have felt as if it ran on tracks, and in only one direction; for instance, its rider had to come to a halt and use his arms to steer whenever he wanted to turn a corner.

Count Sivrac did not patent his invention, so it was quickly copied by blacksmiths, wheelwrights and horse-shoers, who made it available to the general public and set a fashion that was even followed by the newspapers. Those who loved riding the celeripede even had a place to meet in Paris, where they shared their enthusiasm and watched races at breathtaking speeds. It was also used by companies during the first years of the nineteenth century for home deliveries—a kind of pre-modern courier service.

16 The Celerifere or Celeripede was the bicycle's first forerunner. Built by joining a wooden axle and two wheels, it did not have pedals or a steering wheel and was so stiff that every vibration was directly absorbed by the rider.

17 The Celerifere, or Cheval de bois, as it was initially called, was introduced by the Frenchman Mede de Sivrac. The name derives from two Latin words, "celere" and "fero," meaning "fast transport" – a nod to man's instinctive desire for speed.

FIG. 1. THE FRENCH CELERIPEDE.

THE HOBBY HORSE, 18[...]

KASSLER'S BICYCLE, CIRCA 1820

THE ORIGINAL 1817 DRAISINE

THE DRAISINE, 1820 REFINEMENT

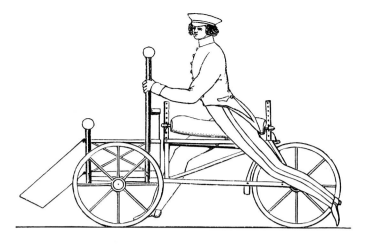

18-19 TOP THE HOBBY HORSE OR DANDY HORSE WAS AN ENGLISH IMPROVEMENT ON THE DRAISINE BY DENNIS JOHNSON.

18-19 BOTTOM WITH THE DRAISINE, THE CONCEPT OF THE STEERING WHEEL WAS INTRODUCED, MAKING IT THE FIRST FORERUNNER OF THE BICYCLE TO HAVE SUCH A MECHANISM. BARON DRAIS' ORIGINAL MODEL, DATED 1817, WAS CONSTANTLY RENOVATED DURING THE FOLLOWING YEARS.

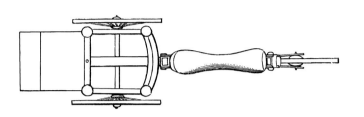

19 THE FIRST DRAISINE RACES TOOK PLACE IN GERMANY, AIDING THE DEVELOPMENT OF THIS 40 KG VEHICLE, WHICH WAS GRADUALLY IMPROVED AND STREAMLINED—AND MADE LIGHTER.

THE CELERIFERE, 1821 REFINEMENT

Despite all this, many believe that the first real forerunner of the bicycle is the vehicle designed by Baron Karl Friedrich Christian Ludwig Drais von Sauerbronn, an officer in the Prussian army, twenty-five years after de Signac.

The Draisienne, as it was called, can be traced back to 1818. This wooden machine stood 2.4 meters long, and could be steered, because it included a handlebar which pivoted on the frame, making it possible to turn the front wheel independently from the supporting structure. As with the celeripede, the rider had to use his feet to drive this vehicle (also known as a "swift-walker") forward, using alternating movement. Drais asked his French agent to patent his invention, and then set up a workshop and school in Paris so that people could learn how to use this new machine. Though the steering principle was revolutionary, its application was somewhat hampered in earlier models, in particular because of its size and weight (approximately 40 kilograms). In contrast to the celeripede, however, the Draisienne seemed to be a truly viable method of transport, even though its early days were marked by negative publicity, due to its inherent risks. Following a disastrous exhibition in Paris, the Baron became the butt of many jokes by French satirical commentators, who drew sketches of him struggling to push his heavy invention. A small victory came outside Paris and later in London, where the designer Dennis Johnson unveiled a version of the Draisienne made from iron and including features such as a padded leather saddle for comfort. This model, which was decidedly lighter and became known as the hobby-horse, was sold in two different versions: one for men and one for women. Even this model, however, did not remain popular for many years. Attempts were made to re-launch the vehicle at sporting events, the first of which was held in Germany in 1819. These helped to improve stability and reduced the overall weight. Yet its destiny remained unchanged: ultimately, the heavy weight and poor maneuverability of the Draisienne, like the celeripede, offered no credible alternative to traveling on foot.

In Italy, the Draisienne was received with suspicion and was even banned by the police in September 1818 following an announcement against the use of similar vehicles at night that read: "Given that it has proven to be the case that velocipedes may cause harm to pedestrians, the authorities hereby declare that it is forbidden to use them on city streets and in the main plazas, though riding them in ramparts and plazas in quiet neighborhoods is tolerated. Offenders will be punished with the confiscation of their machine."

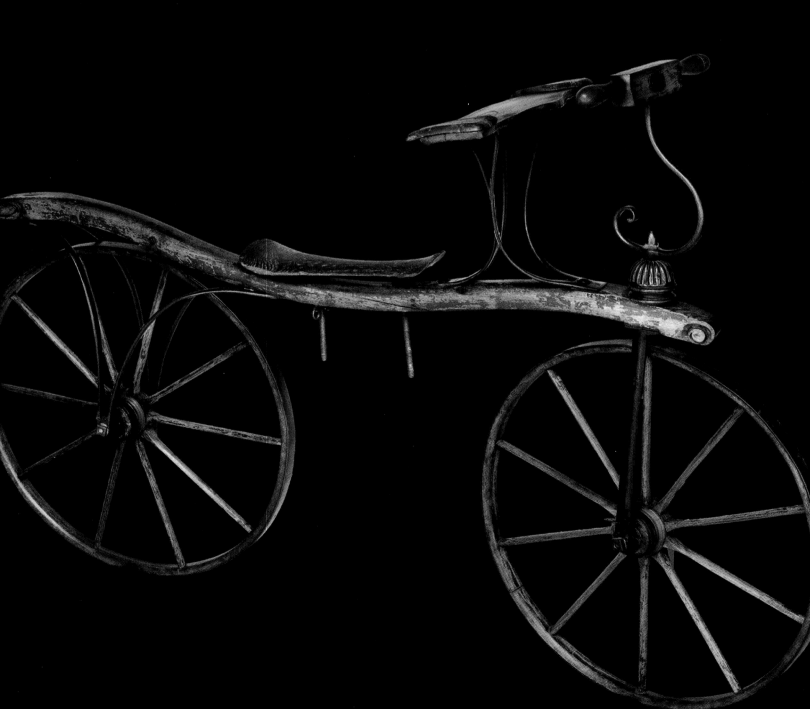

21 top Dennis Johnson's Draisine was soon modified for women; in addition, he created a school whose specific purpose was teaching them how to ride it.

21 bottom A woman's Hobby Horse was similar to a man's, the only difference being the shape of the frame, which permitted female riders to use it while wearing the ample gowns favored at the time.

PEDALS: THE MICHAUDINE

In 1839, a Scottish blacksmith named Kirkpatrick MacMillan invented the first bicycle that could be driven without touching the feet on the ground. In fact, MacMillan had the intuition to direct power from the legs directly onto the wheels. He built a model with asymmetrical wheels powered by a lever system that was driven by the legs themselves. The system operated around the back wheel which provided the power. The front wheel was left free for steering. This machine was faster and less tiring to ride than the German baron's model, which had appeared twenty years earlier. Its frame was made from wood that had been bent using iron, and it had wooden wheels. Its total weight was approximately 25 kilograms, and it could travel at speeds of up to almost 20 kilometers an hour. Unfortunately, during its first public exhibition in June 1842 in Glasgow, a young boy was run over by it, and the inventor was made to pay compensation. Betraying similar problems encountered by previous models, the machine enjoyed only limited success, and its Scottish inventor never submitted a patent. Yet MacMillan's invention was important, since it introduced the fundamental concept of focusing balance at the base of future models.

The invention of pedals was a contribution of Pierre Michaux, a carriage mechanic, and his son Ernest. Pedals were discovered in 1861 (some claim the date was 1855) and coincided with the appearance, in Paris, of the first model made completely from iron. This model was made in four sections and was known as the "michaudine" in homage to its builder. Legend has it that the idea behind the discovery came while Michaux was working on one of his customer's Draisiennes. The young Ernest Michaux first fixed two cranks to the front fork with the aim of improving its comfort and allowing the rider to sit back and rest his feet once the vehicle was moving. This triggered another idea, which made the vehicle even more comfortable and rapid: a newly designed lever that could be attached to either the back or front wheel, which the rider would turn with one hand to go faster while using his other hand to steer; meanwhile the feet were used to keep balance. In fact, this lever worked only in theory. But still, it reflected an important new concept in the evolution of the bicycle..

Soon, the collaboration between father and son Michaux resulted in another new development: the application of two *biellette* to the front wheel's pivot. By pressing down on these two support areas, it was possible to turn the wheel. The Michaux also invented a straight fork which could be fitted to the Draisienne, and attached rudimentary triangular pedals to the front hub. Almost two meters long and weighing 30 kilograms, this new vehicle made its debut on the Champs Elysées in Paris by the owner of the old Draisienne, which had actually been taken to the Michaux family workshop merely for repairs. Two models were subsequently produced, in 1861, but this figure rose quickly in the next few years. In 1865, some four hundred "michaudines" were in circulation. (Nevertheless, for the next twenty years or so, the most common term to describe them remained "velocipede.")

Once the persistent difficulties of balance had been overcome, velocipede riders in Paris became increasingly endeared with this new invention. Indeed, luminaries such as Alexandre Dumas, Claude Debussy, and Charles Dickens all became owners of this new vehicle. In the meantime, the Michaux family came up with yet another modification: a pallet brake on the back wheel that was activated with a fine wire. Given that the pedals drove the front wheel, each stroke moved the bicycle forward at a distance resembling the wheel's dimensions, which made many people believe that it was necessary to increase the size of the driving wheel in order to go faster.

With time, the michaudine began to make so much money that its inventors decided to enter into partnership with the Olivier bankers and set up a company called Compagnie Parisienne. As early as 1869, however, the Michaux family sold their shares under the impression that they had only sold up their workshop and not the patent. But it was not so, and when they started to build bicycles again in 1879, the *Compagnie Parisienne* successfully brought action against them, forcing them to pay a costly fine. This marked the end of involvement in bicycle-making for father and son, but their legacy as inventors of the pedal—and as the first to engage in large-scale production of bicycles—remains unchanged.

Vélocipède Michaux 1869
don de MM.rs Olivier de Sanderval et Frédéric Dumesnil

& LUKKOW
& Peintre

155 Faubou
PA

COMPAGNIE PARISIENNE.

THE HIGH WHEEL AND THE SAFETY BICYCLE

24 LEFT THE VELOCIPEDE WAS USED BY WOMEN LIKE THE FRENCH ACTRESS AND SINGER BLANCHE D'ANTIGNY, WHO INTRODUCED A SPECIAL RIDING GARMENT FOR THE ACTIVITY.

24 TOP RIGHT BROOKS SADDLES WAS BORN IN BIRMINGHAM IN 1866, IN THE FAMILY WORKSHOP OF A SADDLE MAKER. VERY SOON IT BECAME A MUST NOT JUST FOR RIDERS OF BRITAIN'S NOTORIOUS "BONESHAKERS," BUT FOR EUROPEANS ACROSS THE CONTINENT.

24-25 DESPITE ITS GREAT WEIGHT AND BALANCE PROBLEMS, WHICH EARNED THE VELOCIPEDE CONSIDERABLE POPULAR DISTRUST, IT REMAINED A SOUGHT-AFTER ITEM AMONG GENTLEMEN OF THE ERA, AND COMPETITIONS AGAINST OTHER MEANS OF TRANSPORT WERE ORGANIZED TO DEMONSTRATE ITS VIABILITY.

25 BOTTOM AS PIERRE LALLEMENT VIED WITH MICHAUX FOR OWNERSHIP OF THE HIGH WHEEL OR "PENNY-FARTHING," A VERY SIMILAR VEHICLE WAS PATENTED IN THE USA, IN 1866.

The origins of the velocipede sparked a whole series of claims about its authorship. The debate is still open, since at the same time the Michaux model was introduced, two yet very similar versions appeared. The first was designed by the Frenchman Alexandre Lefebvre in 1843 but only came to light in 1864, when its creator moved to the United States. This model, which still exists and can be seen at the San Jose History Museum in California, relied on a pedal-based system which revolved around the rear wheel. Another Frenchman, Pierre Lallement, unveiled his own velocipede model the same year, though he patented it in 1866, when he too emigrated to the United States. The British received the michaudine with suspicion: although they would not admit it, they were piqued that this pedal system had been introduced in France rather than Great Britain. Praise was lavished on their improvements to the French machine, which was given the disparaging nickname "boneshaker" because of the violent vibrations produced by its iron-covered wooden wheels on cobblestone streets.

In an attempt to achieve maximum comfort, Clement Arder (who it said to have completed the first engine-powered flight in 1890) became the first person to cover the wheels in rubber, in 1868. In reality, he was simply putting into practice a solution thought up by the Englishman R.W. Thompson in 1845, which consisted of fitting rubber tires to bicycle wheels. At the time, his idea was not commercially successful and was thus abandoned. Two years before the Englishman John Boultbee Brooks made his contribution to the rider's comfort by drawing on the experience he had learned working with his father, a manufacturer of horse saddles, to start a production line of bicycle saddles for the "boneshakers" of the time. Soon, products that bore the Brooks brand became known for their quality and charm which still mark them out in the cycling world today. In 1869 Jules Suriray decided to compete with the English brand by initiating production of leather saddles too. The evolution from velocipede to bicycle continued unabated. In 1866, the Englishman Edward Cooper designed the first wheels to be made entirely from iron with flat circles, while in 1869 a disused sewing machine factory in Coventry produced lighter models whose frames and forks were made from iron. Also worthy of mention are the first attempts to introduce rear traction to compensate for the problems posed by the front wheel and the difficulty in pedaling and steering at the same time (another limitation was speed).

André Guilmet, a Parisian watchmaker, designed an interesting model in 1868 which in practice allowed the pedals to be controlled centrally. They were positioned almost directly below the seat and rotated on their own axle, thus producing power by turning the chain, which was in turn linked to the rear wheel-hub. The prototype was developed with Eduard Meyer, a deliberate choice, since the German, who was living in Paris, had made his name with three important breakthroughs: replacing heavy wooden supports with metal-tube frames, using padding with holes inside the hub, according to Jules Suriray's patent, and building concave iron circles to fix the first full-leather pads. The fruits of this Franco-German partnership constituted a revolution of sorts, since they heralded the introduction of a method of transport which was completely different to everything that had transpired up till them and was essentially the same as the modern version. Unfortunately the Franco-Prussian War, which broke out in 1870, disrupted the plans of these two designers and halted the budding partnership. André Guilmet died on the front, while the German-born Meyer was quickly side-lined, losing friends and French associates. Their project sank into oblivion, and the evolution of the bicycle was set back a good decade.

It was the "high bicycle," known in France and Italy as the Grand-Bi, which emerged triumphant at the end of the war. It was essentially a natural progression from the boneshaker models, but this time with pedals. In structural terms, the high bicycle relied on a front wheel which was much larger than the rear wheel, and powered the vehicle when the pedals were pushed.

Such direct transmission, as stated earlier, meant that the velocipede moved forward proportionately the dimension of its wheels, meaning that the only way to increase its speed was to make the dimensions of the engine-wheel excessively large. Nevertheless, the larger the front wheel's diameter, the more dangerous the machine became, since maintaining balance proved increasingly difficult. Consequently, riders often fell off and injured themselves. All the same, the velocipede was still modestly successful. James Starley from England was the first person to invent the high bicycle proper, patenting it in 1870 along with his associate William Hillman. It was named "Ariel," an evocative label inspired by the moon of Uranus – then recently discovered and made famous by Alexander Pope's poem "Rape of the Lock."

To improve his design, Starley replaced a system of radial spokes, which were also introduced in 1870 by another Englishman, a certain Grout, with one that used tangent spokes, providing better stability and resistance to the wheel. Thanks to this model, which was known as an "ordinary" or "penny farthing" bike, the English cycling industry, with factories based in Coventry, Birmingham and Manchester, enjoyed a substantial period of growth and became a world leader in terms of both numbers and the quality of product. The high bicycle was widely distributed in France via the production center in Beaulieu, and models were branded by Peugeot and named "Grand-Bi." For the French manufacturer, born at the beginning of the nineteenth century (though first distinguished by its lion logo only in 1858), it was the first model in half a century of activity in various fields that gave it renown. It was produced in the Fils des Frères Peugeot workshop in Paris on the Avenue de la Grande Armée.

26 top As the High Wheel gained traction in the cycling world, improvements such as metal tubular frames and full tires appeared. Between 1870 and 1880, this vehicle was largely used in track racing competitions.

26 center The Briton Starley introduced the first wheels with tangent rays, a solution that guaranteed greater comfort than wheels built with radial rays—this despite the fact that the use of solid tires rendered the concept of comfort little more than an illusion.

26-27 The nickname Penny Farthing stems from the comparison of the large wheel to a penny and the small one to a farthing. Its main drawback was precisely this enormous difference in the wheels' diameter.

27 top Using a High Wheel entailed substantive difficulties—besides riding it, one had to mount and dismount it without tipping over, or falling. Worse, its height made it hard to stop quickly in the case of a traffic emergency.

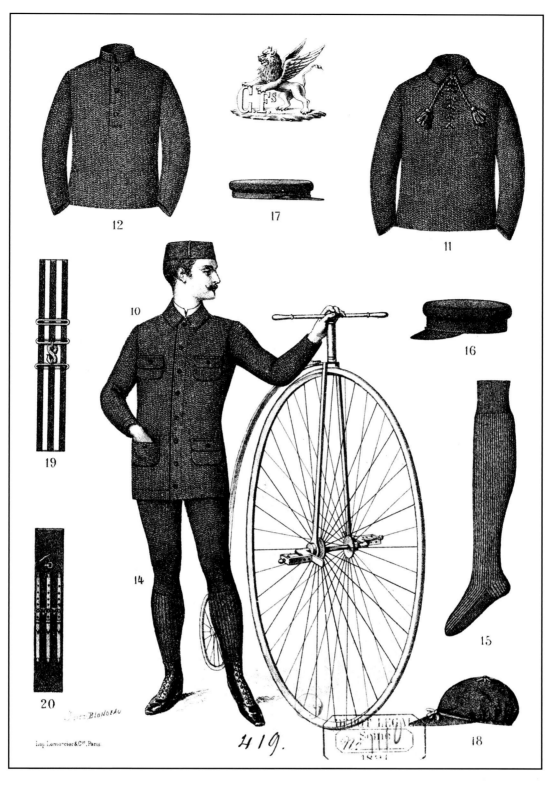

29 bottom CLIMBING ONTO A HIGH WHEEL WAS A PROBLEMATIC OPERATION THAT DEMANDED A CERTAIN SKILL. IN ORDER TO FACILITATE THE MANEUVER, A STEP WAS INTEGRATED IN ITS FRAMEWORK.

28 THE HIGH WHEEL'S SPEED VARIED WITH THE SIZE OF THE FRONT-WHEEL'S DIAMETER. THUS THE LATTER CONTINUED TO GROW—AND WITH IT, ITS GENERAL DANGEROUSNESS TO THE UNPRACTICED USER.

29 TOP PEDALING ON THE HIGH WHEEL FOR COMPETITIVE REASONS REQUIRED THE USE OF PRACTICAL ATTIRE WHICH, EVEN THOUGH IT ALLOWED A CERTAIN ELEGANCE, MUST HAVE AT LEAST MINIMALLY OBSTRUCTED AN ATHLETE'S MOVEMENTS.

From 1876 onwards, Colonel Albert Pope monopolized production of the "ordinaries" in the United States with the Columbia models. These appeared four years after the "movement for good roads" campaign started, so called because its exponents fought to improve the American transport system. The movement's success drove the United States to modernize its transport network and led to an increase in Columbia models on the market to the extent that Pope soon branched out into motor car manufacture.

The drawback of the high bicycle was its speed, which made it particularly unsafe. Stopping and starting was also difficult given the large diameter of the front wheel—it was impossible to put one's feet on the ground quickly. Generally speaking, cycling was dangerous.

It was mainly used on road exhibitions when there was little traffic, and during competitions in cycling stadiums. It never found a niche as a city vehicle. The elderly and women preferred stable tricycles and quadricycles to the high bicycle because these could be used without having to pay too much attention to balance. Added to all this, the bicycle was still chiefly a luxury enjoyed by the well-off.

One solution to instability came in the form of the Star model, manufactured in the United States in the early 1880s. Its design essentially meant that the size of the two wheels was inverted, with a small wheel at the front and a large wheel at the rear. Critics poured scorn on the new vehicle, claiming that the dangers had not been overcome but only circumnavigated.

30 ALBERT POPE'S BOSTON-BASED COMPANY WAS THE MOST RENOWNED HIGH WHEEL MANUFACTURER IN THE UNITED STATES; AND HIS MOST POPULAR MODEL WAS THE COLUMBIA.

31 LEFT THE AMERICAN-MADE STAR WAS THE WEST'S ANSWER TO EUROPE'S HIGH WHEEL. IT OVERCAME THE LATTER'S STABILITY PROBLEM BY INVERTING THE DIFFERENCE IN THE WHEELS' DIAMETER. FORWARD MOTION WAS PRODUCED BY PEDALS AND TRANSFERRED BY MEANS OF A SYSTEM OF LEVERAGES.

31 RIGHT THE NUMBER OF ACCIDENTS ASSOCIATED WITH THE HIGH WHEEL WAS HIGH AND INCLUDED DRAMATIC INSTANCES OF RIDERS FALLING OFF THE FRONT (HEAD OVER HEELS), BACKWARDS, OR SIDEWAYS.

Between 1870 and 1880, spherical cushions, solid tires and hollow-section steel frames became standard, while attention focused on various efforts to ensure that transmission could be achieved using a system of belts and gears: in practice, this meant applying the concept of chains and cogwheels—both of which had existed independently, of course, long before the velocipede had appeared. The French duo Vincent and Sargent, the American Shergold, and the Englishman Lawson all worked on this idea simultaneously. As had been the case with the boneshaker model, a debate ensued over who had made the discovery, with each country claiming that it belonged to their respective nationality. Disputes aside, the essential point is that the way in which velocipedes were driven underwent a definitive change by the end of the nineteenth century, heralding the end of the velocipede and the beginning of the bicycle: pedals became attached to cogwheels which transmitted movement to the pinion of the rear wheel. Enormous front wheels were no longer necessary because speed was no longer tied to their diameter. This solution helped to make up for the time lost when Guilmet and Meyer's prototype disappeared.

In 1876, the ancestor of the compass brake, which is still found on bicycles today, was developed. Another significant modification was made the following year: the first multiplier gears with chain-transmission fitted to the front wheel were distributed, a solution which had been tested many years earlier, but without success.

32 TOP THE KANGAROO MODEL WAS A MARRIAGE, DESIGN-WISE, BETWEEN THE HIGH WHEEL AND THE ROVER. THE FRONT WHEEL WAS STILL LARGER THAN THE REAR, BUT THE CHAIN DRIVE RENDERED THE ENTIRE SYSTEM SAFER.

32 CENTER RIGHT BY THE END OF THE 19TH CENTURY, TRICYCLES WERE PREFERRED TO HIGH WHEELS IN MANY QUARTERS, DUE TO THEIR GREATER ACCESSIBILITY. COMPARED TO THE VELOCIPEDE, THE TRICYCLE WAS REGARDED AS FAR SUPERIOR, BOTH IN PRACTICALITY AND SAFETY.

32 BOTTOM BESIDES BEING MORE STABLE AND EASIER TO MANEUVER ON THE STREET, TRICYCLES WERE ALSO MORE COMFORTABLE, SINCE THE STRUCTURE OF THE FRAME ALLOWED FOR WIDER DISPERSION OF VIBRATIONS.

33 ALMOST A CENTURY AFTER THE CELERIFERE'S INTRODUCTION, THE VELOCIPEDE INDUSTRY COULD BOAST A WIDE TYPOLOGY OF MODELS, FROM THE BONESHAKER TO THE HIGH WHEEL, AND THE TRICYCLE TO THE UNICYCLE.

6. Renn - Bicycle „Invincible".

13. Humber - Tricycle.

8. Saal - Bicycle.

12. Sicherheits - Bicycle „Rover".

10. Manuped.

2. Tandem - Tricycle von Humber u. Comp.

11. Reitmaschine nach Freiherrn von Drais.

3. Touren - Bicycle „Leipzig".

5. „Sociable" für 2 Personen, verwandelbar in ein Tricycle.

1. Touren - Tricycle „Invincible".

7. Gepäck - Transport - Dreirad.

9. Otto - Bicycle.

4. Monocycle.

14. Renn - Tandem - Tricycle „Invincible".

34 IN 1885 JOHN KEMP STARLEY PRODUCED HIS GROUNDBREAKING ROVER, A MODEL WHICH, THANKS TO ITS EQUAL- SIZED WHEELS, TIRES, AND CHAIN DRIVE, DEFINITIVELY MARKS THE BIRTH OF THE MODERN BICYCLE AS WE KNOW IT.

35 TOP THE INTRODUCTION OF THE SAFETY BICYCLE WAS FOLLOWED WITH GREAT INTEREST BY VELOCIPEDE OWNERS. ASIDE FROM ITS LIGHT WEIGHT, WHICH WAS PARTICULARLY WELCOME DURING CLIMBS, ITS SAFETY AND STEERABILITY BOTH ADDED TO ITS POPULARITY.

35 CENTER JOHN KEMP STARLEY MOUNTED ON A ROVER: THIS WAS THE LAUNCHING POINT FOR THE NEXT CENTURY AND A HALF OF MATERIAL AND PRODUCTION INNOVATIONS.

35 BOTTOM LEFT THE DWARF ROADSTER, OR PETIT COUPE, WAS SIMILAR IN STYLE TO THE SAFETY BIKE BUT WITH RETAINED THE STAR'S WHEEL PROPORTION. ITS FRONT WHEEL WAS IN FACT SMALLER THAN THE REAR ONE.

35 BOTTOM RIGHT THE NAME SAFETY DERIVED FROM THE HIGHER SECURITY PERCEIVED (AND INDEED GUARANTEED) BY A LOWER WEIGHT DISTRIBUTION AND FROM THE USE OF EQUALLY SIZED WHEELS.

THE ROVER SAFETY BICYCLE (PATENTED).

Safer than any Tricycle, faster and easier than any Bicycle ever made. Fitted with handles to turn for convenience in storing or shipping. Far and away the best hill-climber in the market.

MANUFACTURED BY

STARLEY & SUTTON,

METEOR WORKS, WEST ORCHARD, COVENTRY, ENGLAND.

Price Lists of "Meteor," "Rover," "Despatch," and "Sociable" Bicycles and Tricycles, and the "Coventry Chair," Illustrated, free on application.

The development of the Kangaroo model, which dated back to 1878, represented an enormous stride forwards for safe cycling. This new machine, designed by John Kemp Starley, the nephew of James Starley, brought a radical change to the bike's structure. In 1885, Starley launched a vehicle known as the Rover, which was large and had direct steering, equally-sized wheels and a diamond-shaped frame, allowing that the cyclist to balance perfectly. The Rover, which was also known as the safety bicycle, took after the Kangaroo in terms of the rear traction, which meant that a multiplier chain could be used. The American version of the Rover was produced by Columbia by Albert Pope; he also manufactured the Columbia Charles, which relied on a cardanic-joint shaft.

Towards the end of the nineteenth century, as safety became an increasingly important issue, the bicycle became popular as a means of military correspondence. From 1887, the British Army conducted large-scale experiments using volunteer cyclists; meanwhile, France, following Britain's example, equipped several territorial units with folding bikes that had been designed by an officer. Great Britain and France were soon followed by the United States and Italy.

36-37 The bicycle was rapidly adopted by the armed forces of several nations – and not only as a means of transport, but even as a barrier behind which to entrench oneself and resist an attack.

DUNLOP AND
LATER MODIFICATIONS

espite all the technical progress that had been made, the drawback caused by vibrations as the wheels traveled over poor roads had still not been overcome. In 1885, the American Charles Goodyear discovered the process of vulcanizing rubber by chance when he saw a mixture of latex and sulfur melt together over a heater. He studied compounds formed by fortuitous circumstances and realized that this particular procedure ensured that high-quality and long-lasting products could be created, and that this quality meant it could be used in new fields, such as medicine and vehicle tire manufacture. His discovery was applied to velocipedes by John Boyd Dunlop, a veterinarian from Belfast, and it solved the problem of making saddles comfortable. The Dunlop brand was thus born on the last day of February 1888.

In an attempt to make a wooden tricycle with full tires (one he had given his son as a gift) move better, the Scotsman – he lived in Ireland but was not Irish – had the idea of covering the wheels with rubber tubing filled with air. Legend has it that the inspiration came when he put on rubber gloves used for veterinary work, but it is more likely it came from his son's football. Dunlop first decided to cover the three wheels on his son's bicycle with inflatable padding. He made a small tube from vulcanized para rubber, filled it with air using a basic valve and attached it to a wooden disk. It proved to be a success: when Dunlop asked his son Johnny to test the invention, he was able to cycle for a substantial length of time on the uneven roads around his house without feeling almost any bumps or holes.

This new invention was soon widely distributed, and the following year, the Irishman W. Hume, owner of a velocipede factory, presented the first pneumatic tire model at the International Bicyclette Humatic Exhibition. From 1890 onwards, all the main production houses who had been given exclusive rights to fit Dunlop pneumatic tires adopted the name bicycle.

The veterinarian's products proved extremely successful, but their main defect was that they were difficult to repair. Two Frenchmen – André and Edouard Michelin – helped to solve this problem when they introduced tires that could be dismantled in 1891. Their idea was to use a mechanical device instead of glue to attach the tubular tire to the wheel, thus making it much easier and quicker to repair punctures. One year later, Giovanni Battista Pirelli, who was born in Milan in 1872 and went on to found the Pirelli production chain, made further improvements to the Dunlop design when he invented a removable, heel-shaped cover, which made it even easier to change a tire. He went on to develop a special tubular tire for cycle racing.

40-41 IN 1891, THE MICHELIN BROTHERS INTRODUCED A NEW IDEA: REMOVABLE TIRES. THE SYSTEM WAS SO SUCCESSFUL THAT THEIR CLERMONT-FERRAND-BASED ESTABLISHMENT WAS SOON EXPANDING—AND THEY BECAME LARGE SCALE EMPLOYERS.

40 BOTTOM LEFT DUNLOP'S BUSINESS INCREASED SO RAPIDLY THAT IN 1889, THE FIRST ESTABLISHMENT FOR THE SERIES PRODUCTION OF PNEUMATIC TIRES OPENED ABROAD, IN DUBLIN.

40 BOTTOM RIGHT DUNLOP INITIALLY PRODUCED PNEUMATIC TIRES FOR BICYCLES ALONE. IT WAS ONLY LATER, AT THE START OF THE 20TH CENTURY, THAT THEY TOOK WINGS IN A NEW FIELD: THAT OF THE AUTOMOBILE.

41 TOP LEFT GIOVANNI BATTISTA PIRELLI, FOUNDER OF THE PIRELLI FIRM (EST. 1872), MODIFIED DUNLOP'S DESIGN AND CAME UP WITH A COVER FOR A DISMOUNTABLE BICYCLE.

41 TOP RIGHT MICHELIN MADE USE OF EVOCATIVE IMAGES TO DESCRIBE THE QUALITY OF ITS PRODUCTS, LIKE ONE OF BIBENDUM (A.K.A. "BIB, THE MICHELIN MAN") PEDALING NIMBLY AMID GLASS BELLS.

41 BOTTOM LEFT THE CONTINENTAL BRAND, BORN IN HANOVER IN 1871, STARTED PRODUCING PNEUMATIC BICYCLE TIRES IN 1892, AND GERMAN SALES SOON REACHED AND SURPASSED THOSE OF MICHELIN AND DUNLOP.

41 BOTTOM RIGHT IN 1893, JOHN F. PALMER PATENTED A PNEUMATIC TIRE WHOSE SHELL WAS COMPOSED OF PARALLEL (NOT INTERTWINING) FIBERS, AND IN ITALY, "PALMER" QUICKLY BECAME THE SHORTHAND TERM FOR SUCH TUBES.

42 EARLIER COMPETITIONS WERE EXHIBITIONS OF SKILL AND BALANCE. CHARLES "MILE-A-MINUTE" MURPHY AND FRANK ALBERT, FOR EXAMPLE, COMPETED AGAINST EACH OTHER IN A DISTANCE RACE, PEDALING ON A TRAINING ROLLER.

43 TOP THE RALEIGH BICYCLE COMPANY WAS ESTABLISHED IN NOTTINGHAM ON DECEMBER 1888. THE NAME OF THIS HISTORIC BRAND DERIVES FROM THE STREET WHERE BICYCLE FRAMES WERE ONCE PRODUCED.

43 BOTTOM FRAMES OF THE DANISH PEDERSEN BRAND WERE CHARACTERIZED BY PAIRS OF TUBES THAT CONVERGED TO FORM A TRIANGLE; DUE TO THIS PARTICULAR SHAPE, PEDERSON BIKES WERE AFFECTED ONLY BY STRESS CAUSED BY COMPRESSION.

During the same period, a small workshop was set up in Raleigh Street in Nottingham for manufacturing three-pointed frames for the safety bicycle. Frank Bowden, a successful lawyer who had been converted to cycling, bought the company and founded the Raleigh Cycling Company in December 1888. Bowden was not yet aware that his creature was about to become the world leader, enjoying a production scale which rivaled that of the United States and Asia in the twenty-first century.

The three-pointed bicycle frame became common when Mikael Pedersen, a Dane who had moved to England, produced a 1893 model that was completely different from those that had preceded it. It was based on the cantilever system used in the Forth Bridge, a railway bridge near Edinburgh, Scotland. The purpose of the triangular-shaped frame and fork was to combine maximum resistance with minimum weight. This principle had been widely applied to bridges and other processes where lightness and sturdiness were of the essence; it was thus ideal for creating a product whose weight was evenly distributed. The frame was made from tube pairings, which were joined in the central movement housing and other parts and always formed a triangle. This design solution made the bike stable and gave the lateral rigidity needed to transmit (and withstand) the energy generated by pedaling.

It would be wrong to think that the bicycle was distributed only in Europe; and it would be even more misleading to believe that the only velocipedes used in the United States had been imported. In 1895, for example, Ignaz Schwinn and his associate Adolph Arnold founded Arnold, Schwinn & Company in Chicago. The first model they produced was the Roadster, a single-speed racing bike weighing 8.5 kilograms, an astonishing amount for the time. Charles "Mile-a-Minute" Murphy's

bike was also a Schwinn. He used it to follow the tracks of a locomotive along the Long Island Railroad in 1899 and reached the impressive speed of 96 kilometers per hour.

Two important innovations should be mentioned before we leave the nineteenth century, taking place respectively 1897 and 1898. The first of these was the Englishman Reynolds' patenting of the first set of tubes of different thicknesses. Established in 1841 in England, Reynolds essentially became the most important production house for steel tubes for use in frames. The second innovation came from Ernst Sachs, a German, who produced the free wheel, which finally enabled cyclists to stop pedaling from time to time, to enjoy their descents and runs without their legs whirling in circles.

The first Army cyclists appeared by the end of the century. By 1900, four companies of *bersagliere* cyclists already existed in Italy. In 1909, *la Bianchi*, a historic Italian factory based in Milan whose origins can be traced back to Via Nirone in 1885, was commissioned to produce the first folding bicycles for the cycling units in the Italian Army.

Following a series of tests and technical improvements, this request led to the production of the first dual suspension model in 1915, a folding bicycle whose structure was similar to the one that had been developed in 1909, but with the addition of telescopic rear covers and a spring-loaded fork for the front, as well as ample section pneumatic tires for better handling on uneven road surfaces.

PLAYER'S CIGARETTES

44 TOP LEFT PEUGEOT IS ONE OF THE OLDEST COMPANIES IN THE BIKING WORLD. THIS LEONINE FRENCH BRAND SUPPLIED THE FIRST BICYCLES USED BY THE FRENCH MILITARY IN ITS WARTIME CAPACITY AS A COURIER SERVICE.

44-45 THE DIFFUSION OF THE BICYCLE AMONG DIVISIONS OF THE ITALIAN ARMED FORCES OCCURRED RAPIDLY, ESPECIALLY DURING THE GREAT WAR, WHEN THE ITALIAN *BERSAGLIERI* (SHARPSHOOTERS) USED IT FOR TRAVELING IN THE MOUNTAINS.

44 BOTTOM LEFT IN 1905, THE BRITISH FIRM BSA PRODUCED A BICYCLE THAT WAS EQUIPPED WITH FIRE-FIGHTING EQUIPMENT. THE CUSTOM-BUILT FRAME COULD HOLD A SIREN, A FIRE HOSE, AND AXE.

44 BOTTOM RIGHT ONCE LOADED WITH BAGS, BACKPACKS, AND RIFLE HOLDERS, A *BERSAGLIERI* BICYCLE COULD WEIGH SOME 30 KILOS. SOME MODELS WERE EQUIPPED WITH RUDIMENTARY SUSPENSIONS IN THE REAR, AND EVEN IN THE FORK.

45 BOTTOM THE LIGHT GERMAN INFANTRY *JÄGER*, FAMOUS FOR HAVING A DIVISION OF CYCLISTS FOR EVERY BATTALION, INCREASED ITS NUMBER 80-FOLD WITH THE BREAKING OUT OF THE FIRST WORLD WAR.

PROGRESS AND THE BIRTH
OF THE LEGENDARY RACES

46 TOP THE BICYCLE ALLOWED WOMEN TO MOVE FREELY,
THANKS TO MODELS ESPECIALLY BUILT TO ALLOW FOR USE WITH
SKIRTS. IN DUE TIME, WOMEN CYCLISTS WERE NO LONGER AN
ANOMALY, BUT A COMMON SIGHT THROUGHOUT EUROPE.

46 BOTTOM BY THE START OF THE 20TH CENTURY, THE BICYCLE
WAS BECOMING A POPULAR MEANS OF TRANSPORT FOR DAILY
USE – BUT PEOPLE OF MEANS WERE ABANDONING IT FOR THE
AUTOMOBILE.

46-47 AS A RECREATIONAL VEHICLE, BICYCLES WERE POPULAR
AMONG ALL CLASSES, INCLUDING THE WEALTHIEST.

47 TOP THE BICYCLE'S INCREASING VISIBILITY IN THE CULTURE AT
LARGE OPENED A SIGNIFICANT BUSINESS ARENA, AND SOON
RETAIL SHOPS SPECIALIZING IN WHOLE BICYCLES, PARTS,
ACCESSORIES, AND REPAIR BECAME WIDESPREAD.

In the twentieth century, the history of the utilitarian bicycle evolved as the history of the racing bicycle. Innovation was centered on designing, experimenting, and perfecting models used by cycling champions before they were applied to the production line. The early twentieth century brought no technical developments of note, but rather a form of social progress: the bicycle began to play an increasingly important part in people's daily lives. Indeed, once a stable, efficient model had been found, large scale production began and an incredibly volatile market was born. Companies employed cycling champions to improve their share on international markets, and the best publicity showed these champions showing off their bikes to the awe-inspired public. Several important factories were set up at the turn of the nineteenth-twentieth centuries, and their names would henceforth be identified with unforgettable steps in the history of the technical evolution of the bicycle and the legendary achievements of certain cycling heroes.

47 BOTTOM UNTIL ASSEMBLY-LINE CONSTRUCTION TECHNIQUES, WHICH PERMITTED A NOTABLE REDUCTION IN PRICE, THE BICYCLE REMAINED THE POSSESSION OF A CERTAIN ELITE. AFTER THAT MOMENT, IT QUICKLY BECAME THE MOST POPULAR VEHICLE OF THE WORKING CLASS.

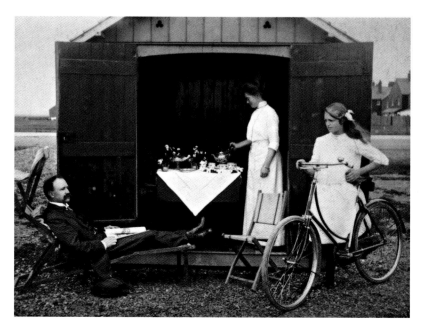

We have already seen that the history of the bicycle from the twentieth century onwards is closely tied with cycling competitions first and the road second, but these competitions already existed during the last forty years of the nineteenth century and were seen as a kind of struggle against time and man. The first competitions consisted of contests between well-off young people who would spend their free time competing with each other, but before long, traveling fairs and markets sprang up whose main purpose was to provide entertainment and amusement for the public. When spectators began betting money on the races, an induced economy was created which inevitably led to the first professional cycling.

The first real race took place in Paris's St. Cloud Park on May 31, 1869. The winner was an English friend of Michaux, James Moore, who cycled 1,200 meters in 3 minutes and 50 seconds, some 20 meters ahead of two French riders. On November 7, 1869, another immensely difficult contest for its time was fought: 123 kilometers. About 100 people took part, including six women. The course ran from Paris to Rouen on roads that were in such a state of ruin that two thirds of the competitors retired from the race. Once again, the winner was James Moore, who took 10 hours and 45 minutes to complete the course. A race from London to Brighton took place in England in 1869; this was the first proper international competition. Three English men competed with as many French men. The French won and took their place alongside "the Englishman from Paris" James Moore. In Italy, Padua hosted two high-speed events the same year, both of which used the Piazza Vittorio Emanuele as the finishing line. Antonio Pozzo and Gaetano Testi won respectively. Races also took place at Ukkel in Belgium and in Germany, where they were known for their high-speed short tracks, even before Dunlop pneumatic tires were introduced. More races were held in Italy in 1870, including the Florence to Pistoia run, 33 kilometers long, which was won by the American Rynner van Hestet. He rode a michaudine with air-filled rubber tires.

By the end of 1880s, national federations in England, France, Belgium, the United States, Germany, Italy and the Netherlands had been set up, and the first priority for these new institutions was to organize national championships. In 1890, the International Cyclist Association was founded; it was superseded in 1900 by the International Cycling Union (UCI), the federation that still governs cycling competitions today.

The first six-day race was held in the north London suburb of Islington in 1878. It was a race against the clock in which only one professional cyclist rode around the track. David Stanton was the first person to bet that he could ride 1,000 kilometers on a high bicycle for 18 consecutive hours a day. He set off at 6 a.m. on the morning of

February 25 and completed the race in 73, hours riding at an average of 13.5 kilometers per hour. The first six-day race in which more than one competitor took part was held in November the same year. The rules were the same as for the first event.

The formula for the six-day race in England was changed in 1881: participants now had to compete without a break for as long as they could until tiredness overcame them. However, this method of competing brought heavy physical and mental sacrifices and consequently many cyclists, despite being well paid, distanced themselves from the events.

48 The first competitions on British soil took place on indoor tracks in velodromes, a solution which guaranteed ease of handling. Athletes on the starting line were not divided by category, and often even competed on very different bikes.

48-49 The starting shot at a Penny-Farthing race, held in 1890 in New York.

49 top In an era when the bicycle was still a novelty for the ordinary public, the most improbable exhibitions, like races against a train, were organized to show off the vehicle's still under-appreciated potential.

Six-day races proved particularly popular in the Untied States, especially in New York and Illinois, where competitions were restricted to 12 hours in a 24-hour period from 1898. The following year, however, the practice of one competitor competing against the clock was abolished – once again to protect the competitors' health – and was replaced by the version where two competitors raced against each other. The first race to take place under these new rules was held in Madison Square Garden in New York in 1899. From then on, the term *madison* became associated in English-speaking countries with a cycling race in which two cyclists competed against each other, while the same event became known as a "*course à l'américaine*" in French-speaking countries.

Professional competitions held in cycling stadiums became immensely popular in the United States, thanks to the efforts of Arthur Zimmerman "the Flying Yankee"of New Jersey, and Marshall "Major" Taylor, the second black man after the boxer George Dixon to take part in any

global competition. They became so popular that people began to treat them as superstars, and they commanded astronomical fees for their time as well as filling stadiums to the point that by the 1930s, the cycling race was the most popular, most widely followed sport in the United States. The lesson of the six-day race was that these competitions tested a cyclist's resistance to the track, competitors and above all himself; they challenged the participant to reach a personal record which could be used as a reference point on which other cyclists could try to improve. In 1893, the Frenchman Henri Desgrange set a new hour record in Paris by cycling 35.325 kilometers. Beating the hour record soon became the goal for all cyclists. From the first attempt through to efforts in twenty-first century, the world's best cyclists have taken turns at getting their names into the record books, including cycling legends Fausto Coppi and Eddy Merckx. The importance of these achievements, however, should not overshadow their use as demonstrations of the improvements made to

50-51 THE LEGENDARY PARIS-ROUBAIX, A COMPETITION LATER NICKNAMED THE "HELL OF THE NORTH," WAS FIRST HELD IN 1896. ON EASTER SUNDAY, APRIL 19, AT 5.30 A.M., THE COMPETITORS SHOT OFF, GIVING BIRTH TO THE STILL-UNRIVALLED QUEEN OF ALL CYCLING CLASSICS.

51 TOP CHARLES TERRONT WON THE FIRST PARIS-BREST-PARIS, A BACK-BREAKING RACE OF SOME 1,200 KILOMETERS, USING MICHELIN PNEUMATIC TIRES WHOSE RESISTANCE PROVED SUPERIOR TO DUNLOP'S PRODUCT.

51 BOTTOM RENE GUENOT LEANS AGAINST HIS BICYCLE BEFORE THE START OF THE 1911 PARIS-ROUBAIX. THE "HELLISH" QUALITY OF THIS RACE DERIVES FROM LONG COBBLESTONE STRETCHES WHOSE UNPREDICTABILITY, ESPECIALLY WHEN SLIPPERY, EXHAUSTS EVEN THE MOST ACCOMPLISHED CYCLIST.

the bicycle over time. Cycling races were commonly held in Europe, but road competitions captured people's imaginations globally. 1891 marked a turning point in the way races were organized: it was at that time that the legendary names which still inspire awe in cyclists and enthusiasts today began to appear on the international scene.

The Bordeaux to Paris race was first held on May 23 1891 and was organized by the French magazine Le Véloce Sport and the Vélo Club Bordelais. At 577 kilometers, the course was already arduous, but it was made even harder by the dire conditions of the dug up, cobbled roads. The race was won by George Mills from England, who reached Paris in 26 hours and 34 minutes. His fellow countryman Holbein came second and was one hour behind him. The grueling Paris-Brest-Paris race was also held for the first time in 1891. The winner was Charles Terront, who completed the 1,200 kilometer-long course in 71 hours and 16 minutes on a Humber bicycle with Michelin pneumatic tires, without even pausing to

catch his breath. His closest rival was Pierre Jiel-Laval, who rode on a Clément bike with Dunlop pneumatic tires, and completed the race nine hours later. The race was held regularly every ten years until 1951, from which time it took place every four years and became a cycle-tourism rally which was renamed as the Olympic Games Cycling.

1892 was the year of the first Liège-Bastogne-Liège race. Léon Houa won this lethal Belgian race the first three times and over the next century all the greatest cycling champions found their name added to the record books for this classic competition, which was commonly referred to as the doyenne. The same year that the modern-day Olympic Games were held for the first time in Athens in 1896, another little-followed competition appeared: the Paris-Roubaix. The German Josef Fischer was the first person to win it when he traveled 280 kilometers in the "inferno of the north" (the name given this challenging race) at an impressive average speed of 30.162 kilometers an hour.

In 1903, the first edition of the race that in time would become the world's most famous, prestigious cycling competition, the Tour de France, was held. To Henri Desgrange, editor of the newspaper "L'Auto" and already an hour record holder from 1893, the race was the realization of one of his oldest ideas, which until then had never come to fruition: a staged race across France. Desgrange was a former cyclist and wanted to create an itinerant event which would reveal the fascination of cycling to the host country and, to make it even more appealing, he named his event "Les géants de la route" (Kings of the Road).

When it was born, the Tour de France was engulfed by a multiplicity of problems, but once established it became incredibly successful; it became a classic by the very next year. The first race began on July 1, 1903, stretched over a distance of 2,428 kilometers, and consisted of six stages. The winner was Maurice Garin, who averaged 25.3 kilometers an hour. Riding a heavy bicycle and with only one gear, and pedaling for laps that averaged 400 kilometers in length over untarmacked roads, competitors faced indescribable obstacles and challenges. The second race was held in 1905 and took in some challenging climbs, including the Ballon d'Alsace over the Vosges, at 1,178 meters above sea level. It was in 1907, when cyclists had to climb up the Alpine pass and over the Pyrenees – whose 2,000 meter high slopes were impossibly steep – that the race became for the first time truly legendary, fascinating millions of fans and drawing them to the streets in throngs no smaller than today's.

52 MAURICE GARIN, A PRINCIPAL PLAYERS IN THE FIRST EUROPEAN COMPETITIONS, WAS ITALIAN BY BIRTH BUT FRENCH BY ADOPTION. GARIN WON THE 1903 TOUR DE FRANCE (THE FIRST ONE), TWO PARIS-ROUBAIX RACES, AND ONE BORDEAUX-PARIS RACE.

52-53 CYCLISTS LEAVING PARIS AT THE START OF THE 1906 TOUR DE FRANCE. THIS COMPETITION OF "LES GÉANTS DE LA ROUTE" OBTAINED A REMARKABLE POPULAR SUCCESS AND WAS SOON THE MOST IMPORTANT CYCLING RACE IN THE WORLD.

54 top The first Giro d'Italia was held over eight stages of some 300 km each. The so-called Pink Race was organized by the *Gazzetta dello Sport*, a newspaper.

54 bottom left Lucien Petit-Breton was the winner of the first edition of the Spring Classic, the Milano-Sanremo.

In the wake of the magnificent French Tour de France, three new races emerged in Italy and became famous for their length and scenic beauty. The first was the Giro di Lombardia. It was the idea of Armando Cougnet and took shape for the first time in October 1905. Since it was held in autumn, commentators and fans alike nicknamed it "la classica delle foglie morte" (the race through the golden leaves). The itinerary was regularly altered over the years, taking in various paths through the region of Lombardy, but the symbol of the race quickly became – and still is – the "Ghisallo," an ascent from Bellagio, the pearl of the Lake Como, up to the small church of Madonna del Ghisallo, which has been the "protector of cyclists" since 1948. Giovanni Gerbi, a cyclist from Italy's Piedmonte region who was nicknamed "the red devil" because he regularly wore scarlet-colored clothing which made him stand out from the group, was the first person to win the Lombardy race. The second classic Italian race, which was more impressive than the first, was the Milan to Sanremo race. The rack was 295 kilometers long: one of the longest races of all the tournaments and was renamed "il mondiale di primavera" [the spring competition] for its difficulty.

Chronologically, the last competition that appeared was the Giro d'Italia. In practice, like the Milano-Sanremo race, it was simply a modified car race course with laps that were organized by the Italian newspaper *Corriere della Sera*. Rumor has it that *La Gazetta dello Sport* was tipped off by Angelo Gatti Dell'Atala and over time beat *Corriere*, which, in partnership with the Bianchi factory, was planning a cycling version of the event. The Giro dates back to 1909, when the race set off from Milan on May 3 and finished in the same city eight laps and 2,448 kilometers later with Luigi Ganna dell'Atala as the winner. The rich Italian landscape, full of demanding climbs over the Apennines and the Alps and taking in long stretches of relatively flat land that offered a balanced mixture of difficult and gentle laps, ensured that this would become one of the most important sporting fixtures in the world. Indeed, it placed it close to – even on a par with – the Tour de France.

Motivated by the plethora of emerging cycling competitions, researchers studied further ways to reduce the weight of the bicycle, and consequently the effort required to reach top speeds. Around 1911, the average weight was 14 kilograms: the tires weighed 550 grams, there were steel tubes, one pinion and iron wheel frames. Several advances were made by the winner of the race: a handle-bar with lower, more "sporty" hand-grips and foot-rests. Lucien Petit-Breton was the first to grasp the importance of gear changes, and he turned up at the Giro d'Italia on a Fiat bicycle with a rear wheel-hub which was twice as large the normal size and contained a complex, spring-loaded expansion mechanism that made it possible to change down through the gears automatically. In fact, there had been talk over changing gears at the end of the nineteenth century, but it was only in the wake of Petit-Breton's experiment that cycling was revolutionized for good. 1911 also saw the birth of the Catalunia cycling competition, which took place in Barcelona and Valencia and was won the first time by Sebastià Masdeu from Spain. The race covered a distance of 365 kilometers and was divided into three stages.

Twenty-four years later, in 1935, the Vuelta competition was held for the first time. A professional movement was gathering pace in Germany the same year, leading to the first competitions of the Deutschland Tour, which covered a distance of approximately 1,500 kilometers through the Reich territories. Due to the economic and political difficulties which were engulfing Germany, especially the catastrophe of the First World War and the financial crises of the 1920s, the race was not held regularly in the years leading up to 1931. It did, however, take place regularly in the lead-up to and the aftermath of the Second World War.

In 1913, another competition was held in Belgium for the first time which would soon become famous worldwide, although this time in the Flemish-speaking region: the Fiandre Tour. In addition to this race, which has been characterized by its "walls" (relatively short but fearsome uphill stretches marked by lethal inclines and paving) the Gand-Wevelgem and Freccia Vallone competitions made their debut in 1934 and 1936 respectively, completing the landscape of Belgian races.

In England, competitions where cyclists lined up on the start line and set off together as a group were not allowed. Instead, each cyclist competed against his own time and that of the other competitors. The types of bicycles used for this kind of timed event were often similar to those used in the cycling stadiums: gears were only fitted when changes in the terrain required speed changes. Not long after, the First World War broke out, bringing normal ways of life to an abrupt halt and, inevitably, the history of the bicycle and cycling. The revival was initiated by Costante Girardengo, known both as a cycling champion and a technician. He made a few simple modifications which later rationalized this method of transport: he installed the first leather basket to the handlebars of a bicycle and even researched a new kind of mudguard. Inspired by the champions, fashions began to emerge, increasing production as a result and encouraging many smaller-scale producers who wanted to see the bicycle distributed on a larger scale and sold at a cheaper price.

A CHANGING CYCLE

IN THE BEGINNING: A TURNING WHEEL

The racing bicycles which appeared at the turn of the twentieth century were made from steel tubes of different thicknesses and assembled using metal joints. The tubes used in most models were produced either by the Italian company Columbus or the English company Reynolds, whose 531 Series, which appeared in 1935, became the de facto standard and held a monopoly on most of the industry. Still, most wheel frames were made from wood, which proved robust and resistant enough on most of the roads where they were used. It was not until 1937 that aluminum wheel frames were fitted to specialized racing bicycles. Using aluminum increased wheel longevity, and once its use became standard for races throughout the world, it was rolled out for large-scale production of home and tourism bicycles. As for gears, bicycles of this period were fitted with only one pinion on the rear wheel, which may have been an 18 and turned at some 5 meters 45 centimeters when linked to the gear ratio, or a slightly more agile 19, which turned at 5 meters 17 centimeters. This undoubtedly proved very tiring on the knees and made it difficult to maintain high speeds on upward inclines. And so the first multiple free wheels began to appear; they had two separate pinions at either end of the rear wheel hub. Cyclists had to perform an operation known as "turning the wheel" in order to change gear. To climb hills easily, the wheel was dismantled and reassembled at the top. It was a simple but uncomfortable process that entailed not least the risk of stripping the wheel nuts. Only established champions could rely on spare parts being available; for most, a breakdown signaled the end of the competition – and consequently, retirement for all the other competitors. Indeed, this issue was so important that cyclists would not only train physically for a race, but also practice fitting a wheel in the shortest possible time. This laborious technique was, however, the norm in those days and was widespread despite its drawbacks. The best cyclists could do it in under 15 seconds. The masters of this operation were without question Henri Pelissier of France, Ottavio Bottecchia from Italy and the Belgian Lucien Buysse. They rode bicycles from Saint Etienne and won a total of four Tour de France in a row, from 1923 to 1926.

57 Fausto Coppi, arguably the greatest cycling champion of all time, and unquestionably a man of numerous incomparable feats.

58 top Henri Pellisier won the 1923 Tour de France on an Automoto. His archrival in the race was the Italian Ottavio Bottecchia, who rode the same model.

58 bottom Clarence Kingsbury, Ernest Payne, Leonard Lewis Meredith, and Benjamin Jones made up the British quartet that won the team pursuit race at the 1908 Olympics in London.

59 Ottavio Bottecchia, here crossing an alpine pass, won two consecutive Tour de France titles—1924 and 1925.

le Tour de France 1913

Moyeu

..eur

3

ESSES

·COMIOT

It would be wrong to believe, however, that no one had tried to find a solution to this problem of having to undertake such a complex operation during a race. Testing and development of the first gear-change models took place well before the end of the nineteenth century, but they were hampered by the reticence of cyclists, who saw the first advances as unreliable, given the excessive friction caused – a cause of increased fatigue – and the fact that some race organizers banned their use. Consequently, improvements in gear changing systems were held up. Gear change mechanisms were not allowed in many Italian competitions until the 1930s, and they were not permitted at the Tour de France until 1937. Once the restriction was removed, the average speed for the entire course rose exponentially.

The first stage of development led to the creation of gear systems contained entirely within the rear wheel hub, whose functioning was based on the principle of the epicyclical gear that James Watt had designed for his steam engine. The next stages involved developing the cog mechanisms and adapting to them all possible pressures to make sure that they could resist the power of the pedals. The first patent concerning a duel-speed wheel hub, developed by the Englishman William Reilly, was not filed until 1896. The updated version, which had been increased to incorporate three speeds, took off and was mass-produced by engineers Henry Sturmey and James Archer, who went on to design and then patent their own version of a wheel hub with its own gear change system in 1902. The newly-founded Sturmey-Archer company was a division of the enormous English firm Raleigh, which was owned by the lawyer Frank Bowden. The invention was born in the workshops of Nottingham and was fitted to all new English bicycles as soon as it was released onto the market. However, there were other bicycle manufacturers who had had the same idea, especially given that the two-times winner of the Tour de France, Lucien Petit-Breton, rode the Grande Boucle in 1913 on a three-speed bicycle. In 1903, this English brand was developed, and various different models were released onto the market, including a six-speed wheel hub. Sturmey-Archer remained a part of Raleigh's until 2000, when it ran into economic difficulty and was dismantled and then ruthlessly liquidated by its parent group.

60-61 LUCIEN PETIT-BRETON, ONE OF THE FIRST PROFESSIONALS TO APPRECIATE THE IMPORTANCE OF THE GEAR BOX, ARRIVED AT THE 1913 TOUR DE FRANCE WITH A BICYCLE WHOSE REAR HUB INCLUDED A 3-SPEED STURMEY-ARCHER GEAR.

60 BOTTOM STEEL (LEFT) WAS USED IN RACING WHEELS FROM 1937 ON; UNTIL THEN, BICYCLE WHEELS WERE MADE OF WOODEN RINGS SPECIALLY TREATED TO RESIST BUMPS. BY THE EARLY 20TH CENTURY, THE RACING BICYCLE (RIGHT) WAS ALREADY HIGHLY EVOLVED, BUT IT STILL LACKED MANY OF TODAY'S STANDARD ACCESSORIES, SUCH AS THE GEARBOX, DUAL-PIVOT CALLIPER BRAKES, AND AERODYNAMIC HANDLEBARS.

61 BOTTOM THE BANTAM, INTRODUCED IN 1893 BY THE CRIPTO CYCLE COMPANY, STOOD OUT BECAUSE OF ITS PRIMITIVE GEARBOX, WHICH MAXIMIZED THE EFFECT OF THE EPICYCLOIDAL GEARS IN THE FRONT HUB.

62 TOP FROM 1900 TO 1910, THE TORPEDO WAS IN VOGUE, THE OBSESSIVE SEARCH FOR SPEED HAVING CAUSED A SHIFT IN THE WAY AERODYNAMIC FRAMEWORKS WERE TESTED AND DESIGNED.

62 CENTER ALONGSIDE EUROPE'S PROFESSIONAL RACES, WHICH WERE SO POPULAR THAT THEY WERE CLOSELY FOLLOWED BY SPECTATORS ACROSS THE CONTINENT, A CIRCUIT OF UNORTHODOX FIELD TRACK COMPETITIONS SPRANG UP TO EXPLORE ALTERNATIVE USES OF THE BICYCLE.

62 BOTTOM UNLIKE CARS, BICYCLES DO NOT OFFER SHELTER FROM RAIN; HENCE THE DEVELOPMENT, AROUND 1940, OF HULLS TESTED WITH WATER-REPELLENT MATERIALS SO AS TO GUARANTEE BETTER PROTECTION.

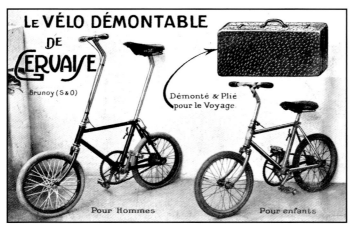

62-63 The increasing popularity of the bicycle led to its use in almost every conceivable way, including tight-rope walking exhibitions at circuses where cyclist and bike were suspended in mid air.

63 bottom The concept of the folding bicycle was finally realized in 1928, when two different models (one for adults and one for children) were launched on the market. Both could be easily dismantled and stored in a case.

AN AID FOR THE CHAMPIONS: VITTORIA-MARGHERITA AND SUPER CHAMPION

We have seen that the change in speed was first opposed by cyclists and then banned by race organizers. Yet it was not prohibited in *all* competitions: in the 1927 World Competition, which saw Alfredo Binda take the gold medal, an automatic version was unveiled. This too was received with suspicion: mistrustful of an unknown component which was not yet entirely reliable, few cyclists chose to fit it to their bicycles.

Italy did not invent any groundbreaking gear change devices until the early 1930s, when it released the Vittoria. Officially unveiled in 1931 by the Turin-based company Cavaliere Ufficiale Antonio Nieddu, this new mechanism comprised a spring-loaded bar with a chain stay and three gears fitted to the real wheel hub. It was activated by a lever that was fitted at pedal-height. Once activated, it released the mechanism making it possible to change gears. Cyclists had to shift the chain manually while pedaling backwards at the same time in order to move from one pinion to the other. Following this discovery, another variation was developed for traveling and town-riding velocipedes. It was known as the Vittoria Turismo, existed in two models – one for racing, one for entertaining – and both operated on the same principle.

At the beginning of 1935, the Vittorio-Margherita gear change system was developed, an improvement on the previous model which had maintained the lever with the chain-holding pulley positioned behind the bottom bracket on the lower stays. It was tightened manually along the small bar in the toothed semi-arch positioned above the bottom bracket, between the oblique tubes. There were still three pinions, but the novelty was that the chain was fitted a wire-command that activated the small metallic fork positioned on the lower stays of the rear triangle. This was comprised of a series of more or less taut bars, and served as a gear shifter. But there were problems with this version too, such as the need to back-pedal to tighten the chain. The leverage was too widely spread, and mud and dirt caused blockages. Competitors had to overcome this drawback by using naphtha and oil to get the bike going again. In the years that followed the Second World War, this model was updated by placing the fork below the frame's lower stays, so as to make it act on the rear part of the chain. The Vittoria-Margherita shifter was used for a decade and proved particularly successful in Italy, where it was considered to be the *non plus ultra* of components. It was selected by many cycling champions, one of whom, Gino Bartali, won the 1938 Tour de France on a Legnano fitted with a Vittoria-Margherita gear shifter.

> *The introduction of the gearshift was the last piece of the puzzle which completed the bicycle, rendering it a vehicle that could now to surpass increasingly greater difficulties.*

64 The Margherita Gearbox, officially introduced in 1935, represented the evolution of the Vittoria model proposed by the Turin firm. Gino Bartali was one of the few professional riders to exploit the new mechanism from its inception.

64-65 The twin presence of cycling greats Gino Bartali and Fausto Coppi ignited Italian and foreign races in the first decades of the 20th century. Bartali, "the tenacious Tuscan," won the 1938 Tour de France thanks to his performance in the Alps.

65 top Alfredo Binda boasted, among his laurels, 5 Giro d'Italia, 3 world championships, and 2 Milano-Sanremo victories. In 1930 he was paid to stay out of the Giro by organizers who wanted to give new competitors a chance to win the race.

The Super Champion model, known in England as the Osgear, was produced in Paris during the same period. While the Vittoria was the first true gear change system, the Super Champion was the first model to become universally known in cycling competitions. Its name is less grandiloquent in comparison with those brands to which "official" historiography attributes fame, yet its use became decisively widespread during competitions, even if for a limited time. It was the only mechanism allowed in the 1937 Tour de France and the Belgian Eloi Meulenberg's victory that year in the road-based World Championships, which took place in Copenhagen.

Although the Simplex Champion du Monde and Vittoria-Margherita devices were both produced at the same time, professional cyclists were allowed to use neither mechanism. Those who wanted to wear the yellow vest in 1937 could alleviate their fatigue only by using the Super Champion model.

The Super Champion was produced in Paris by a company owned by Oscar Egg, who had made his name as a professional cyclist before World War I. He was a three-time hour record holder

66 TOP A LATE-THIRTIES BIANCHI EQUIPPED WITH SUPER CHAMPION GEAR. NOTE THE SPRING-LOADED CRANK ARM MOUNTED BENEATH THE CENTRAL MOVEMENT BOX.

66-67 1937 SAW THE FIRST WIDESPREAD USE OF GEARBOXES IN THE TOUR DE FRANCE; BEFORE LONG, THEY LOST THEIR NOVELTY TO BECOME A FUNDAMENTAL COMPONENT OF EVERY RACING VEHICLE, ESPECIALLY THOSE USED IN MOUNTAIN STAGES.

67 TOP ARRIVING AT A LEVEL CROSSING, 1937 TOUR DE FRANCE CYCLISTS DISMOUNT AND CROSS THE RAIL TRACKS ON FOOT.

67 BOTTOM ROGER LAPÉBIE WON THE 1937 TOUR DE FRANCE AFTER A CLOSE BATTLE AGAINST THE BELGIAN SYLVÈRE MAES; THE LATTER ULTIMATELY ABANDONED THE RACE AFTER THE 17TH STAGE, LEAVING THE PLACE OF HONOR TO THE ITALIAN MARIO VICINI.

(1912, 1913, 1914). Egg was inspired by the first version of the Italian Vittoria-Margherita, and his gear change system was in fact made of a spring-loaded chain-stay fitted to the bottom bracket. A pedal backwards was needed to move the chain from one pinion to the other and shift gears.

This model was known simply as the Champion and was released in 1932. Three years later, after some technical progress, it popular throughout Europe. Its popularity increased further still when the fork that moved the chain was repositioned in the rear part of the bicycle so that it operated below the chain and eliminated the need to pedal backwards.

In 1934, gear change systems produced by the company of this former French cyclist sold 45,000. But that was nothing in comparison with the 300,000 which had been sold by 1936, and the one million sold in 1939.

Only "Le Simplex" could claim such a widespread fan base and represent a serious contender. It was continuously produced in England until the mid-1940s, with the result that it held a near monopoly on cycling competitions. The Super Champion project made the product simple to produce and easy to fit and maintain. The lever that caused motion had a "stop" for each gear, even if the cyclist had to lightly pass over it and turn back to the previous position to make the change. The chain cover was initially fitted just behind the bottom bracket unit, but it was moved to the lower part of the oblique tube onto a soldered support at the back of the movement box as early as 1936.

The tourist version of the Super Champion was identical to previous models, while racing versions had a shorter holding unit (some cyclists nonetheless preferred to keep the standard measurements).

The fork that moved the chain from one gear to the next was fitted to a fastened clip on the bottom bracket and activated using a control cable. Some versions were produced with a chain guide to guarantee that the chain remained in line, and a protective casing was fitted to protect the wheel spokes on all Super Champion gear change systems, so that the gear fork could not become stuck inside these when the bicycle was moving, which would have caused the cyclist to fall off.

This was initially applied only to the three-speed version, but over the years it was extended to the five-speed variant. In the wake of the Second World War, Egg's models fell out of favor with European cyclists and sales further tapered off when the Simplex Tour de France model was launched, even though it could be found in catalogues until 1965.

68-69 A GROUP OF ENTHUSIASTS WAITS FOR THE ACTION AT PLEYBON, BRITTANY, DURING THE 1939 TOUR. THE SPECTATORS ARE STANDING IN FRONT OF THE BICYCLE SHOP OF PIERRE CLOAREC, AN AVD CYCLIST WHO WAS RACING IN THAT YEAR'S *GRANDE BOUCLE*.

70-71 A GROUP PILE-UP DURING A RACE IN MILWAUKEE, IN 1934. AT THIS TIME, MANY RACES WERE HELD IN VELODROMES OR HIPPODROMES, BECAUSE GUARDING AN INDOOR RACE COURSE WAS EASIER THAN DOING SO AT A STREET EVENT.

70 BOTTOM THE FIRST MOTORIZED BICYCLES, KNOWN AS *DERNY*, MADE THEIR APPEARANCE IN FRANCE AT THE END OF THE 1930S. THEY WERE USED BOTH FOR PACING THE TRACK, AND AS AN INCENTIVE FOR CYCLISTS TO INCREASE THEIR SPEED.

71 TOP THE GOLD MEDAL IN THE TEAM PURSUIT RACE IN AMSTERDAM'S 1928 OLYMPIC GAMES WAS TAKEN BY THE ITALIAN TEAM: CESARE FACCIANI, GIACOMO GAIONI, MARIO LUSIANI, AND LUIGI TASSELLI.

71 BOTTOM A LONG BUT CLOSE-KNIT LINE OF CYCLISTS FLIES AROUND THE PARISIAN VELODROME BUFFALO DURING A 1928 SIX-DAY EVENT. BECAUSE OF ITS DIFFICULTY, THIS FORM OF TRACK CYCLING WAS ESPECIALLY APPEALING TO SPECTATORS OF THE ERA.

CAMPAGNOLO'S IDEA

The concept of gear shifts was by this time well established and widely accepted. It was simply a matter of developing the ideas of Vittoria and Oscar Egg to drive progress forwards. This time, it was a former Italian cyclist who had a brainwave. His name was Getullio Campagnolo, or "Tullio," and he had cycled with Alfredo Binda, Learco Guerra, and Costante Girardengo. While climbing the face of Croce d'Aune in the Dolomites, Campagnolo was allegedly forced to retire due to the cold and mud, which prevented him from loosening the wheel nuts. In November 1927 he decided that something about the bicycle had to be changed.

His expression "something's gotta change behind!", uttered in the Venetian dialect, became famous. And so, at the back of his father's hardware store, he developed a new method for releasing the wheel. He patented his design, which accelerated and rationalized the wheel-turning operation, at the beginning of 1930.

Yet this man from Vicenza did not limit his efforts to producing a new wheel release system for the hub. He turned his attention to the actual manufacturing of gear shift mechanics. Having spent many years studying models already available on the market, he designed a rod change system in 1936 that was officially recognized (ten years later) by the name "Cambio Corsa."

Campagnolo patented his new chain-free gear shifter. The first version of the mechanism was controlled by two levers, approximately twenty centimeters in length, which were attached to the right-hand side dropout. The first bar blocked the wheel, which continued to turn on the frame's tooth-guide, while the second moved the chain from one pinion to the next. The Cambio Corsa suffered, however, from the same drawback as its predecessors in that once the first lever had been released, a backwards pedaling motion was required to adjust the wheel after the desired gear had been selected.

The 1948 Italian film *Bicycle Thieves* by Vittorio De Sica shows many clips of cycling competitions in which the bicycles are fitted with Campagnolo's Cambio Corsa. In 1949, this former cyclist made another modification to his product and removed one lever. At that point, all that was necessary were two separate movements which freed the wheel and moved the chain. When cyclists needed to shift gears they had to make the rod perform a half-movement to release chain tension. Then, shifting the rod for the duration of the race, they moved the chain from one pinion to the next while simultaneously pedaling backwards. When selecting a lower gear, the hub would slide over the frame's dropouts, shortening the wheel base. On the other hand, if the cyclist opted for a higher gear, the hub would move downwards, extending the bicycle's stretch. As soon as the final maneuvers were complete, the rod was returned to its original position in order to retain the chain and complete the operation. The Vicenza factory produced two versions of its product: one with a short lever, known as the "Corsa," and one with a long lever, known as the "Sport."

Obviously, it remained counterproductive for cyclists to break momentum to change gear, especially on an uphill climb. Gino Bartali was one of the few cyclists who managed to successfully pedal backwards while maintaining his speed. Bartali, who was from Tuscany and called *le pieux* ("the pious") by the French, won the Tour de France in 1948, ten years after the first victory on a Legnano fitted with the Campagnolo Cambio Corsa.

72 Campagnolo's Roubaix derailleur gear was renamed in 1951 after Fausto Coppi's victory in the Paris-Roubaix classic. Despite his victory, he claimed to be dissatisfied by the gear's performance.

73 Gino Bartali (with Legnano's team car) cleans and fine-tunes the gearbox pinions of his bicycle. Having the right gear ratio was a fundamental necessity in beating a rival like Coppi, especially during a climb.

74-75 BARTALI WON THE TOUR TWICE, WITH A DECADE IN BETWEEN HIS VICTORIES: IN 1938, USING VITTORIA-MARGHERITA GEAR; AND IN 1948, USING THE CAMBIO CORSA GEAR OF HIS VICENTINE CAMPAGNOLO.

75 COPPI WAITS FOR THE START OF A 1951 GIRO D' ITALIA STAGE NEXT TO HIS BIKE, WHICH IS MOUNTED WITH THE PARIS-ROUBAIX GEAR. (THE *CAMPIONISSIMO* HAD TO SATISFY HIMSELF WITH FOURTH PLACE IN THE GENERAL CLASSIFICATION THAT YEAR.)

In October 1949, Campagnolo designed a new version of the Cambio Corsa known as the "Roubaix," though its name changed the very next year to Paris-Roubaix in homage to Fausto Coppi, who came in at the same time as André Mahe in the eponymous French race.

The Roubaix functioned in a similar way to the Cambio Corsa in the sense that,like the first Campagnolo model, it comprised a lever that ran the length of one of the upper stays of the rear triangle. Moreover, because it did not have a chain stay, it was once again necessary to kick the pedals backwards to change speed. Its only novelty was that the quick-release was oval, rounded and threaded. The Roubaix and Paris-Roubaix replaced the Cambio Corsa, but they were not destined to last long; significant progress in cyclists' demands coupled with competition among rival manufacturers led to the production of new products which were simpler to use.

By the end of 1949, a prolific manufacturing year for the Vicenza-based company, a dual-cable gear shifter was unveiled at the Milan Fair: the "Gran Sport." It was a pilot model for the version launched universally in 1951. This new mechanism used one cable to move the chain over the higher gears and another to pass them over the lower gears. This first model was not widely distributed. Given that only ten were manufactured, it was essentially nothing more than a prototype. The Super Sport meanwhile heralded a turning point in comparison with previous Campagnolo models and led the way for the dazzling rise of the Italian brand, which was soon to demolish the competition and storm the market.

THE FRENCH SIMPLEX

The "Simplex," a spring-loaded gear shift system that appeared after Campagnolo's invention but differed from the Italian version in that it did not require backwards pedaling, was becoming increasingly popular in France at the same time.

It clearly represented a major step forwards, given that products manufactured by the Vicenza plant were soon built in a similar way to fight off competition. Its founder Lucien Juy, a trader from Dijon, launched the first gear shift system under the name Le Simplex in 1928. This mechanism used one single pulley to tighten the chain, and two plates to move it from one pinion to the other.

The entire gear mechanism was held tight by a spring that kept the chain tight and prevented it from coming off.

The Simplex model was one of the first of its kind to have a spring positioned in the pin at the top of the gear housing, a solution that was to become integral in modern indexed gear shifting systems. Juy tried to convince the Alcyon team to use his invention in the 1928

Paris to Roubaix race; but the cyclists refused to test an unproven product in such an important competition. This setback did not deter the French merchant, who continued to make improvements to his design and so dedicated that many cyclists used the Simplex in the early 1930s at the increasingly dominant French competitions. The visibility triggered by these competitions led to an increase in production, to the point that Juy was able to claim that he had produced 40,000 in

SIMPLEX présente ....
la création
la plus
MARQUANTE
complément indispensable
d'un dérailleur moderne
le
GALET "Universel-Caoutchouté"
Brevets S. G. D. G. Modèles déposés
C'est une création "Le Simplex"

Adaptable sur
tous nos modèles
en service
Livrable sur
Demande
pour
nos modèles actuels

SILENCE TOTAL pendant la marche
DOUCEUR de roulement incomparable
RÉDUCTION de l'usure de la chaîne
Rendement et durée supérieurs
au galet acier

76 TOP AND 76-77 THE FRENCH JEAN ROBIC WAS A STURDY CYCLIST WHO EXCELLED IN STAGE RACES. HE WON IN THE FIRST *GRANDE BOUCLE* AFTER THE SECOND WORLD WAR, USING A BIKE WITH SIMPLEX GEAR. HE TOOK THREE STAGES IN ALL, AMONG THEM THE CLASSIC 195 KM LUCHON-PAU STAGE THROUGH THE PYRENEES, WHERE HE OVERCAME THE OBSTACLES PRESENTED BY SUCH LEGENDARY PEAKS AS THE PEYRESOURDE, ASPIN, TOURMALET, AND AUBISQUE.

77 IN 1939 SIMPLEX STARTED TO USE RUBBERIZED ROLLERS FOR ITS GEAR BOXES, GIVING THE PRODUCT A GENTLER, SILENT GEAR CHANGE, AND CAUSING SIGNIFICANT REDUCTION IN THE WEAR AND TEAR OF THE CHAIN.

1933 alone. The same year, an impressive four races in as many French championships were won using the new Simplex model, which by then had three speeds.

Two years later, the Dijon manufacturing plant released the commemoratively named "Champion de France" model, which had a modified arm in order to move the chain more efficiently over the gears. This new design shot to fame and remained the leading Simplex model at competitions for eleven years. Despite the ease with which the

gears could be shifted, the Champion de France did not, however, become as popular as its competitor the Super Champion, which was the only model allowed in the 1937 Tour de France.

In 1936, this French company unveiled its Champion du Monde model, which was probably the first gear shift mechanism available in five pinions. In addition to the gear box, a special hub was designed that made it possible to install the free wheel body using an octagonal adapter. The Simplex Champion du Monde was also the first to use a chain measuring 3/32 inches.

The manufacturer now began making a series of models for touring and city bicycles. Given its proven track record of smooth-running operations, which came as a result of the many victories won on the racing track, these new products became enormously successful in many sectors throughout the whole of Europe (though not in Great Britain, where other manufacturers were favored).

As for the racing models, production of the Champion du Monde model continued even after the Second World War and was particularly successful in France and Italy. In an effort to make continuous improvements to the design, the pulley was modified, thus bringing precision to the gear-changing process.

Furthermore, now that the gear shift pulley had been moved closer to the freewheel by means of a spring-loaded pin, changing from one gear to the next became substantially easier.

Unfortunately, however, the first version was not as successful as anticipated given that the gear shift cage was made of two parts. (Because of this, the mechanism was produced using only one part the following year.)

As soon as its use was permitted in the Grande Boucle, the next model – the Tour de France – became a standard-bearer for professional cyclists and even overtook the Super Champion as the favored mechanism.

Following the Second World War, Campagnolo and Simplex competed to become the favorite brands for cycling champions and manufacturers alike. Nevertheless, the eternal battle between France and Italy meant that Italian manufacturers preferred to fit the Campagnolo design, while their French counterparts opted for those models designed by Lucien Juy. In both cases, the Simplex product, which was made using a spring and pulleys to hold the chain tight and operated using a dual cable, enjoyed a large success compared with those produced by the Venice-based company, at least until the Campagnolo Gran Sport model was released. In 1945, Paul Maye won the Paris-Roubaix race on a bicycle fitted with a Simplex gear change mechanism, and in 1947 the Frenchman Jean Robic, who was known by his nickname "glass head" due to his tendency to wear a protective helmet during races, won the Tour de France. Even the highly successful champion Fausto Coppi switched from a Campagnolo to a Simplex, which led to his victory in the Grande Boucle in 1949, using the French design. Coppi, who was known as the "Heron" and came from a town called Castellania, stood out from the crowd because in those days cyclists who entered the Tour de France rode using a national brand, using the Cambio Corsa or, as was the case with Bartali, the Cervino di Nieddu. When he took part in the Inferno del Nord the following year, Coppi resorted to using the Italian mechanism since the Campagnolo used previously at Roubaix did not have a pulley. This helpful device meant that it was virtually mud- and dust-proof, and worked well in a challenging race such as the Roubaix.

78-79 Fausto Coppi was paid handsomely to become a promoter of Simplex Gear. The Campionissimo was the only Italian to compete in the 1949 Tour de France using all French products.

78 bottom left Fausto Coppi won his second Tour in 1952—and took the yellow jersey by the 10th stage. Some months earlier, he had also won the Giro d'Italia, thus adding to his belt that year two consecutive achievements held only by the very best "thoroughbred" cycling champions.

78 bottom right Coppi signs autographs for fans before the start of a Grande Boucle stage in 1949, the same year he won in the overall classification with a lead of almost 11 minutes over his eternal rival Gino Bartali.

79 Fausto Coppi, Lucien Lazarides, Apo Lazarides, and Jean Robic on the Tourmalet during the 11th stage of the 1949 Tour.

The Italian cyclist Fiorenzo Magni was one of the key players in the Campagnolo-Simplex rivalry. Magni asked his mechanics to replace a Cambio Corso mechanism, which he was contractually obliged to use, with a Simplex model before attempting a high-altitude leg of the 1949 Tour de France. The next day he won the Pyrennies leg on a Willier-Triestina bicycle fitted with the French Simplex and took the yellow jersey. Campagnolo only realized that he had made the switch when they saw the photographs in the newspaper.

The Campagnolo manufacturers sent a telegram to France to congratulate the Italian cyclist, who was then forced to abandon the Simplex. Legend has it that this was the incident that drove Campagnolo forward, following cycling races while modifying their patents based on the advice of participants. Soon they had abandoned the Cambio Corsa and Roubaix in favor of developing a spring-loaded gear shift model, a prototype of which came to light in 1949 and entered production in 1951 by the name "Gran Sport." Fiorenzo Magni was one of the first was one of the cyclists to use it on his bicycle.

80 TOP MAGNI EARNED THE NICKNAME "LION OF FLANDERS" AFTER HAVING DISPLAYED UNUSUAL TENACITY AND TACTICAL SENSE IN THREE CONSECUTIVE FLANDERS TOURS, IN 1949, 1950, AND 1951.

80 BOTTOM LEFT MAGNI, THE DEFINITIVE THIRD MAN OF ITALY'S GOLDEN AGE OF CYCLING, WHOSE THREE VICTORIES AT THE GIRO D'ITALIA (AND AS MANY NATIONAL CHAMPIONSHIPS) ALLOW HIM THE RIGHT TO STAND NEXT TO HIS COUNTRYMEN COPPI AND BARTALI.

80 BOTTOM RIGHT FIORENZO MAGNI BEING HELPED BY HIS TEAMMATES AFTER A FALL DURING THE 1956 GIRO D'ITALIA. IN THAT RACE THE TUSCAN CYCLIST ARRIVED SECOND, MORE THAN THREE MINUTES BEHIND CHARLY GAUL.

80-81 FIORENZO MAGNI AT THE 1949 TOUR, WHEN HE HAD HIS MECHANICS EXCHANGE THE CAMBIO CORSA HE HAD BEEN USING (PER CONTRACT) WITH THE SIMPLEX.

THE EAST: NO WAITING AND WATCHING

There is no question that the changes and developments in the bicycle's history took place predominantly in Europe for more than a century, but in the early twentieth century it was Japan which took the lead by releasing two new brands, both of which were to become market leaders in the 1960s, first in the United States and later in Europe.

The Maeda Ironworks Company, which was to later known as SunTour in the West, was set up by Shikanosuke Maeda in Kawati-Nagano in 1912. It began by manufacturing free wheels for bicycles, which were known by the numbers 888 in the first series, as well as gear mechanisms for agricultural machinery. Since the First World War had put an end to the importation of foreign bicycles to Japan, it was an ideal time to begin production of bike parts. During the 1914-1918 conflict, an industrial center was set up in Osaka to manufacture weaponry. It was converted into a bicycle production plant when the war came to an end on the false assumption of what was occurring at Saint-Etienne in France and Birmingham in England. In this context, in 1921, the entrepreneur Shozaburo Shimano established Shimano Iron Works, which became a giant in the world of bicycle manufacture. At the outset, the factory only produced one-speed free wheels, but then its founder declared that his goal was to make Shimano products the best in Kansai, then in all Japan and finally the whole world. With Japanese flair and efficiency, the export rate guaranteed the company a period of stable growth starting in 1931 and culminating in 1940, when its name (and focus) changed.

During the Second World War many Japanese industries were taken over by the government for the production of munitions; Maeda was one of these. It was razed to the ground in 1945 during the bombing raids that destroyed Japan's economic centers. As the war came to an end, production had to be reinitiated, but the industry in Osaka was not diminished. At that time, the needs of more than seven million bicycle owners shifted towards one-speed models to make up for the lack of motor vehicles and fuel on which to run them. People became interested in this type of bicycle because gear shift systems had not yet been developed locally. Meanwhile, single-mechanism models such as the British-manufactured Sturmey-Archer and BSA were rarely imported, and only during the post-war boom.

In 1949, Junzo Kawai, the new chairman of the newly refurbished Maeda, traveled to Europe to witness firsthand the technical progress made by Europeans in the field of gear shift mechanisms. This dynamic entrepreneur returned to Japan in the company of several freewheel and gear-shift cycling champions. On his return he decided to bring production in his company in line with international standards. The real turning point came, however, when a number of cycling competitions between the United States and Japan were held in Japan. American cyclists used French bicycles, fitted with Simplex mechanisms that had been used in the Tour de France. This product did not pass unnoticed by local engineers, who then suggested that identical mechanisms should be sold on the Japanese market using the same technology as those manufactured by Lucien Juy. This led to the birth of a Japanese manufacturing industry for gear shifting mechanisms and multiple-pinion free wheel bicycles. Shimano and Maeda were the first to appreciate the importance of this innovation and capitalized on this world-leading position. They were followed by brands such as Cheruvino, Dia and Sanko, who soon either lost their way or restricted themselves to producing parts on a small-scale.

In the mid-1950s, various manufacturers unveiled models that were clearly imitations of the Simplex mechanism. In 1956, both Shimano and Maeda, which used the name SunTour on its product for the first time, released their first external gear change mechanisms for touring bikes whose design was inspired by transalpine models. Similarly, several Japanese models were developed using a body-shifter (which used the tension in a spring from pulleys to keep the chain tight) and a dual-cable which shook when the gear needed to be changed. This newfound interest in Japan for racing bikes became significant in the 1950s and opened the market to gear shifting systems and free wheels, but the demand for external mechanisms only lasted a few years, because Japanese cyclists switched their preference back to internal mechanisms once again. Once again, Shimano rose to the occasion and produced the first rear hub with an integrated three-speed mechanism in 1957. Meanwhile, Maeda sought to improve its SunTour model by making it more efficient and more precise. From this time on, these two Japanese manufacturers followed different roads; their decisions reflected different approaches to the world market and varying degrees of success in the global sale of bicycle parts.

82 AMERICAN SOLDIERS STATIONED IN OKINAWA DURING AND AFTER WORLD WAR II ORGANIZED RACES WITH BICYCLES REQUISITIONED FROM THE JAPANESE INFANTRY.

83 TOP THE FIRST WORLD WAR STOPPED THE IMPORTATION OF BICYCLES INTO JAPAN, NECESSITATING THE BIRTH OF A DOMESTIC MANUFACTURING INDUSTRY.

83 BOTTOM LEFT THE SHIMANO IRON WORKS, WHICH WAS STARTED IN 1921 BY THE ENTERPRISING SHOZABURO SHIMANO.

83 BOTTOM RIGHT IN THE PERIOD FOLLOWING JAPAN'S DEFEAT IN THE SECOND WORLD WAR, THE COUNTRY SAW A VIRTUAL BOOM IN THE USE OF BICYCLES BY CIVILIANS.

84-85 In the wake of the destruction caused by the Second World War, the bicycle assumed a vital role in cities like Berlin, where the scourge of bombardments (and zones set up by occupational forces) made long-distance travel on highways unfeasible.

85 top The reconstruction of Europe after the Second World War also saw the coming of age of the bicycle as the most popular means of every-day transportation.

85 BOTTOM AS GERMANY'S CITIES WERE BOMBED INTO OBLIVION DURING THE SECOND WORLD
WAR, FLEEING CITIZENS LEFT HOUSE AND HOME—AND MOST OF THEIR BELONGINGS. BUT NO
MATTER THE SITUATION, NO ONE LEFT WITHOUT HIS BICYCLE: NOT SURPRISINGLY, IT WAS ONE OF THE
MOST PRIZED POSSESSIONS THE AVERAGE FAMILY HELD ONTO.

86-87 DURING THE SECOND WORLD WAR, THE BICYCLE INFANTRY ASSUMED A VITAL ROLE, AS IN
HOLLAND, WHERE THE DUTCH ARMY USED ITS MAIN REGIMENT TO PATROL NATIONAL BORDERS.

CYCLING'S TAILOR'S SHOP

THE RECONSTRUCTION OF THE PEDAL

The outbreak of World War II in 1939 brought an end to international sporting events for more than five years, and cycling competitions began again only once the hostilities were over, in 1945. The first Giro d'Italia, evocatively tagged *Giro della Rinascita* ("the Reborn Giro") was held in 1946 and won by Gino Bartali. The first Tour de France held after the war took place in 1947 and was won by Jean Robic. Despite the profound damage caused by a five-year period of intense conflict, there was a universal desire to start afresh. One aim was to reunite peoples across the nations that were still divided by the hatred and desire for revenge at home and abroad. Cycling competitions held in many different nations brought various nationalities and ethnicities together, and the fact that these competitions were held regularly was an incentive to the cycling community to roll up its collective sleeves and get on with the sport, even if while rebuilding what the war had destroyed. This competitions once again began to take place, even before competing environments were fully restored. The damage caused by the conflict could be seen most easily in the road conditions. The cyclists who took part in the 1946 Giro d'Italia, for example, staged a protest to vent their exasperation with the number of holes and pits in the roads—and the increased likelihood of injury from falling off bikes at high speeds. During the Naples to Rome stage, competitors made their unhappiness clear by actually bringing the race to a complete halt. A heated discussion between competitors and race organizers followed, with the latter attempting to explain that the state of the road surfaces could not be attributed to the race judges and that the race leg should continue. After much squabbling, hunger won through when many cyclists came to realize that if they continued their protest or retired from the race they would forfeit a meal and payment. For many cyclists, the prize money from competitions was the only means they had to support their families. And so the competitors were forced—by their own need—to get back on the road to Rome.

89 During his professional cycling years, Eddie Merckx was served by the best European artisans, including Colnago and De Rosa.

90 bottom left and 90-91 By the 1960s, European competitors, tired of competing on rough roads whose conditions (especially on newer, speedier vehicles) were downright deadly, began to protest publicly and agitate for safer courses.

90 top The Swiss Hugo Koblet during a stage of the Tour de France 1951. He won the race with a 22-minute lead over the Frenchman Raphaël Géminiani, and a 24-minute lead over Lucien Lazarides.

Roadbed and surface improvements had, of course, been under-way all over Europe since the aftermath of the First World War, not on-ly with an eye to repairing the damage but also improving the entire network by replacing ancient paving stones with more modern surface materials that could withstand the weight of motorized vehicles. Indeed, thousands of miles had been brought up to the standard of to-day's smooth roads, so that they could no longer be fairly called, as Alfredo Binda had described them, "dried-up river beds." But the Second World War wiped out more than twenty years of progress, leav-ing the impression that the improvements made in the past had nev-er occurred at all.

The restoration of cycling routes marked a return to normalcy and economic revival. After years of deadly air raids, during which the fear of open spaces had taken an enormous psychic toll on the public, Europe's highways and byways once again vibrated with people who, free from the shadow of war, could once again breathe freely outdoors.

This newly rediscovered freedom to *be* could be felt not only in peo-ple's daily routines, but also on cycling tracks. In the years leading up to 1950, cycling became one of the most recognizable facets of post-war reconstruction and forgiveness in Europe.

At the same time, cycling grew to become the most sensational and closely-followed sport on the continent. People would pour onto the street from factories, offices, schools, and homes to watch their fa-vorite competitor ride past. There was no sense of discrimination, be-cause no one had to buy an entrance ticket.

Everybody felt welcome to a cycling events; nor was there a merito-cratic selection procedure to establish who could take part and who couldn't. Anyone willing to test his mettle in the saddle could join in. Spectators lined the streets to watch the competitors cycle past, shar-ing in their dreams, hopes, and aspirations for a better world and for liberation from the darkness of conflict, suffering, and economic and social hardship.

92-93 A group waits for the start of the opening stage of the 1956 Tour de France, in front of the Cathedral of Reims. After 223 km, at the finish line in Liège, victory smiled on the French sprinter André Darrigade.

93 top left Spectators watch while their heroes take a break at the start of the 5th stage, Dieppe-Caen, in the 1953 Tour. In those days cyclists and spectators were able to communicate directly—there were no dividing barriers between them.

93 top right The French Andre Darrigade crashes into a race judge who was too close to the track, in the last stage of the 1958 Tour.

93 bottom Jean Forestier is the first competitor to arrive on La Sentinelle in the 16th stage of the 1956 Grande Boucle, which ran from Aix-en-Provence to Gap.

94-95 IN THE SWELTERING HEAT OF MID-JULY, THERE IS LITTLE AS GOOD AS A BUCKET OF WATER. HERE, DURING THE 1953 TOUR, THE DANE JAN NOLTEN IS THE RECIPIENT OF A SPECTATOR'S GENEROSITY.

94 BOTTOM FIREMEN WATCHING THE GRANDE BOUCLE TRY TO RELIEVE THE OPPRESSIVE HEAT SUFFERED BY RACERS AT CHARLEROI-METZ, IN THE 1957 EDITION OF THE TOUR DE FRANCE.

95 BOTTOM LEFT HEAT EXHAUSTION IS PROBABLY A CYCLIST'S WORST ENEMY AT THE TOUR DE FRANCE.

95 BOTTOM RIGHT SPECTATORS ATTEMPT TO BRING RELIEF TO PERSPIRING CYCLISTS DURING A STAGE OF THE 1957 TOUR.

SCHOOLS COMPARED:
ITALY AND FRANCE TO THE
CONQUEST OF THE MARKET

O nce the gear shifter had been introduced, the racing bicycle and its appearance remained largely unchanged for many years, despite continuous improvements being made to its working and the weight of each part. The number of gears increased to five, while the gear shifter was coupled with the derailleur. Cyclists could now rely on a dual gear wheel – a dual plateau – which brought the number of possible couplings between gears to ten. The two French manufacturers Simplex and Huret were the first to use a derailleur in the early 1950s.

This part was renamed the "suicide lever" by cynics because cyclists had to push on a small bar running along the length of the handle bars to make it work. In other words, the first derailleurs required the cyclist to take one hand off the handle bar, which during the heated moments of a contest was particularly unnatural and caused unpracticed riders to fall off their mount.

Until the 1940s, the market for manufacturing gear shifters was largely populated by small- and medium-sized businesses, each with its own model and different from others in some minor respect. From the mid-1950s onwards, these manufacturers hit hard times and disappeared, leaving only a handful of producers to enjoy the profits. Only Simplex and Huret survived in France.

Huret's Tour de France model was fitted to Stella models and led the market up to 1955 in the Grande Boucle under Frenchman Louison Bobet's leadership. Named in honor of the founder's mother, Stella bikes were manufactured in Nantes by the Fountineau family.

Simplex products remained the most popular and were used in competitions throughout the world, even though the technology of the models was never updated, and one of its historic competitors was on the brink of overhauling this particular accessory so dear to cyclists. In Italy, Tullio Campagnolo had patented a parallelogram gear shifter which was launched under the name Gran Sport. It replaced the Cambio Corsa and Paris-Roubaix, whose technology had by this time been overtaken and which were slow to adopt to the new demands of cyclists for designs that guaranteed speed and precision.

96 Lousion Bobet signs autographs while waiting for the start of the 8th stage (Vannes to Angers) in the 1954 Tour. The classy Bobet was one of the most popular French cyclists among the transalpine public.

96-97 Louison Bobet won the Grande Boucle three consecutive times: 1953, 1954, and 1955. A well-rounded cyclist, he excelled not only in the mountain stages but also during time trials.

97 TOP LEFT HARSH TRAINING ALWAYS PRECEDES VICTORIES, AS DOES THE THANKLESS DEDICATION OF *DOMESTIQUES* AND THE SLEEPLESS NIGHTS OF MECHANICS PAID TO GUARANTEE, WITH THEIR WORK, THAT EVERY COMPONENT IS WORKING IN THE MOST EFFICIENT MANNER.

97 TOP RIGHT IN THE EARLY 1950'S, THE DOUBLE CHAIN WHEEL WAS INTRODUCED, A NOVEL SOLUTION WHICH, COMBINED WITH 5-SPEED GEAR, INCREASED THE NUMBER OF POSSIBLE MATCHES BETWEEN CROWNS AND GEARS TO TEN.

The contrast between French and Italian models reached record levels on the cycle track and was epitomized by two Swiss cycling champions: Ferdi Kubler and Hugo Koblet. Kubler, who won the Tour de France in 1950 and the rainbow jersey (denoting a world cycling championship) the following year, used Simplex mechanisms. Koblet won the pink jersey in 1950 and the yellow in 1951, using a Campagnolo device. Campagnolo continued to make improvements to the Gran Sport model, beginning in 1952 with the second generation, which was called the Gran Sport Extra. The third, definitive version, which had a revamped case and pulleys, was released in 1953 when the suffix "Extra" was dropped from its name. This gear shifter, coupled with the first derailleur produced by the Vicenza-based company, set a new trend and quickly became the most popular fitting of cycling champions. In 1953, Fausto Coppi won the World Cycling Championship in Zurich on a Bianchi bike fitted with the Gran Sport gear shifter. Charly Gaul from Luxembourg, who was famous for his ascent up snow-clad Monte Bondone in 1956 and his success in the 1958 Tour de France, also used this Italian product.

98 THE SWISS CYCLIST FERDI KUBLER AT THE END OF THE 15TH STAGE OF THE 1951 GIRO D'ITALIA, WHICH RAN FROM BRESCIA TO VENICE OVER DUSTY, BUMPY TERRAIN.

99 TOP FERDI KUBLER BEING INTERVIEWED BY A JOURNALIST AFTER HIS VICTORY IN CAEN-SAINT-BRIEUC, THE 5TH STAGE OF THE 1954 GRANDE BOUCLE. KUBLER ARRIVED SECOND, AFTER LOUISON BOBET, IN THE OVERALL CLASSIFICATION.

99 BOTTOM KUBLER LEADS A BREAKAWAY GROUP ON THE ASCENT OF THE TOURMALET IN THE 12TH STAGE OF THE 1954 TOUR, A HEROIC ACTION, BUT NOT ENOUGH TO REMOVE BOBET FROM FIRST PLACE IN THE GENERAL CLASSIFICATION.

100 TOP LEFT GAP, 1951, AT THE END OF THE 19TH STAGE OF THE TOUR DE FRANCE: THE SWISS CYCLIST HUGO KOBLET POSES IN THE YELLOW JERSEY WITH JUBILATING FANS. BESIDES WINNING THE OVERALL 1951 TITLE, KOBLET WON 4 STAGES.

100 TOP RIGHT LOUISON BOBET, FERDI KUBLER AND HUGO KOBLET SEEK SHELTER UNDER AN UMBRELLA AT THE END OF THE BREST-VANNES STAGE OF THE 1954 TOUR. IT RAINED SO HARD DURING THE RACE THAT MANY CYCLISTS DONNED CAPES.

100 BOTTOM HUGO KOBLET, IN YELLOW JERSEY, AND ABDEL KADER ZAAF QUENCH THEIR THIRST AFTER FINISHING THE LAST STAGE OF THE 1951 TOUR. THE FRANCO-ALGERIAN CYCLIST WAS THE ONLY NORTH-AFRICAN REPRESENTATIVE TO FINISH THE RACE.

100-101 A GROUP OF CYCLISTS ENTER THE PARIS VELODROME, FINISHING POINT OF THE 1951 TOUR DE FRANCE. THE VICTORY IN THIS LAST STAGE WENT TO THE FRENCHMAN ADOLPHE DELEDDA.

102 Fausto Coppi won the 1953 World Road Championship in Zurich on a Bianchi equipped with Gran Sport Gear—the first victory to thrust him firmly into the limelight as a true champion.

103 top left Fausto Coppi and Primo Bergomi take a post-competition break. The *Campionissimo* was deadly even in velodrome races, where he won the rainbow title twice while trying to break time records.

103 top center Coppi receiving a congratulatory bunch of grapes from his adversary Luigi Casola during the 1952 Giro d'Italia. The *Campionissimo* won the overall classification that year, wearing the pink jersey for 10 of 20 stages.

103 top right Fausto Coppi (in yellow jersey) leads the ascent to the Puy de Dôme, a stage of the 1952 Tour de France, with Stan Ockers in hot pursuit. By winning the title, the Italian champion consolidated his classification supremacy over the Belgian.

103 The victorious Coppi is triumphantly borne through the streets of Lugano in 1953, after winning the rainbow jersey—and having beaten his eternal rival, Bartali, who, due to bad luck and obstinacy, never managed to become a world champion.

> *The postwar period, from the 1940s to the 1970s, can be defined as the golden age of cycling for European brands, for during that time, they set the standard (particualrly French and Italian names) for all others.* "

104 TOP CHARLY GAUL IN ACTION DURING THE 1956 TOUR DE FRANCE. BESIDE TWO STAGE VICTORIES, THE LUXEMBOURGIAN WON THE POLKA DOT JERSEY, WHICH IDENTIFIES THE BEST CLIMBER.

104-105 CHARLY GAUL, GILBERT BAUVIN, AND FEDERICO BAHAMONTES STRUGGLING UP THE OEILLON, DURING THE GRENOBLE-ST. ETIENNE

STAGE OF THE 1956 GRANDE BOUCLE. (THE FINAL VICTORY IN THIS STAGE WENT TO STAN OCKERS.)

105 TOP LEFT CHARLY GAUL GIVES HIS BEST ON MOUNT BONDONE AT THE 1956 GIRO D'ITALIA. THE LUXEMBOURGIAN TOOK OFF IN A SNOW STORM BUT WON THE STAGE AND THE PINK JERSEY—AND HUNG ONTO IT ALL THE WAY TO MILAN.

105 TOP RIGHT IN THE WAKE OF AN APOCALYPTIC SNOWSTORM THAT PLAGUED THE ENTIRE CLIMB TO MOUNT TRENTINO, DURING THE 1956 GIRO, CHARLY GAUL IS CARRIED AWAY, HAVING SUCCUMBED TO A BOUT OF HYPOTHERMIA WHICH TOOK HIM OUT OF THE RACE AT THE END OF THE MERANO-MONTE BONDONE STAGE.

106 CENTER THE "GENTLEMAN" MODEL, CREATED BY THE EXPERT HANDS OF RENÉ HERSE IN THE 1950'S, BUT DESIGNED (DESPITE ITS NAME) FOR EVERYDAY USE. THE DISTINCTIVE CHARACTERISTIC OF THIS BICYCLE WAS ITS INVERTED BRAKE LEVERS.

106-107 ANOTHER TOURING MODEL BUILT BY RENÉ HERSE AND EQUIPPED WITH DERAILLEUR GEAR MADE BY BOUILLER AND RAIMOND'S FRENCH COMPANY, CYCLO.

106 TOP LEFT THIS 1964 COLNAGO RACING BICYCLE WAS BUILT WITH COLUMBUS STEEL TUBING JOINED BY MEANS OF MICROFUSED BRAZE-WELDED JOINTS; IT IS EQUIPPED WITH CAMPAGNOLO'S NUOVO RECORD DERAILLEUR GEAR.

106 TOP RIGHT A TOURING MODEL OF THE 1950'S, HAND-BUILT BY THE FRENCH CRAFTSMAN RENE HERSE. (NOT ONLY THE FRAME, BUT ALSO THE MAJORITY OF THE COMPONENTS, WERE ASSEMBLED BY THIS SKILLED TRANSALPINE BUILDER).

The economic boom that swept through Europe in the years immediately after post-war reconstruction gave new impetus to developments in the manufacture of motor cars and large industries, fuelled by
market demand, and overlooked the bicycle, which could not compete
with the benefits of the car, for some time. It was the beginning of a
change in people's attitude towards the bike, which was already over-
shadowed by an era of large-scale car manufacture. Car and motorbike manufacturers offered discounts and incentives for those people
who wanted to trade in their bicycle for a motorbike or moped. The bicycle remained in vogue as a piece of sporting equipment for competitions, but people who used one to go about their daily life were
mocked by friends with motorcycles. Nonetheless, even in its darkest
years, which began with the inexorable increase in popularity of the
scooter and motor car and the looming oil crisis, the bicycle continued
to evolve—if slowly, then still surely. One significant step forward came
with the introduction of materials previously used only in aviation, for example aluminum alloys and titanium, which began to appear in the cycling world in the mid-1970s. In 1962, Cino Cinelli produced the
Unicanitor saddle, the first to have a plastic cover. It was a revolutionary
discovery because until then saddles, such as the Brooks and Ideale

versions, were made entirely from leather and required lengthy treat-
ment to protect them against water and debris, with the result that they
were uncomfortable for cyclists after long races. The introduction of
plastic saddles made the manufacturing process simpler and ensured
that the shape of the saddle would not be distorted by use over time.

The following year, the same manufacturers released the first racing bike aluminum handle bar onto the market. This product had the
same curved shape as earlier models, but the fact that it was made
from an aluminum alloy, unlike traditional models made from steel, represented an important step forwards in reducing the bike's weight without compromising the sturdiness of this vital component which cyclists
cling to during uphill climbs and during time trials.

Racing bike parts such as the brakes and tubes, were introduced
into line production. As usual, the races themselves were the bench
test of progress. After the war, aluminum wheels were also fitted to touring bikes. People wanted their bicycles to resemble those of their favorite champions as closely as possible. Many accessories were improved, and bicycles became lighter as a result. Racing bikes became
eight kilograms lighter and standard bikes by ten kilograms.

The 1950s and 1960s saw the success of the Italian manufacturers.
New names popped up on the Italian and foreign markets, most of
them named after former cyclists who at the end of their sporting careers channeled the experience they had gained from years of competitions into bicycle manufacture.

Cino Cinelli was one such cyclist turned manufacturer. Others in-
cluded Ernesto Colnago, Ugo De Rosa, Faliero Masi and Giovanni
Pinarello, who put their names to famous brands such as Bianchi,
Olympia, Atala, Gloria, Legnano, Umberto Dei, Maino, and Stucchi.
Special mention should go to Tullio Campagnolo, who made a come-
back despite the extraordinary success of Simplex products.

The Italian bicycle industry grew alongside other large European
manufacturers from Great Britain, France, and Germany. In 1958, for example, France and Germany maintained the same level of production
as Great Britain, which was losing its market share. Italian bicycles were
even exported to countries that used the dollar, which until that point
had proven unprofitable and impenetrable.

These so-called Italian "designers" bought increasingly large market
shares, but it would be wrong to believe that products produced in other countries, especially transalpine nations, were not successful.
Manufacturers based north of the Alps were alive and well with brands
such as Caminade, Caminargent, Le Chamineau, Royal-Fabric, Alex
Singer and René Herse especially good at making a name for themselves. From 1940 until his death in 1976, Herse in particular was considered to be the greatest exponent of French cycling handicraft. His
innovative style led him to employ ground-breaking frame manufacturing techniques, including joints soldered with silver. Herse's attention to
detail resulted in a higher-quality product, because he was not only a
frame-maker but an all-around manufacturer too. Indeed, he developed a series of parts which separated the pedals from the hub and
the levers from the brakes.

Cycling competitions continued to be the main showcase for products manufactured north of the Alps, which remained largely popular. The Frenchman Jacques Anquetil, one of the most charismatic figures of his time, won two of his five victories at the Tour de France – 1957 and 1961 – using a custom-built bicycle fitted with the very best technologies that France could offer. The frame was manufactured by Helyett, set up in 1926 and one of the most important racing bike manufacturers of its time, along with other transalpine producers such as Alcyon, Automot and Mercier. The gear shifter and derailleur were produced by Simplex, the pedals by TA Specialities, the brakes by Mafac, and the wheel hubs by Atom. Initially, the crank was supplied by TA Specialities, but successive models used a Stronglight product instead. (In the 1930s this French company, which is still successful today, had launched the first four-pivot crank, a piece that substantially simplified fitting the bottom bracket and maintaining the entire mechanism.)

Following tests and subsequent adjustments, a new model of pedal crank – the 57 Super Competition – was released in 1957; it was made from an aluminum alloy and designed to be fitted immediately onto the dual plateau.

The levers which provided movement had five arms and a 122 millimeter pin turn, making it possible to use even 38-tooth rims. This proved particularly helpful for extremely steep climbs. French manufacturers did not sit idly by, however, and soon joined the competition with Stronglight.

The next year, 1958, the Italian manufacturer Campagnolo launched its first four-pin crank on the Record series. Having noted the success of the French model, especially its method for coupling the arm with the bottom bracket, Campagnolo designed its pedal crank in a similar (if it not identical) fashion. The first product was called a Record and became part of a comprehensive group of parts that included a gear shifter (Cambio Sport), a derailleur, a steering section, bottom bracket, wheel hubs, pedals and seat posts. The Legnano Tipo Roma Olimpiade model, named in honor of Ercole Baldini's victory at the 1956 Olympics in Melbourne, was fitted entirely with Italian-made parts.

108 top Leading the team up a climb during the 1963 Tour de France are the first two of the overall classification: the French Jacques Anquetil and the Spanish climber Federico Bahamontes, the Eagle of Toledo.

108-109 Edward Sels in the velodrome of the Parc des Princes, in Paris,

during the final stage of the 1964 Tour de France. The Belgian won four stages that year, and wore the yellow jersey for two days.

109 bottom left Anquetil discusses race tactics with his team's athletic manager, the former cyclist Raphaël Geminiani. The Norman racer won

the first two Tours on a Helyett, before moving on to Gitanes.

109 bottom right Anquetil, winner of the 1961 Tour, and one of the most charismatic figures of his time, receives applause from the crowd during his victory lap in the velodrome of Paris's Parc des Princes.

110-111 TOM SIMPSON TAKES TO THE PODIUM AT LASARTE, AT THE END OF THE RACE THAT MADE HIM A WORLD CHAMPION. THE GREATEST SUCCESS OF HIS CAREER, IT ALSO EARNED HIM THE BBC'S SPORTS PERSONALITY OF THE YEAR AWARD.

111 TOP ST. GAUDENS, 1962: TOM SIMPSON IN THE YELLOW JERSEY AT THE END OF THE 12TH STAGE OF THE TOUR. SIMPSON WAS THE FIRST BRITON TO WIN THE TOUR.

111 BOTTOM TOM SIMPSON AT THE *PARC DES PRINCES* VELODROME IN PARIS DURING THE LAST STAGE OF THE 1964 TOUR DE FRANCE. SHORTLY AFTER THIS, QUEEN ELIZABETH II KNIGHTED HIM FOR HIS ATHLETIC ACHIEVEMENTS.

112 THE POPULARITY OF THIS FOLDING BICYCLE WAS REVIVED IN THE 1960'S THANKS CHIEFLY TO AN INTELLIGENT MARKETING CAMPAIGN, AND PERHAPS ALSO TO THE MUSICALITY OF ITS NAME, GRAZIELLA.

113 TOP THE FOLDING BICYCLE WAS HIGHLY VALUED FOR ITS COMPACT SIZE, ITS SOLIDITY, AND ITS EASE OF HANDLING. ITS U-SHAPED FRAME WAS CHARACTERIZED BY A CLASP THAT ENABLED ONE TO FOLD THE ENTIRE MIDSECTION.

113 BOTTOM LEFT THE GRAZIELLA WAS WIDELY REGARDED AS A SYMBOL OF FREEDOM AND ANTI-CONFORMISM; AND TO AN ITALIAN IN THE 1970'S, OWNING ONE MEANT BEING IN TUNE WITH THE SPIRIT OF THE TIME—THE SPIRIT OF COLOR AND LIGHT-HEARTEDNESS.

113 BOTTOM RIGHT THE GRAZIELLA'S WINNING CARD WAS ITS EXTRAORDINARY MANEUVERABILITY. HERE INGRID BENNING, A MODEL, SHOWS HOW EASY IT IS TO PUT IT IN ITS LARGE CARRYING BAG, ONCE THE FRAME IS FOLDED AND THE HANDLEBAR AND SADDLE ARE TAKEN OFF.

The threat to French-made products came not only from Campagnolo, but also from a group of accessory manufacturers including Ofmega and Magistroni (Officine Meccaniche Giostra), who made cranks, steering columns, and bottom brackets; Universal, who produced brakes; and Regina, whose chain and wheel Oro series competed with the French-made Sedis, then owned by Sram. Also worthy of mention is Cinelli, as well as Ambrosio, who manufactured handle bar attachments; and Nisi, who made wheels in competition with Mavic (a French manufacturer since 1926) and Super Champion.

In 1962, the French champion Anquetil, or "Master Jacques," changed teams three times in a row and rode the Tour de France finale on a Gitane bike fitted with Campagnolo parts. Louison Bobet also turned his loyalty to Campagnolo in 1956, forsaking Huret. This is not unremarkable, as Bobet's standing as a national champion had been enhanced, up to then, by his reputation for using only French products. But the fact that cyclists were opting for Italian-made products was unquestionable proof that they were better made. (They were less expensive, too.)

Meanwhile, the concept of a folding bicycle to be used for everyday activities was becoming increasingly popular and widespread, with the result that more city bicycles were manufactured. In actual fact, the concept of folding bikes had arisen in Great Britain in the late eighteenth century. More than a century later, during World War I, Italian soldiers had been equipped with bicycles that could be transported like backpacks and used to cross Alpine mule tracks. Manufacturing a folding yet resistant frame was a headache, but the problem was solved many years later in 1962 by Teodoro Carnielli, who produced the Graziella model. The winning formula of this bicycle was its incredible practicality. Its robust frame, which could be folded thanks to a central hinge and the absence of a horizontal rod, its small wheels, padded saddle and handle bar – both of which could be easily removed, and whose connecting frame tubes were slightly thicker to ensure resistance – meant that the bicycle could be easily transported, even in the passenger well of a motor car. The same year saw Alex Moulton, an English engineer who had worked on motor car suspensions, including those for the Mini, launch a bicycle fitted with 16-inch wheels and front and rear spring suspension. He believed that this new structure was capable of revolutionizing the bicycle market. His models were indeed widely distributed, but the revolution he foresaw never materialized.

In 1967, Campagnolo released the Nuovo Record gear shifter, which replaced the Record model launched in 1963. Its name had been around since the late 1950s and was inscribed on certain accessories such as the dual-multiplier crank. The Nuovo Record was not, in fact, substantially different in its function, but its body was made from aluminum rather than chromium bronze. Initially, the gear shifter was part of the Record group, which from 1969 onwards could be defined as complete, since the manufacturer had also begun to produce brake parts. The following years saw additional parts added to the range (derailleur, pedal cranks, wheel hubs, etc), but these differed from the Record parts chiefly in the material used to produce them rather than the way they worked. Steel and bronze were systematically replaced with aluminum, and in 1974 Campagnolo made a bottom bracket axle and the wheel hub rod from titanium. The crank, initially made from 151-milimeter turn bolts, was soon reduced to 144 millimeters, thus enabling the use of an internal 41-tooth ring, although the standard version soon became 42-tooth.

The 1960s and a large part of the 1970s were largely dominated by the Belgian Eddy Merckx. Nicknamed "the Cannibal" because of his great thirst for victory, he rode throughout his career as a professional cyclist on Gotha European bicycles, which were in the same league as Superia, a brand that had debuted alongside Peugeot, Masi, Marcel Van der Este, Colnago, and De Rosa. These experts followed on the tails of the best cyclist of modern times – he surpassed Fausto Coppi in the number of victories won – and answered each one of his stubborn requests for new and more inventive frames along the way. Merckx excelled in what can be considered cycling's golden age, given the extremely high number of very successful competitors on all fronts (a number that further underlines his prowess). To wit, the cyclists found lined up on at the starting tape in those years often included Felice Gimondi, Luis Ocaña, Roger De Vlaeminck, Freddy Maertens, and Francesco Moser.

The cycling elite showed just how strong and well-rounded Merckz was, and this can be seen in all kids of competitions: races divided into stages, direct races, and track events. Indeed, his victories included the three main races divided into stages: the Tour de France and the Giro d'Italia – both of which he won five times – as well as the Spanish Vuelta, which he won in 1973. Merckx won 426 victories all in all, and completed every major world cycling competition: he won the Flanders Tour twice, the Paris-Roubaix three times, the Lièges-Bastogne-Lièges five times, the Giro di Lombardia twice, and the Freccia Vallone three times, and also set the record at the Milano-San Remo race for the highest number of victories won by a cyclist in a direct race. He wore the rainbow jersey as world cycling champion three times and stripped Ole Ritter of the hour record in Mexico City in 1972 over a distance of 49,431 kilometers on a bike that was specially made by Ernesto Colnago, surpassing the Dane's record by 779 meters. Merckx's record only beaten in 1984, by Francesco Moser.

116 Eddy Merckx at an individual time trial ion Bordeaux, during the 2nd half of the 5th stage of the 1977 Tour. Now nearing the end of his career, the Cannibal finished the Grande Boucle in 6th place, 12 minutes behind Thevenet.

117 Felice Gimondi, wearing the rainbow jersey, on the slopes of the Mottarone in 1973. The Champion from Bergamo is rode a Campagnolo-equipped Bianchi, the brand he was always associated with.

118 Three breakaways set
the pace at the Stelvio
Pass on Coppi, during the
1975 Giro d'Italia. In that
edition the pink race ended
right on the peak of the
mountain, without
continuing to the
traditional finish line
in Milan.

118-119 A group of
cyclists tackles the
hairpin turns on the
Trentin side of the Stelvio
Pass during the last stage
of the 1975 Giro d'Italia,
which started in Alleghe.
Though the race began
on June 7, the cyclists
still had to pedal between
walls of snow.

BETWEEN CRISIS AND INNOVATION

In the early 1970s, the cycling world experienced a new boom. The greatest growth was felt especially in the United States, and some have sought to link it to the oil crisis triggered by the Arab-Israeli conflict. In fact, it was much more likely due to an unexpected demographic shift – the coming of age of baby boomers' children – and to a growing awareness of pollution, global warming and city traffic. Of course, the shortage and cost of fossil fuels only helped in winning new converts – and drawing old fans back – to cycling as a viable method of transportation, and not just a sport.

By 1970, French and Italian manufacturers had established themselves on the global market. Simplex and Huret had increased their production thanks to the Prestige (Simplex) and Allvit and Jubilee (Huret) models.

Campagnolo was not far behind with its Super Record, the smaller Valentino models, and the recently launched Gran Turismo, and was becoming increasingly dominant, not only in the competitive arena but also in the field of gear shifters for touring and city bikes. At the beginning of the decade, the giants of French manufacturing – Motobecane, Peugeot and Gitane (the latter two supported the best British cyclist of the time, Tom Simpson) – were competing for the upper hand in the world market.

Their advances in transalpine products were achieved in the face of medium-range products targeted for export, especially to the US, and by means of favorable taxation on French merchandise headed overseas.

In 1970, Cinelli patented the M71, the first quick-release pedal in history. And so began the long evolution of a bicycle part that would radically alter the way bikes were pedaled to become an essential, irreplaceable component on professional and amateur vehicles. The new design, which was more efficient and a lot safer than toe-strap pedals, simplified the process of taking one's foot off the pedal and placing it on the ground if necessary.

A metallic plate was fitted to the sole of one's shoe to connect up perfectly with the pedal. The M71 model, which was reissued in 1972, was not as widely distributed as its Italian manufacturer would have liked, and it was not until the 1980s that this bicycle part actually saw global sales. (Until 1976, Italian bicycle manufacturers struggled with limited exports, the oil crisis, and production problems related to unsupportable raw material import costs.)

120-121 THE ATTEMPT TO MOTORIZE A GAS PUMP CONNECTING IT TO A BYCICLE WAS A NATURAL BYPRODUCT OF THE SEARCH TO FIND ALTERNATIVE TRANSPORTATION SOLUTIONS DURING THE 1970S, WHEN FUEL RATIONING BECAME A REALITY IN MANY PARTS OF THE WORLD.

121 TOP THE OIL CRISES OF THE 1970'S FORCED ITALY'S GOVERNMENT TO IMPOSE A PERIOD OF OBLIGATORY ENERGY SAVING KNOWN AS AUSTERITY, DURING WHICH THE USE OF PRIVATE MOTOR VEHICLES WAS FORBIDDEN ON CERTAIN DAYS, SUCH AS CAR-FREE SUNDAYS. NO WONDER THAT, IN ADDITION TO RESORTING TO PUBLIC TRANSIT, MILLIONS REDISCOVERED THE PREVIOUSLY ABANDONED BICYCLE.

In 1971, the bicycle boom reached the United States. Certain Italian and French manufacturers became so tired of trying to meet ever increasing demands that they inevitably gave in to local industries. Others who benefited were companies in nations with state-run economies, as well as those in developing countries which, for environmental or political reasons, were able to muster competitive strengths that outshone Italian and French counterparts.

It was this climate that Maeda, SunTour and Shimano exploited to the maximum to impose their products. In 1964, for example, SunTour produced the Gran Prix, its first inclined parallelogram gear shifter, a technique which is still used today.

In 1966 it launched its first derailleur, the "Spirit." Shimano opened a plant in New York in 1965 and in partnership with Schwinn products set out to conquer the American market with its Sky-lark gear shifter. To the annoyance of European competitors, Japanese manufacturers focused their activities on producing low-cost models and developing a better quality-cost ratio than their rivals Huret's Allvit and Svelto, Simplex's Prestige, and Campagnolo's Valentino.

Another winning formula was the marriage of a fully compatible Japanese gear shifter with the cost-effective Alpine touring bike model then fashionable in the US. It relied on 52- and 40-tooth cogs and a five-speed free wheel with pinions on a 14-, 17-, 20-, 24- and 28-tooth scale. (European gear shifters were better suited to racing.)

Even though French and Italian producers felt the sting of Japanese competition in the United States market, the battle in Europe was fought between France and Italy alone.

The most successful Italian manufacturers at that time were the founders of the Bianchi family, with the Chiorda and Atala brands, the Gios family from Turin, the Wilier family from Trieste, and rising stars Masi, Colnago, and De Rosa.

The latter three established themselves by riding the wave of the Merckx legacy. Of course, the tradition of making bicycles to suit the needs and whims of professional patrons and promoters did not end in the 1970s; on the contrary, it blossomed as talented industrial designers inspired by such impressive champions as Gianbattista Baronchelli, Franco Bitossi, Michele Dancelli, Rik Van Looy, Gastone Nencini, and Moreno Argentin drove production in new directions.

122 BOTTOM LEFT GATHERED ON THE STONY GROUND OF MONT VENTOUX, A FORMIDABLE PEAK KNOWN AS THE GIANT OF PROVENCE, SPECTATORS AT THE 11TH STAGE OF THE 1972 TOUR ENCOURAGE CYCLISTS AS THEY TACKLE THE ASCENT.

122-123 THE FRENCHMAN CHARLY GROSSKOST SPRINTS DURING A TIME TRIAL IN THE 11TH STAGE OF THE 1970 TOUR DE FRANCE. (LATER FORCED TO WITHDRAW FROM THE GRANDE BOUCLE, HE NEVER MADE IT TO PARIS.)

123 TOP LEFT THE CYCLO-CROSS USUALLY TAKES PLACE BETWEEN NOVEMBER AND FEBRUARY, HELPING ROAD RACERS IMPROVE THEIR RIDING ABILITY.

123 TOP RIGHT GROSSKOST IN DIVONNE-LES-BAINS DURING AN INDIVIDUAL TIME TRIAL AT THE 11TH STAGE OF THE 1970 TOUR.

In France, Bernard Thevenet won the Tour de France in 1975 and 1977 (against champion rivals such as Luis Ocaña of Spain and Lucien Van Impe of Belgium) on a Peugeot PX010 bike fitted with Reynolds 531 series tubes and transalpine accessories. As for the parts, the crank was still made by Stronglight and the gear shifter by Simplex (the Super LJ model, the first ever to be made from delrin).

It had Super Champion wheels, Maillard wheel hubs, Mafac brakes, and an Ideale saddle. This model was one of the most popular among professional cyclists, who respected its trustworthiness, but it was also a favorite among amateurs and aspiring racers thanks to its modest price and ample distribution network.

Riding the crest of the wave alongside Peugeot was Gitane, which had made its name known to the public by manufacturing Jacques Anquetil's bikes for his three Tour de France victories between 1962 and 1965. Both producers tried to keep the cost of the bicycles down and extend their distribution network and played a successful role in the global market. Unlike other European manufacturers, they also capitalized on the cycling boom taking place in the United States in the early 1970s and asserted themselves in the collective thought of American cyclists as producers of reliable, light-weight vehicles. It was not only "Master Jacques" who had a Gitane bike: 1976 also brought victory to the Belgian Van Impe in the Grande Boucle race. Van Impe, a great climber, shared the title of "king of the mountains" for many years with Federico Bahamontes of Spain, who was known as "l'Aquila di Toledo." (The latter had worn the yellow jersey in 1959 on a Coppi bike.)

Despite all this, the story of the bicycle remained rooted in Europe – even as the competition grew more ruthless. For one thing, the Japanese cycling industry still chipped away at its old monopoly and successfully broke into the US market. For another, the success of products in the US that were stamped "made in Europe" made the hard times of the late 1970s even harder.

In 1974, Teledyne launched the first large-scale titanium frame production line. Speedwell, based in Great Britain, had already experimented with titanium in cycling in the 1960s. Frames were soldered by the Italian company Lamborghini, but so few parts were manufactured that it was essentially a small-scale, private operation.

The following year Gary Klein made aluminum frames that were soldered and thermically treated and displayed at the New York International Exhibition. This young American began studying aluminum alloys in 1973 using the results of an experiment that led to the manufacture of a prototype developed at MIT (Boston) by Shawn Buckley, along with his students Marc Rosenbaum, Mark Tanquary, and Stan Stone. The same year, Exxon Graftek designed the first frame made of carbon-fiber tubes linked together with steel joints. Although there were still problems relating to structural resistance, this model paved the way for composite-fiber manufacturing throughout the world.

Thanks to the rich variety of products in America and the farsightedness of certain key players, these three innovative materials – titanium, aluminum, and carbn-fiber – entered production in the cyapce of just two years, increasing the possibilities for every frame-maker. But it was a different phenomenon altogether which would soon revolutionize the cycling world.

124 GIMONDI WON THE RAINBOW ROAD TITLE IN 1973 ON A CAMPAGNOLO-FITTED BIANCHI. FREDDY MAERTENS CAME IN SECOND, ON A DURA-ACE VEHICLE, THUS SECURING THE JAPANESE COMPANY'S REPUTATION AS A WINNING BRAND.

124-125 THE FRENCHMAN BERNARD LABOURDETTE (TEAM BIC) CROSSING THE FINISH LINE WITH HIS ARMS RAISED, IN THE POURING RAIN WHICH-PLAGUED LUCHON-GOURETTE, A SEMI-STAGE OF THE 1971 TOUR.

125 BOTTOM LEFT A SMALL CAGE OVER THE PEDALS RENDERED PEDALING MORE EFFICIENT BY GLUING A CYCLIST TO HIS BIKE. IN THE CASE OF A FALL, HOWEVER, IT WAS HARD TO FREE ONE'S FEET QUICKLY AND REGAIN BALANCE.

125 BOTTOM RIGHT RACERS AT EASE BEFORE THE START OF THE 20TH STAGE OF THE 1970 TOUR.

MADE IN THE USA: AN AMERICAN REVOLUTION

FROM THE STING-RAY TO THE BMX

Between 1963 and 1975 the American bicycle market was stormed by a phenomenon which initially affected youngsters and later had worldwide effects: the introduction of new production possibilities which allowed for innovation, and the secondary wave of activity set off by manufacturers who understood the profits to be made from them.

There was also the process of democratization. Take, for example, the popularity of the innovative Sting-Ray model, first manufactured by Schwinn in 1963. Its arrival on the market clearly signaled that the bicycle had become an icon of its time; and it took a world that had become fed up with racing bike purists by storm.

The original idea for the Sting-Ray, as was often the case in those days, originated on the streets. In the early 1960s, the great manufacturers of motorized vehicles were offering personalized machines: sports cars, known as "muscle cars", with powerful V8 engines and firm suspension; not to mention Harley Davidson-style motorbikes.

Young people living on the West coast of the United States were inspired by this movement and began to personalize their own bikes based on motor vehicles. The most commonly used parts were Easy Rider-style handlebars, known as ape hangers, and long, banana-shaped saddles in the shape of sissy bars, which derived from motor vehicles and could also serve as a small carrier.

In 1962 the young engineer Al Fritz, who had worked for Schwinn, heard about this very Californian trend through a friend. He was curious to learn more about it, and decided to observe it first-hand. Inspired by what he had saw on his travels up and down the West Coast, he envisaged a new bicycle modeled on the creations he had seen and then presented them to manufacturers.

Fritz's project centered on a model which favored personalizing almost all aspects of the bike, leaving youngsters the freedom to design their own two wheels as adults had done with motorcars and motorbikes.

The idea went down well with the bosses at the Chicago-based manufacturer, which caught on to its enormous potential for profit and so decided to begin manufacturing the model. Its name – the fruit of a search for something striking – is of course borrowed from the flat, triangular-shaped (and deadly) fish.

The first models to appear were the J-38, which was launched in 1963 and was received with mixed opinion. Adults found its appearance less than fashionable and were sure that is was destined to be unsuccessful.

Meanwhile, youngsters approved of the new aesthetic. They were especially enthused by the endless possibilities of personalizing it,

which in turn opened the door to further imaginative design ideas and a rush to answer unforeseen individual riding needs. The Sting-Ray sold 40,000 copies in its first year, after which stocks ran out. Far greater sales had been anticipated by its manufacturer by then, but its distribution was impeded due to a shortage of parts: Schwinn simply could not meet public demand. (The first parts to run out were the 20 inch tires.)

Its characteristic high resistance, reliability, and an ability to absorb shocks from jumps led the Sting-Ray to dominate the American market for more than a decade. Each year new colors were introduced. In 1964 a model for women known as the Fair Lady was released, covered in flowers and painted pastel. Its handlebar was fitted with a basket. Quaint as it might sound today, the version soon became just as popular as the first.

The most commonly sold Sting-Ray models were those in the Krate series. The first model was launched in 1968 and, given its in-

Photographed at 20th Century Fox Studios

22

127 BORN IN THE 60'S, THE BMX ALTERED
THE CYCLING WORLD FOREVER BY INJECTING A
FRESH BREEZE OF JUVENILE RECKLESSNESS
INTO THE SLIGHTLY STILTED ENVIRONMENT OF
PURISTS AND PROFESSIONALS—AND
REORIENTING THE RETAIL INDUSTRY TO A
YOUNGER, HIPPER MARKET.

128-129 SCHWINN'S BEST-SELLING STING-RAY
MODELS BELONGED TO ITS KRATE SERIES.
LAUNCHED ON THE AMERICAN MARKET IN 1968,
THEY WERE SOON IMMENSELY POPULAR.

129 TOP THE STING-RAY WAS THE BRAINCHILD
OF AL FRITZ, DESIGNER OF THE SCHWINN, WHO,
AFTER NOTING HOW CALIFORNIAN YOUTHS OF
THE 1960S CUSTOMIZED AND DECORATED THEIR
BIKES, ALTERED HIS OWN DESIGNS ACCORDINGLY.

novative design, proved extremely popular; so much so that seventy percent of all bikes sold that year in American were Krate Sting-Rays or similar competitor models. In only two years, sales reached the one million threshold, and it soon attained cult status. The Krate was different from earlier Sting-Ray models in that its wheels were asym-

metrical; that is, the front wheel measured 16 inches and the rear 20. It comprised a Springer fork, and the rear shock-absorbers were integrated into the sissy bars. Its gear shifter lever, known as a Stik-Shift, was placed on the horizontal tube, which moved the five-speed Huret, Shimano and SunTour gears, the first products by Shimano and SunTour to be sold in the US.

The success of the Krate model drove Schwinn to market a tandem version known as the Sting-Ray Mini-Twinn, which had two integrated gears and was almost identical to the single-seat model, apart from the size of the front wheel, which at sixteen inches was larger, and there was no spring-loaded fork.

Krate's success began to diminish in 1974, when a national committee inspecting the conformity of commercial products imposed a ban on the Stik-Shift lever, practically invalidating one of the most typical features of this model.

Classic models, however, continued to remain popular with enthusiasts and collectors. Krate series models, particularly the rare Orange Krate, Apple Krate, Pea Picker and Grey Ghost models (all produced only in 1971), attained cult status and appeared in specialist magazines.

A new market for such pre-used bikes, hidden away in basements and second-hand shops, was now born as cherished models went on sale for thousands of dollars.

Sting-Rays were not simply a passing trend, however. BMX competitions were becoming increasingly popular – especially with the Bicycle Motocross – and this ensured that the bicycle would survive.

As the races became increasingly demanding, the strain on every individual bicycle part made it necessary for manufacturers to give each one attention.

Bikes improved in quality, but there was a side-effect: they also became more standardized, and there were fewer opportunities to customize them.

130 top The "Grey Ghost," which appeared in 1971, is one of the most sought-after models by collectors of such vehicles. Cultish devotion to certain bicycles can drive the price above $2,000 in certain markets.

130 bottom The Sting-Ray was characterized by bright colors and by snazzy components such as "ape hanger" handlebars, banana-shaped saddle with "sissy bars," and front springer fork.

131 TOP KRATES WERE
VALUED FOR THE ENDLESS
PERSONALIZATION
POSSIBILITIES THEY PROVIDED,
AND FOR THE ARRAY OF
AVAILABLE ACCESSORIES THAT
MADE CUSTOMIZATION A
WHOLE WORLD OF ITS OWN.

131 BOTTOM THE SCHWINN
STING-RAY WAS
CHARACTERIZED BY ITS
"EMBOSSED" CANTILEVER
FRAME, AND BY ITS SINGLE-
PIVOT SIDE-PULL CALIPER
BRAKES (THOUGH SOME
MODELS HAVE DUAL-PIVOT
CALIPER BRAKES ON THE REAR
WHEEL).

The BMX was officially born on 10 July 1969 when a group of teens from Palms Parks, near Los Angeles, tried to copy their motocross heroes using bikes in a race along a road with tight corners and many bumps. The idea was so popular that dirt-track races were soon being organized regularly, giving rise to what was known as the "pedal cross" race. The following year, races took place in nearby Long Beach, where the thirteen-year-old Scott Breithaupt, considered by many to be the real father of this sport, made his mark. He was soon organizing races that revealed the true scope of possibilities for this new kind of cycling.

Bruce Brown's documentary *On Any Sunday*, which hit American movie theaters in 1971 with scenes of young men on Sting-Rays emulating motocross champions, and starred Steve McQueen, lit the spark for cycling races across the entire West Coast. In 1973, the National Bicycle Association was founded. Its role was to supervise the organizing of races, which reached a peak in 1974. In the meantime, the sport became definitively known as BMX racing.

Unlike previous models, bicycle frame structures changed drastically, becoming more compact so that they could enable cyclists to get out of trouble quickly. Handlebars and saddles were modified to do away with their chopper effect, and accessories especially made for use with motocross models were introduced. Bicycle wheels still measured 20 inches, but they were fitted with firmer, thicker rubber. Meanwhile, certain brands undertook to rationalize spring-loaded rear shock absorbers fitted to Krate models. These innovations paved the way for the mountain bike. Manufacturers continually sought to find the perfect balance between robustness, a capacity to resist knocks and good handling.

BMX racing, which had successfully combined enjoyment with athletic exertion, reached its peak in 1974. With larger segments of the public becoming interested, Bicycle Motocross News, a magazine, was launched. The NBA organized the first national BMX competition in Los Angeles the same year. The Japanese manufacturer Yamaha, which had recently released a BMX "moto bike," sponsored the event and spent $100,000 in prize money and glittering promotions.

BMX racing became so popular among young Americans that even the cult magazine "Sports Illustrated" – the most widely read American sports publication – took an interest in motocross bike competitions and began to serve as a sounding board for this increasingly common sport. Riding this wave of popularity, the National Bicycle League (NBl) was formed in Florida and soon came to represent the movement in the eastern parts of the United States.

Bike manufacturers, smelling success, all added BMX models to their catalogs. Additional companies, Kawasaki and Suzuki included, drew on years of experience in motor-powered models to manufacture bicycles.

European motocross riders who had traveled to the United States to train discovered the BMX and took the phenomenon back to Europe, thus opening up a new market for American producers. Before long, European manufacturers such as Moto became were churning out their own models in an effort to compete with imports. (As early as 1968, the British manufacturer Raleigh had understood the importance of this new movement and begun production of its "Chopper" model.

The Chopper had a particularly angular frame, an ape hanger handlebar, a banana-shaped sissy bar saddle, a Sturmey-Archer hub, and five integrated gears.)

In 1976 Bob Osbourne launched the magazine *Bicycle Motocross Action*, which soon became a bible for the BMX movement and kept its cult status for more than thirty years. One year later, yet another organization, the American Bicycle Association, was set up – the first to have a truly national scope.

132 THE BMX TOOK THE LIMELIGHT AFTER APPEARING IN SEVERAL POPULAR MOVIES, INCLUDING A 1971 DOCUMENTARY STARRING STEVE MCQUEEN, "ON ANY SUNDAY," AND STEPHEN SPIELBERG'S WILDLY POPULAR 1982 FLICK "E.T."

133 THE SCHWINN HORNET WAS INSPIRED BY THE MOTOR VEHICLES USED AT MOTO-CROSS COMPETITIONS. THIS MODEL WAS CHARACTERIZED BY ITS FAKE TANK, LONG SADDLE, AND THE NUMBER PLATE ON THE HANDLEBAR.

Meanwhile, bicycles themselves evolved to meet new performance demands, and became even more agile and aggressive, designwise. In 1984 Vanderspeck organized the first BMX contest on a halfpipe – a ramp shaped like a half-tube which had been used up until that point only by skateboarders. He also joined forces manufacturers like including Skyway and Boss to improve and rationalize freestyle BMX riding, and in doing so altered the structure of the bike frames and sections of tubes to ensure greater support during athletic maneuvers. The early 1990s were a time of stagnation for the BMX movement. True, it was officially recognized by the International

In the late 1970s and early 1980s, some professional cyclists began looking for new ideas and started to use their bikes for acrobatics. Initially, this new form of cycling led to technical improvements in racing, but the use of ramps – known as quarterpipes or simply quarters – for cycling almost instantaneously opened the door for a new kind of bike rider; one who relied on aerial maneuvers and force. The Californian Bob Haro was one of the first pioneers to make a substantial contribution to this new discipline. But he soon abandoned the sport to dedicate himself entirely to freestyle and also began to manufacture specialized frames for that sport.

The 1980s saw the spread of BMX and freestyle cycling to the rest of the world. In 1982, the International Bicycle Motocross Federation was organized, and the first freestyle world championship was held in Dayton, Ohio the same year.

Soon other races and championships sprang up, and competitors everywhere used their skills and mastery of the form to stupefy spectators in as many new ways as possible. In 1983, freestyle acquired its own federation – the American Freestyle Association – which oversaw two separate disciplines: quarterpipe and flatland. The latter was carried out without ramps and involved carrying out acrobatic yet somewhat static maneuvers that nonetheless require incredible balance. A leading flatland exponent was Dave Vanderspek, who founded the Curb Dogs bikers and skaters group (also known as "Vander, Radner, and the Flying Dutchnman"). He invented the historic Vander Roll, a forward somersault. And so began a new era of experimentation involving dynamic yet static maneuvers and balancing acts.

Cycling Union (UCI), which used its institutional status to represent the sport. But a very real challenge remained: ensuring extreme technical ability and dealing with the arrival of the mountain bike, which was not only more interesting and simple for the general public to use, but also – even more important – more profitable for manufacturers to produce.

During this period of change, it was, not surprisingly, almost solely the diehard enthusiasts who soldiered on with their work, pushing technical boundaries to higher levels and widening possibilities for the bicycle.

136 TOP DAVE MIRRA AFTER HIS DISASTROUS CRASH AT THE 2003 GRAVITY GAMES. THE
ACROBATIC STUNTS CARRIED OUT DURING FREESTYLE COMPETITIONS DEMAND UNNERVING RISKS, AND
PUSH CYCLISTS TO SUCH LIMITS THAT THE SMALLEST MISTAKE CAN BE FATAL.

136 BOTTOM A TRICK SEQUENCE IN PROGRESS AT THE 2006 DEW ACTION SPORT TOUR. THANKS
TO THE COURAGE AND CREATIVITY OF FREESTYLE RIDERS THROUGHOUT THE FIELD, STUNTS HAVE
BECOME INCREASINGLY IMPRESSIVE.

136-137 DAVE MIRRA UNDERTAKES A BACKFLIP-TAILWHIP AT THE 2005 X-GAMES IN LOS ANGELES.
THE USE OF BMX'S FOR FREESTYLE RIDING CAME OF AGE IN THE 1970S.

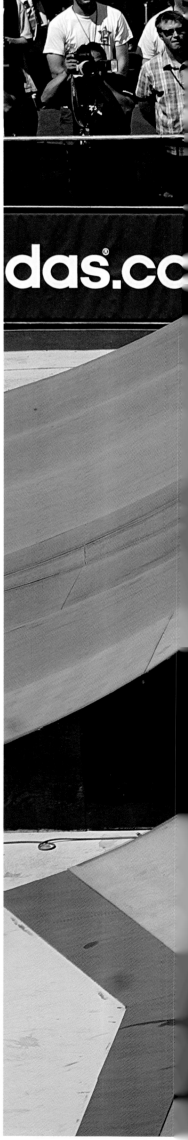

138 DAVE MIRRA ACCOMPLISHES WONDERS AT THE X-GAMES OF SAN FRANCISCO IN 1999. THE BIKER FROM
SYRACUSE IS THE UNDISPUTED DOMINATOR OF THE EXTREME SPORTS OLYMPICS IN THE 90'S AND THE 2000, BEING ABLE TO BOAST
OF THE VICTORY OF OVER 20 MEDALS (15 OF WHICH GOLD).

139 TOP LEFT DAVE MIRRA FLIES—LITERALLY—FOR THE GOLD AT THE 1999 X-GAMES IN SAN FRANCISCO. HIS VICTORY EARNED HIM THE
"FREESTYLER OF THE YEAR" AWARD.

139 TOP RIGHT DAVE MIRRA AT THE X-GAMES OF SAN FRANCISCO IN 1999. MIRRA'S FEATS MADE HIM ONE OF THE MOST FAMOUS RIDERS OF
THE 1990S.

139 BOTTOM LEFT DAVE MIRRA AT THE 1999 X-GAMES, WHEN HE TOOK 91.90 POINTS IN THE FINAL THREE ROUNDS, AND SUCCESSFULLY
COMPLETED HIS SIGNATURE "SPINNING FLAIR" TRICK.

139 BOTTOM RIGHT DAVE MIRRA ON THE HALF-PIPE AT THE 1999 X-GAMES. THE USE OF THIS RAMP WAS INTRODUCED TO THE BMX WORLD BY
DAVE VANDERSPEK AND HIS TEAM, THE CURB DOGS, IN 1984.

THE CLUNKERS AND
THE MOUNTAIN BIKE

The origins of the mountain bike can be traced back to the first thirty years of the twentieth century. In 1915, Bianchi manufactured a folding bicycle for the Italian Army which had high telescopic rafts, a spring-loaded rear fork, and wide-section tires. In 1933, Ignaz Schwinn began producing and selling an incredibly robust bicycle called the Schwinn Excelsior in the United States.

Thanks to its famed indestructibility, it soon became popular with paper boys. Improvements were made to the model in 1938 with the Chicago-based company's introduction of a front brake box, a cantilever frame –henceforth used on other models, including the cruiser – and a spring fork. All these components led the Excelsior to be viewed as the "grandfather" of the mountain bike.

Was there a specific date when simple off-roading officially became known as mountain-biking? It is hard to say for sure, but the evolution reached a visible plateau in California in the late 1970s, when the Canyon Gang, a group of youngsters from Marin County, organized downhill dirt-track races that later became the rage across the country.

Once more, the Schwinn Excelsior proved to be the only bike that was sufficiently robust to withstand the demands placed on it by this use. In contrast, the Varsity model – also manufactured by Schwinn – could not stand the stress caused by the sudden jolts. Gary Fisher, a leading figure in this sport, described these first bikes as "BMXs for grown-up kids," since they combined elements of the cruiser with the light components typical of road bikes to make for a robust model that could be fully customized and used for off-roading. Many people preferred the "ballooner," whose name derives from its wide-section wheels, or "clunkers," a faux-offensive moniker for ugly, retro bikes.

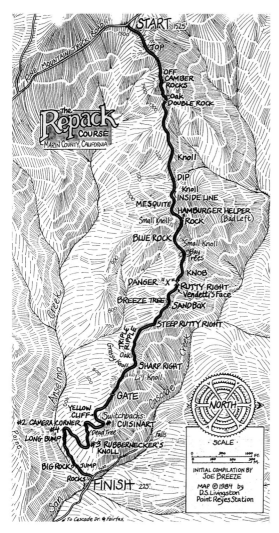

Legend has it that the mountain bike "Big Bang" happened on one of the many fire fighting roads in the Californian hills, where the summer heat is such sweat barely has time to drip down the face before it evaporates. In this climate, the Canyon Gang kids used bikes with coaster brakes requiring a large quantity of lubricating grease to ensure smooth running.

It was this constant need to replenish the grease that had been burnt up on down-hill stretches that gave its name – "Repack," for repackaging the grease burnt up by braking – to the first real mountain bike competition in history.

In October 1976, the first "Repack" was organized by the Marin County Velo Club Tamalpais, on winding roads leading from the peak of Mount Tamalpais (800 m) and crossing the canyon that ends in the town of Fairfax.

The race was only 1,800 meters long, but 400 meters of this was made up of steep terrain. In five minutes and twelve seconds, Alan Bonds became the winner of the first race.

As the dust clouds settled, it became apparent that he was one of only ten competitors to complete the race without falling off or damaging his bicycle.

"Repack" was not only the first race of its kind, but also sparked a series of experiments that helped transform the first rough and ready mountain bike models into an increasingly evolved and sophisticated machine.

The bicycle Bonds used to win his first race was made by the same Californian, using a Schwinn Excelsior frame. The main difficulty lay in adapting it to modern parts. Indeed, agile and pain-staking manual labor was necessary to alter the hub fixtures to make them compatible with integrated-box brakes but not upset the assignment of the various tubes.

Bonds chose to use reinforcement supports for the fork with the aim of preventing them from giving way during jolting downhill stretches. He used an adaptor kit to fit the new crank to the bottom bracket. Finally, he used a quick-release collar to lower the saddle during downhill stretches, thus enabling better control while also preventing the saddle from collapsing.

Over the next few years, new bikers traced their own paths through the Californian hills, and competitions became increasingly popular. At the same time, improvements in steering techniques and balance meant that race times fell and speeds rose.

Setting or beating a record became harder, and races, at first primarily entertaining, became more seriously competitive. Up to 1984, the record was held by Gary Fisher at 4:22. The fastest woman was Wendy Cragg – "Queen of Clunkers" – who completed the race in 5:27.

In the meantime, other bicycles were evolving, too. In 1974, Russ Mahon fitted a gear shifter to his Schwinn bike, and in 1977 Craig Mitchell brought out an innovative model using a Schwinn Excelsior frame. This new model comprised a SunTour Cyclone shifter and command lever, an aluminum crank made by TA Specialités, a Brooks B-72 saddle and Schwinn Uniroyal rubber tires. Joe Breeze, who won ten out of twenty-four Repack competitions, was the first radically to overhaul this type of bicycle. In response to a specific request by Charles Kelly in October 1977, Breeze made a specially structured frame without adjusting any previous models and using chrome or molybdenum 4130 aeronautic steel, a material that was typical of racing models.

The components were all superior in quality and included a fork manufactured by Red Line for 6-inch BMXs, a SunTour gear shifter, and a derailleur with handlebar controls, Weinmann cantilever brakes activated by Magura motor-inspired levers, and 26-inch Schwinn S2 wheels coupled with hubs especially made by Phil Wood using Uniroyal plugged rubber. Joe Breeze won the "Repack" using this model the same year. This bike was bound to be successful, and many versions were made, one of which is still on display at the Oakland Museum.

In sum, mountain bikes were manufactured using advanced techniques and components and put together with the same care used to make road bikes. This helped to dispel the remaining prejudices surrounding them. Indeed, it soon became hard to talk disdainfully about "ballooners" and "clunkers," since the mountain bike

was manufactured using the same techniques applied to racing bikes – and was even lighter, weighing ten kilograms less.

It was not only competition that helped to develop the BMX; the simple pleasure of adventure played its part too, as in the establishment of the Colorado marathon, which ran from Crested Butte to Aspen. The long journey encompassed virtually impassable roads, and culminated with a climb to Pearl Pass (3,800 m). Thanks to the adventuresome nature of the organizers (as to the competitive spirit of Repack's founders, more and more people took an interest in the BMX, and more and more customized bikes took to the roads.

A chronic shortage of fittings for these vehicles slowed large-scale production at first, but by 1979 companies were manufacturing replacement parts for mountain bikes. That same year, Joe Breeze (winner of the 1976 Repack) and Otis Guy (holder of the third fastest speed), introduced themselves to Tom Ritchey, who was building a tandem which these two young Americans would use to travel across the American continent in the search for a new record. Breeze took with him the bicycle he had manufactured in 1977 to show the Californian producer. Ritchey was impressed with the quality of the work and immediately understood the mountain bike's potential for advanced development. Gary Fisher, who had decided not to buy a bike made by Breeze, got wind of Ritchey's interest and suggested that he would manufacture two frames: one for himself to be used in the Repack (which he went on to win in 1979) and a second one that could be sold. In the next few years Ritchey produced new models which did not sell well with buyers from Palo Alto, and so he

142 THE 1981 INTRODUCTION OF THE STUMPJUMPER, BY MIKE SANYARD'S SPECIALIZED BICYCLE COMPONENTS, OPENED THE DOORS TO THE LARGE-SCALE PRODUCTION OF MOUNTAIN BIKES. BUILT IN JAPAN, ITS RETAIL PRICE WAS 750 DOLLARS.

142-143 JOE BREEZE REVOLUTIONIZED THE WORLD OF CLUNKERS AND BALLOONERS WHEN, IN 1977, HE DESIGNED AND THEN CREATED A FRAME WITH COMPLETELY NEW PROPORTIONS; THAT IS, WITHOUT MODIFYING AN ALREADY EXISTING MODEL.

went to see Fisher to ask him to sell them in Marin County. Fisher teamed up with Charles Kenny; they invested around $2,000 to set up a company called MountainBikes. (After Kelly's departure in 1983, it was renamed Gary Fisher Bicycles.) This was the first real mountain bike business, and it opened the door to a market which at that time was completely undiscovered. Few parts were manufactured *en masse*, and were accordingly expensive, but before long Mike Sinyard's new California company, Specialized Bicycle Components, was paving the way for large-scale production. In 1981 this company began manufacturing its Stumpjumper mountain bike, with a frame designed by Tim Neenan of Lighthouse Bikes and manufactured in Japan to maximize the quantity produced and keep costs down. Steel tubing made by Touring was initially used for the joints, but in later models, joints were TIG-soldered. One of the defining characteristics of this bike is its "golf club" handlebars, a modified version of those normally used on BMXs. The original curve on the first Stumpjumper models derived from Magura's motocross bike, with brake levers borrowed from motorcycling models and produced by Tommaselli. The Racer model was initially designed to be fitted to

light touring bikes. The plated-aluminum Cyclotourist crank was made by TA Specialités and imported from France. It was lightweight, which enabled it to be used with short gears, a necessity for tackling difficult off-road conditions. Unfortunately, since this design was specifically targeted for off-road use, the Cyclotourist often broke down. The three-crown crank was linked to a Suntour Arx GT five-speed gear shifter and derailleur. The covers were particularly interesting: Specialized designed a light off-road model with specific fittings for the tires on this mountain bike, putting its experience in tire manufacture to good use. In 1978 it became the first company to manufacture folding covers.

The Stumpjumper, which has been on display at the Smithsonian Institution in Washington since 1990, became *the* standard bearer for future manufacturers and opened the door to new models such as Ben Lawee's Univega, which introduced the Alpine Sport model in the 1980s, around the time that sales of mountain bikes in the United States began to rise exponentially (they overtook road bike sales in 1986). It was the beginning of an increase that would culminate in global market dominance.

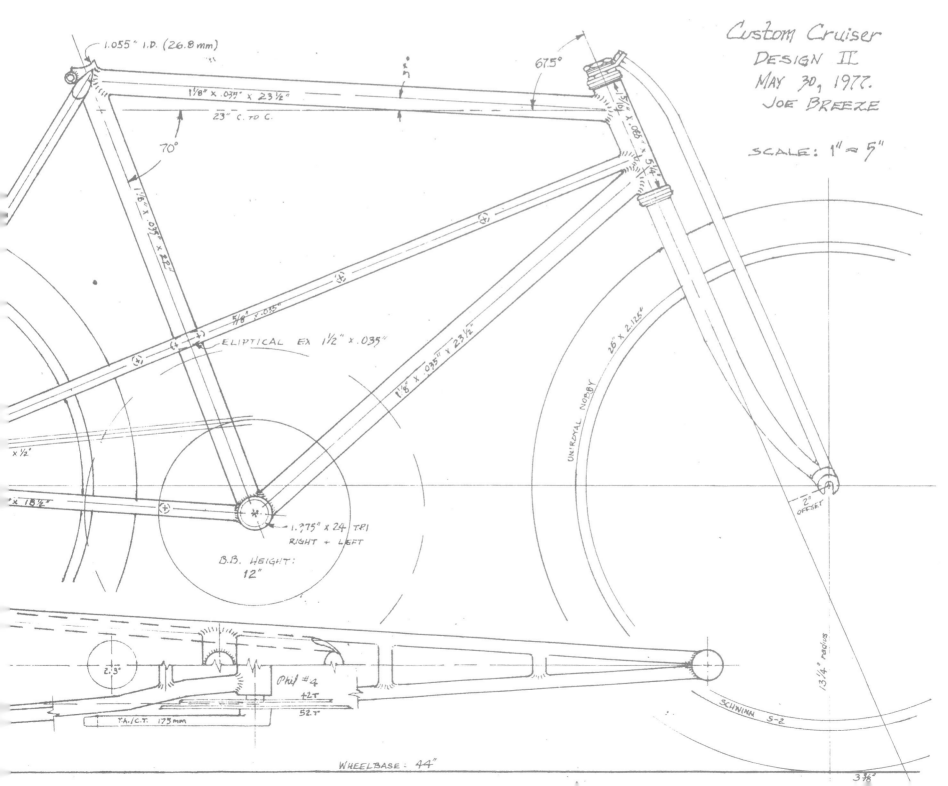

TWENTY YEARS
OF TURMOIL

SHIMANO TO THE CONQUEST OF EUROPE

Shimano had conquered the upturn in the United States in the late 1960s when Schwinn launched the Krate model by using cold-forging techniques, which made improved and fashionably designed products possible. But it was not until the early 1970s, in the wake of the astronomical cycling boom, that this Japanese company became a household name outside the United States, most significantly Europe. Its products saturated the markets and became standard-bearers in just twenty years.

Shimano opened a branch in New York in 1965 and put on an exhibition at the Milan International Exhibition, tackling the European market for the first time in its forty-year operation. Its arrival in Europe was celebrated in 1972 when Shimano Europe was officially opened in Düsseldorf. Milremo became the European distributor for SunTour products the same year, allowing products manufactured in Asia to be imported into Europe.

The following year Shimano opened its first plant outside Japan, in Singapore, and launched the first version of its successful Dura-Ace series into the world market. It was the beginning of a long, successful history for a product which is still considered one of the company's most trustworthy.

145 The mountain bike established itself globally from 1985-1995, as the evolving geometry of its frames (and the introduction of increasingly sophisticated components such as suspensions and disc brakes) increasingly differentiated it from road bikes.

146 and 147 From 1973 on, Dura-Ace occupied the top spot, sales-wise, of the Japanese brand Shimano. At its Tour debut, Flanders bikes equipped with Dura-Ace components took two stages, thanks to Walter Grodefroot.

Gear shifters also appeared in the standard kit (the usual proof of a brand's technical reliability), and the crank offered a twin-option crown (39-52 and 45-54).

There was a gear shifter known as "Crane", a compass-derailleur and compass-brakes, which in terms of efficiency were a serious competitor for Campagnolo's Super Record models. It was also possible to choose between three types of pinion casing: two five-speed gears, with racing or touring teeth, and one six-speed set aimed specifically at competitors. The kit also included two types of hub: traditional or extended flange. Each part had clearly been cold-forged to ensure utmost resistance and precision, and the products boasted an authentic hand-made quality.

The Dura-Ace was clearly a high-quality product, but cyclists preferred turning to French and Italian manufacturers for high-quality products – mostly by tradition: they had always been better. Shimano now came to realize that competing merely on the basis of price would not suffice, and that it needed to invest in research and devel-

opment. Still, the first Dura-Ace signified an important step forwards for Japanese manufacturers as they entered a world dominated by the Italo-French duopoly. The race was now on.

Shimano could not focus its attention on cycle racing to the exclusion of other forms of cycling, however, or neglect to offer a full range of products. After all, in some markets the competition was closed, and buyers still favored SunTour, whose products were considered to be easier to use than Shimano's, while just as efficient and reliable. From 1970 to 1984 the market offered different models which varied in cost and group, but SunTour's GT along with Huret's Duopar – made from titanium – were the favorites, particularly in the United States, because they supported the 34-tooth pinions more appropriate for gears on city bikes and the newly-discovered mountain bike. SunTour was always the first choice, because it worked extremely well, was reasonably priced, and was easy to dissemble and repair.

The effects of the bike boom became more acutely felt in the late 1970s, but Asian manufacturers had already built up a solid reputation in the United States to the detriment of European companies, which had a reputation for being too expensive in relation to their quality. Campagnolo alone was content with its sales, given that by then it had become the market leader of exceptional high-quality specialized racing equipment. SunTour and Shimano triumphed in the low- and medium-cost gear shifter market, with their market shares going from 25% in 1973 to 90% in 1978.

In 1977, Shimano released its Positron model, the first indexed gear shifter to incorporate Positive Pre-Select (PPS) technology, which had been developed in its own laboratories. The system was designed to be installed on low-cost bicycles on the premise that non-professional cyclists often have difficulty aligning the chain manually, a skill which is normally only mastered after many hours of cycling experience. The product was radically redesigned over the course of the following years to make it more functional and attractive, but it never won favor with the public (and this in spite of enormous advertising campaigns) and was thus withdrawn in 1982. Three years later SunTour manufactured the "Mighty Click" model, also indexed, but this too did not prove as popular as its makers hoped.

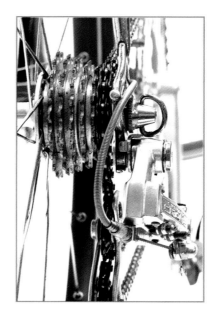

148 TOP THE 14TH STAGE OF THE 1988 GIRO D'ITALIA PROVIDED A SCENE FROM ANOTHER WORLD AND ERA, AS COMPETITORS TACKLED THE ENTIRE GAVIA UNDER DENSE SNOWFALL.

148 BOTTOM BERNARD HINAULT WAS THE STRONGEST FRENCH CYCLIST OF ALL TIMES. THE "BADGER" (HE EARNED THIS ODD NICKNAME BECAUSE OF HIS PUGNACIOUS SPIRIT) WON, OVERALL, 216 RACES, INCLUDING 5 TOURS, 2 GIRI, AND 3 VUELTA.

Shimano released the AX series in 1980. It was a brave attempt to sell a series of complete products (Dura-Ace, 600 and Adamas) with unusual designs. In addition to their striking aesthetic appearance, the shapes for these models had been carefully studied and were supposedly as aerodynamic as possible. The initials stood for "aerodynamic-to-the-max," and stylistically, they did indeed set the product ahead of its time. However, it never proved popular enough to achieve longevity, and was withdrawn after two years.

The period was nonetheless an important one Shimano, because it highlighted the potential of its research and development department. That remains even if Shimano never really made its mark on the market, and particularly on SunTour.

The latter released two gear shifters – the Superbe Pro and Mountech – in 1982, both of which proved to be weakly designed and short-lived. It first put forward the Deore XT group (which spawned a specific production line for mountain bikes) and then (in 1984) updated its market-leading product, the Dura-Ace, which by this time was

supplied with an indexed gear shifter. More than seven years after the first experiment with the Positron, the mechanism was revised and corrected. Cyclists were now able shift gears with precision; and they no longer felt the chain move, because it aligned itself effortlessly to the freewheel without the need of manual correction.

Interestingly, SunTour released a similar system, but it was discontinued and phased out by 1969. Known as the "Speed Click" in homage to Sting-Ray's Krate models, it did not inspire the appreciation it should have for the potential behind its creation, and so left the field wide open for its rival, which reached cycling's top league following the release of the Dura-Ace in 1984. It was now that the indexed gear shifter group became a reference point for all other manufacturers, who from then on found themselves scrambling to follow Shimano. (SunTour, Campagnolo and Simplex had to wait three whole years before releasing their own indexed gear shifter models.) It is important to realize that this was the first inclined-parallelogram shifter to be manufactured by Shimano, since SunTour's patent protecting this manufacturing

technique had by then expired. (From 1986, the Dura-Ace was sold only its in complete gear shifter format, a strategy which prevented accessory manufacturers from competing.)

The late 1980s were dominated by Shimano, which had become the market leader for group gear shifters. Shimano's philosophy dictated that the gear shifter should be the bicycle's "soul." This encouraged frame-manufacturers to manufacture products that were as compatible with Japanese gear shifters as possible. Branches appeared all over the world as the number of professional cyclists increased, and bought Japanese group gear shifters which they attached to their highly specialized racing bikes.

Shimano's leading position was largely due to its enormous capital and the fact that at least 10% of profits were invested in research and development. On the shoulders of this success, Shimano released an off-road indexed gear shifter in 1987, and in 1989 seven- and then eight- gear versions were released. Shimano continued to grow throughout the 1990s, positioning itself once again at the helm of the global market. In 1995, sales reached the billion dollar mark and profits rose to more than $54 million dollars. Its supremacy was again ensured by its high technical standards and designs, such as the integrated gear shifter levers on the brake, which was first tested on the mountain bike and subsequently fitted to all road bikes.

The mechanism, known as STI (Shimano Total Integration), was released in 1990 and became immediately popular because it made cycling a safer activity.

Cyclists no longer had to take their hands off the handlebars to change gears (Shimano released a nine-gear shifter in 1997). This "total integration" was a commercial success since in practice the various bike parts fitted together to form a group shifter, which meant that cyclists could use exclusively Japanese-made products.

Shimano was not always a source of inspiration, however. Instead, it capitalized on existing methods and practices, improving, refining, rationalizing and adapting them to the demands of the modern market, capitalizing on every available opportunity to reach the top.

THE GLOBAL DIFFUSION
OF THE MOUNTAIN BIKE

The mountain biking culture gained momentum through its participants' love for nature and their desire for a pollution-free environment, as well as the powerful emotions that this sport evoked.

In the 1980s people began not only to recognize the importance of protecting the environment, but also to rediscover their bodies, and their need for healthy living. In a world of cars, people longed for a greater closeness to nature and an easier way to escape the confines of built-up cityscapes.

The words "fitness" and "wellness" spread throughout the marketing world – admittedly, just as much the result of 1980s consumer-focused jargon as anything more noble – and spurred on the launching of new products.

The mountain bike soon became the ideal bike to sponsor. No longer aimed exclusively at serious enthusiasts only, it won increasingly large market shares among "regular" people eager to trade concrete and asphalt for off-road experiences, and soon its popularity generated new interest not just in the product itself, but in cycling generally – an interest that had been in decline.

The first limited-edition mountain bikes from the 1970s (made by the entrepreneurs Joe Breeze, Tom Ritchey, and Gary Fisher, et al.) used a mix of components such as Huret Duopar or SunTour GT gear shifters, Simplex derailleurs, SunTour command levers, Magura brake levers or Mafac cantilevers.

Campagnolo Record and Super Record were even used on certain Ritchey models, but generally speaking, Campagnolo never made a breakthrough, even though in 1990 it produced an off-roading series of two Euclid and Centaur complete groups.

In the 1980s, the Specialized Stumpjumper and Univega Alpina Sport – the first large-scale models – gave the market a new direction; these were soon followed by other models that focused the attention of the public on the mountain bike.

Trek, Cannondale, Diamond, Back, the Canadian-based Mongoose, and Japan-based Bridgestone, Raleigh of Great Britain, and small manufacturers such as Gary Klein all interpreted the mountain bike – ("the bike with fat wheels," as Schwinn called it) – in their own way. In the mid 1980s the mountain bike found success in Italy, too, when Rossin manufactured its Marathon model and Cinelli began large-scale production of the Rampichino.

The latter was so successful that its name entered the Italian language and remains widely associated with the mountain bike.

Once they had forced themselves into the US market with the Sting-Ray and the bike-boom of 1971, SunTour and Shimano watched the mountain bike phenomenon closely, waiting for an opportunity to make their mark.

SunTour was the first to take advantage of the new fad. In 1983 it introduced a series of components known as Dirt, manufactured in partnership with Sugino and Dia-Compte, who provided the triple crank and cantilever brake set.

Their venture was so successful that in 1983 almost all mountain bikes were equipped with Dirt parts. Also in 1983, Shimano brought out the Deore SX group, which became popular the next year. Before long the gear shifter market was monopolized by SunTour and Shimano, which from 1987 onwards – when the latter released an indexed shifter for the mountain bike too – became increasingly dominant in the world of cycling. SunTour was the victim of fast changes in the market: its products did not manage to keep up with those released by Shimano, which relied on its research and development center to maintain its vanguard position.

In 1987 a new invention in the field of off-roading changed road and mountain bikes for good. At an exhibition at Long Beach, California, Paul Turner, a mechanic in the Honda motocross racing team, and Keith Bontrager, a bicycle frame manufacturer, unveiled a futuristic model with dual suspension – front and rear – an idea that took enthusiasts and skeptics alike by surprise.

Two years later Turner and his wife, Christi, made further improvements to the model with their friend Steve Simons, the designer behind the suspensions that had revolutionized motocross, and set up a company called Rock Shox intended to make its mark solely with suspensions.

Their first model – the RS1 – was manufactured with aluminum rods and 25.4mm thick brackets. It operated in an open oil bay and measured 50 millimeters.

152-153 AFTER THE INTRODUCTION OF THE FIRST COMPOSITE FORK CROWN IN 1987 BY PAUL TURNER AND KEITH BONTRAGER, SUSPENSION SYSTEMS WERE QUICKLY REFINED, IMPROVING BOTH COMFORT AND RIDEABILITY.

154-155 UNFORESEEN OBSTACLES ONLY ENHANCE A TREK UNDERTAKEN ON A MOUNTAIN BIKE. FINDING ONESELF WADING AN UNEXPECTED TORRENT, FOR INSTANCE, OR BEING SPLATTERED WITH MUD, GIVES THE ADVENTUROUS ATHLETE A FEELING OF FREEDOM AND JOY.

156 Pedaling in direct contact with nature forces one to make unorthodox maneuvers, from jumping ditches and crevices to fording brooks.

157 With the global spread of the mountain bike phenomenon, manufacturers produced one new model and accessory after another, and expanded with each one the limits that had previously made this or that terrain unsuitable for cycling.

Launched in 1990, and used by the first world champions to be recognized by the UCI in Durango, California, the product now gained the attention of the worldwide cycling community, which was anxious to see if the downhill race would be won by cyclists whose bikes were fitted with it. All doubts were dispelled when Greg Herbold and Cindy Devine won the men's and women's races respectively, both using Rock Shox equipment to take the title. The jury was still out on suspension use in cross-country racing, where rigid frame forks were still the preference, in a bid to improve efficiency during climbs and to reduce the weight associated with absorber models. But Ned Overend's victory on a prototype Stumpjumper Epic Ultimate model with a Rock Shox fork removed any remaining doubts the very next day and opened the door to a new market. (A flat elastomers fork also made its debut at the first world championships. It was manufactured by Manitou and fitted to Yeti bikes by another mountain bike legend: John Tomac, who won the first mountain bike World Cup.)

In 1991 Cannondale became the first company to produce a mountain bike fitted with an EST (Elevated Suspension Technology) system for the rear shock-absorbers. The pivot was positioned over the steering column, which reduced the number of shocks, though a drawback remained: the pivot on which the rear section balanced required permanent upkeep because its size was not sufficient to support the stress-bearing zone.

The following year Cannondale brought out its Headshok system for its bicycles. A hydraulic system fitted to the head tube was attached to the large, firm aluminum fork – the Pepperoni. The first Headshok models were fully adjustable: unlike telescopic forks, the sliding relied on rollers rather than bushing, and the runners dug into the fork stem and the steering column. In 1992 Schwinn supplied its professional team with the Paramount model, a fully suspended piece of equipment that used SASS (Schwinn Active Suspension System) technology. The sturdy rear shock absorber, which measured 100 millimeters (50 was typical at the time), was designed by

Eric Buell, who had made his name in motor racing and manufactured parts for Harley Davidson.

Mountain bike sales continued to rise, and in 1993 more than 8.8 million were sold. The following year a discovery brought new technical improvements: Sachs, which manufactured the Sram model, released the first hydraulic disc brake for bikes, known as the PowerDisc. Yet another technical development of the time can be attributed to Horst Leitner, who came from the Tyrol and moved to the United States, where he founded AMP Research. The aim of his invention was to make the rear shock absorber system independent from the pedals. A simple articulated joint on the horizontal bars, known as a Horst joint, helped prevent the suspension from compressing when the chain was in traction during pedaling. The patent was first acquired by Specialized in 1994 and used it for its FSR system, but it can now be seen on other similar bikes.

In 1996, when the mountain bike made its first real debut in Atlanta at the Olympics, the sport entered a new and critical phase, throwing the entire movement that had revolutionized cycling so remarkably over the previous twenty years into the dark. One possible

158 BOTTOM IN 1991, CANNONDALE PROPOSED A MODEL THAT EXPLOITED THE ELEVATED SUSPENSION TECHNOLOGY SYSTEM FOR THE SUSPENSION FORK. THOUGH INNOVATIVE, THE SOLUTION WAS NOT WITHOUT FLAWS, AS IT HAMPERED PEDAL-STROKE FLUIDITY..

158-159 IN THE MID-1980S, TIG WELDING STREAMLINED THE MASS PRODUCTION OF FRAMES IN THE USA, AND AMERICAN MANUFACTURERS BEGAN TO EXPORT ALUMINUM FRAMEWORKS, ESPECIALLY IN THE MOUNTAIN BIKE SECTOR.

cause behind the sudden downturn in the boom fueled by the mountain bike was simply competition from other consumer goods. Still, the sales slump did not stop progress completely: the mountain bike did continue to evolve, modernizing itself to the point that it became almost unrecognizable when compared with earlier models. After steel, manufacturers soon began to use aluminum and alloys, both materials that helped reduce the total weight of the frame by 10-12 kilograms. This weight was further reduced when the first bikes made from carbon hit the market.

Rider comfort was also improved with new solutions, including the optimization of both front and rear suspensions and customization to meet various uses and trip lengths. The number of gears on some bikes rose from 15 to a stunning 27, while the emergence of V-Brakes (and later, hydraulic disk brakes) made them more reliable and efficient than ever. This system was brought to perfection with the SRAM model, which on top of everything, ensured maximum safety. The development of mountain bikes now spurred similar improvements on city bikes, and opened up a whole new market among urban riders.

159 top Besides suspensions, one component that separated the road and off-road sectors was the braking system. In 1994, the SRAM company launched the PowerDisc on the market.

159 bottom The Cannondale Super V was one of the most famous mountain bikes of the early 1990's. Initially made of aluminum, and later composite fiber, it was equipped with the Pepperoni fork crown developed by the Bedford Company.

“ *The introduction of new materials and advanced technologies in the 20th century’s final decades radically changed the bicycle’s shape and components.* ”

160-161 The success of the mountain bike caused decreasing interest in the Cyclo-Cross, and it was soon regarded anachronistic for athletes to compete in cross-country events on bicycles designed for on-road use.

161 top Thanks to its technical superiority, the mountain bike allow a cyclist to conquer almost any off-road obstacle.

161 bottom Nonetheless, there are times when even the best cyclist must dismount and engage the challenges of the course on foot, with one's bike on one's shoulders.

162 TOP A PHASE OF THE DUAL SLALOM RACE AT THE 1988
NORBA WORLD CHAMPIONSHIPS. ALONG WITH CROSS-COUNTRY
AND DOWNHILL RACES, SLALOMS WERE ORGANIZED TO TEST A
BIKERS' STEERING ABILITY.

162 BOTTOM BIKERS IN THE CROSS-COUNTRY RACE AT THE
1998 NORBA WORLD CHAMPIONSHIPS RASIE DUST—AND THE
SPECTER OF HELL, AS RIDERS IN THE MIDDLE OF THE PELOTON
RISK EXTREME DANGERS CAUSED BY POOR VISIBILITY.

162-163 THE AMERICAN VICTOR (AND MEMBER OF THE
MOUNTAIN BIKE HALL OF FAME) JOHN TOMAC AFTER THE
CROSS-COUNTRY RACE AT THE 1988 NORBA WORLD
CHAMPIONSHIPS.

164 TOP THE NEW ZEALANDER TOM HOLLAND ATTEMPTS STUNTS DURING THE HEAT THAT PRECEDES THE DOWNHILL RACE, A PREREQUISITE FOR ADMISSION TO THE 2006 WORLD CHAMPIONSHIP EVENTS HELD IN ROTORUA, NEW ZEALAND.

164 BOTTOM IN DOWNHILL RACES, PROFESSIONAL CYCLISTS WEAR FULL HELMETS AND PROTECTIVE GEAR SIMILAR TO THAT WORN BY MOTORCYCLISTS. WITHOUT THESE, THE SLIGHTEST IRREGULARITIES COULD CAUSE SERIOUS INJURY.

165 A GOOD BIKE MAY BE THE STARTING POINT, BUT IN ORDER TO PREVAIL IN A FOUR CROSS RACE, THE CYCLIST NEEDS TWO OTHER LEGS TO STAND ON: AN EXCELLENT RIDING TECHNIQUE, AND THAT PINCH OF RECKLESSNESS THAT PUSHES ONE TO FIGHT SHOULDER TO SHOULDER, WITH THE MOST FORMIDABLE ADVERSARY.

166-167 The Norwegian Gunn-Rita Dahle, one of the most important cross-country figures of the late 20th Century, and a rider whose Olympic and World Championship victories have earned her a permanent place on the roster of cycling greats.

167 Gunn-Rita Dahle at the 2005 European Cross-Country Championships. In addition to excelling there, she has won several editions of the World Cup, the World Cross-Country, and a few marathon championships.

168-169 JUMPING THE
BUMPS IS ONE OF THE MAIN
SKILLS NEEDED TO GAIN
MOMENTUM AND OUTPACE
ONE'S ADVERSARIES IN THE
FOUR-CROSS. THE JUMP MUST
BE JUST THE RIGHT LENGTH—
CERTAINLY NOT TOO SHORT,
BUT ALSO NOT SO LONG AS
TO RISK LANDING OUT OF
TRAJECTORY.

169 TOP AS CYCLISTS
UNDERTAKE EVER MORE RISKY

MANEUVERS, SOME HAVE
STARTED DESCENDING ICED
TRACKS BUILT FOR
BOBSLEDS—THOUGH NOT
BEFORE FITTING THEIR
VEHICLES WITH ICE TIRES.

169 BOTTOM DESCENDING A
BOBSLED TRACK REQUIRES
EXCEPTIONAL BALANCE, SINCE
RACERS EMERGE FROM THE
PARABOLIC CURVES AT SUCH
HIGH SPEEDS AND SUCH
ELEVATED ANGLES.

170 IN ORDER TO WIN THE LEADING POSITIONS IN THE DECISIVE PHASES OF A RACE AND TO MANAGE TO PREVAIL OVER THE ADVERSARIES, THE COMPETITORS PUSH THEMSELVES TO THEIR LIMIT AND OFTEN EVEN BEYOND. THE GREATEST RISK IS THAT OF FINDING ONESELF ON THE GROUND AFTER A CRASH.

170-171 THE GROWING IMPORTANCE OF THE SPORT AS SHOW HAS BROUGHT TO THE SHIFTING OF THE FOUR CROSS DISCIPLINE ON SNOW TRACKS. THE RIDERS HAVE TO BE VERY CAREFUL TO MAINTAIN THEIR BALANCE DURING THE ENTIRE RACING COURSE.

ALUMINUM AND SLOPING

Light alloys were used by the French company Cycles Aluminum to manufacture frames as early as in 1890, but aluminum bicycles did not appear until 1975, when Gary Klein manufactured alloy frames drawing on the knowledge he had acquired under Shawn Buckley at MIT and through experiments carried out by Marc Rosenbaum, Mark Tanquary, and Stan Stone.

During the same period, manufacturers such as Alan and Vitus worked on light alloys in France and Italy and made their mark by distributing aluminum bikes that relied on consolidated frame-making traditions and an extensive commercial network. Two particularly eye-catching models produced by these manufacturers were the Vitus 979 and Alan's Super Record. Essentially, the manufacturing technique was the same as the one used for steel frames, with tubes bound to the inside of joints.

The complete structure was not achieved using braze welding, which is not possible with aluminum, but by using epoxy resin. The French-made 979 model incorporated a main triangle made from tubes whose external diameter was larger than the internal joints. With the help of the glue, these frames kept their shape, even when there was interference. Just as unusual, the locking mechanism for the saddle did not rely on a classical clamp but rather a screw threaded di-

rectly into the tube – a safeguard against its coming loose. 979's quickly gained a reputation for being light-weight, and incredibly flexible – a quality that improved comfort but also dispersed the energy built up by the cyclist's pedaling, according to its detractors. Nevertheless, Ireland's Sean Kelly used it to win the 1988 Vuelta and the green jersey at the 1989 Tour de France. Both victories shattered the commonly-held view that a rigid frame is always more efficient.

Alan's Super Record model, a natural evolution of the Competition, was the high point for this Italian manufacturer's development of light alloy frames. The tubes were slightly thicker to improve sturdiness and were glued and then fitted closely to the joints –a technique employed to improve resistance. The design of the fork on this model was unique: the stems were large and the head was made from ergal; further, the saddle node joint relied on high stay attachments to improve the bike's resistance.

Gary Klein's most important contribution was the introduction of techniques such as TIG soldering (arch soldering using tungsten electrodes pressurized under inert gases) and thermal treatments to manufacture frames. This technique was soon adopted in the steel industry, as it enabled the tubes to be connected directly using only filling material and without needing joints. TIG soldering on a larger scale was

TRADITIONAL FRAME

GIANT COMPACT FRAME

first introduced by American manufacturers, who began producing and later exporting aluminum frames with oversized tubes in the 1980s, particularly in the field of mountain bikes. These were received with skepticism in Europe because their parts were unusually large compared with those made from steel. But critics quickly rethought their position once these products proved themselves to be as reliable as anything else. In 1983, Cannondale launched its "aluminum for the masses" campaign, bringing the model a new following and rebranding the ST500 sport/touring model. It was extremely successful and was soon followed by the first aluminum mountain bike model – also produced in Bedford – known as the SM500.

The high demand for mountain bikes enabled large American manufacturers to sell their products in Europe. Consequently, they became established market players, aided by the fact that production was relocated to Asia. As they focused their attention on producing mountain bikes (and industrializing the production thereof) they essentially abandoned other forms of bicycles. Over the 1990s, as the miracle of the mountain bike began to fade, even American manufacturers had to refocus their attention on those types of bicycle which were once again coming into fashion. Having made a fortune in the world of mountain biking, it was natural that they should follow the market; regrouping, they concentrated their efforts once again on the road bike. They made their entry into the market equipped with clear goals and excellent production processes refined over time and contrasting sharply with locally made, hand-tailored frames.

Aluminum proved so successful partly because there was a demand for lighter products but also because the material was relatively inexpensive and remarkably malleable, which in turn meant lower manufacturing costs than steel. "Sloping" was introduced to reduce costs

further, thus enabling decisions to be made faster in contrast to craftsmen, who would often spend hours deliberating on the changes that needed to be made to the length or inclination of the tubes.

The term, which derives from "slope," came (in cycling) to stand for the technique that sloped the horizontal tube towards the steering column rather than having it run flat along the bottom.

A frame which incorporated this technology was more compact and as a consequence more rigid and efficient since closing the main triangle generally lowered the vehicle's center of gravity and thus making it more stable and closer to the ground. (The flip side of the coin was that in some cases excessive lowering of the horizontal tube made the rear components excessively rigid, and so reduced the dissipation of vibrations.) This made the whole mechanism overly dry and uncomfortable. A sloping frame brought advantages which were appreciated by some cyclists, given that the bicycle was flung around more and was shorter between the wheels; leading athletes preferred it because they could count on its efficient structure to reduce energy loss. But there were disadvantages too. Soon many manufacturers, who had realized the potential production savings, no longer manufactured the model to measure, instead offering only a serious of standard models which needed adjustment, and capitalizing on those components available to the market.

The most successful model to be fitted with a sloping frame was used for road bikes in the mid-1990s and was produced by a Taiwanese company called Giant, which entered into partnership with professionals from the Spanish Once team. The model became known as the TCR. Even though it was the first to offer this structure, it soon became fashionable and led almost the entire sector in a new direction.

172 THE TCR MODEL BY THE TAIWANESE MANUFACTURER GIANT WAS AMONG THE FIRST TO EXHIBIT SLOPING PROPORTIONS. THIS STYLE OF SOON BECAME THE STANDARD, AS IT ENTAILED ADVANTAGES AT BOTH A TECHNICAL AND ECONOMIC LEVEL.

173 THE MAIN DIFFERENCE BETWEEN A TRADITIONAL AND SLOPING FRAME IS THE INCLINATION OF THE HORIZONTAL TUBE, WHICH MAKES THE FRAME'S TWO OPPOSING TRIANGLES BOTH STURDIER AND MORE COMPACT.

TESTING CARBONIUM

We have already seen that the first attempt to manufacture a carbon frame was made in the United States. In 1975, Exxon Graftek used the same production process to manufacture its own product, only in this case the tubing was made from a combination of materials: carbon-covered aluminum containing epoxy resin. The carbon coating was made to measure and molded around the aluminum tubing, making sure that fibers were correctly placed to maximize resistance.

Before being placed in the furnace, the "sandwich" of fiber and metal was coated with Tedlar coating to compress the composite and protect it from abrasive chemicals. The tubes were then joined together using glue and aluminum. To make the structure stable, it was placed in the furnace once again. It was a brave attempt to bring a new manufacturing material to the world of cycling. The

drawback of the frame was unfortunately the insufficient longevity of the joints; strong glues were still being developed, and in the interim, Exxon Graftek could not undertake large-scale production but had to limit its product to competitions only.

This American company's experiment was once again followed by Alan and Vitus, who applied their expertise in light alloys to the field of composites. Alan used carbon-covered aluminum tubes glued at the joints and bound using screws. The Carbone 9 model manufactured by Vitus used exactly the same method as the one previously employed by its American predecessor.

Peugeot was not far behind these two companies, launching its Prince Reynolds 531 PY-10 model in steel under the new name PY-10 FC, which stood for "carbon fiber." In comparison to rival models, the main triangle was made from three carbon tubes glued to the joints.

174 LEFT IN 1995, THE COLNAGO C40 BECAME THE FIRST BIKE WITH AN ENTIRELY COMPOSITE-FIBER FRAME TO COMPETE IN THE PARIS-ROUBAIX; IT SAW VICTORY THE FOLLOWING YEAR, THANKS TO THE ITALIAN FRANCO BALLERINI, THEN TEAM CAPTAIN OF THE MAPEI CLAS.

174-175 COLNAGO'S COLLABORATION WITH FERRARI ENGINEERING STARTED IN 1986 WITH AN INNOVATIVE CONCEPT BIKE AND WAS CEMENTED OVER THE NEXT YEARS THROUGH THE CO-PRODUCTION OF SEVERAL OTHER MODELS.

The frame was made using a venture joint with Bador and CLB-Angenieux. Since the 1970s this partnership helped to produce Duralinox, a material which was used to make the rear triangle. The bicycle made its debut at the Tour de France and was used by Pascal Simon. In Peugeot's 1983 catalog, the PY-10 was compared to the Space Shuttle – a nod to its advanced technology.

1986 was a profitable year for carbon frames. Look, which had become famous in 1984 for launching the first widely distributed quick-release pedal system, supplied the athletes of the *Vie Claire* team with the KG86 model during the mountain stages, signaling the emergence of carbon products in the transalpine market.

The specialty of this particular vehicle was its composite tubes and joints made from polyamide with reinforced plastic. The American Greg Lemond won the first of his three Tour de France races using this bike after a tough competition from his teammate Bernard Hinault, who had won the fifth edition of the race the previous year. The first fruits of the Colnago-Ferrari Engineering partnership, a prototype which used innovative design technologies for its time, appeared the same year. The frame was developed to ensure maximum sturdiness, and it was indeed this goal that spurred the design team to utilize the same materials as Ferrari uses to make

sports cars. The tubes were made from carbon fiber with epoxy resin while the nodes, as with the transalpine Look, were manufactured with advanced techno-polymers filled with carbon and glass.

The gear shifter mechanism was particularly interesting on this concept bike. The thinking of this manufacturer from Lombardy and his Cavallino technicians was to do away with the derailleur command mechanism and replace it with an incased gear shifter, designed so that it could be fitted between the bulk for the chain crown. Only the crown could be seen from outside the casing, which was unusual, and it did not rotate at the same speed as the pedal axle since a series of gear selectors were fitted between the two enabling the desired gear to be selected. To change gear, it was necessary to replace the only pinion fitted to the free wheel of the rear axle, or change the crown, so adapting it to the varying features of the course (climb, flat stretch, or descent).

Even the choice of brakes was ahead of its time. Designers decided to go beyond the experience of mechanical braking by introducing a hydraulic command which transferred to the normal compass brakes the cyclist's braking action by means of a lever on the handlebar.

In 1986, a magical year for carbon, the first jointless frame was marketed drawing on monocoque body technology from the American firm Krestel. The model was known as the 4000 and was also the first to incorporate aerodynamic section tubes. Kestrel enlisted the help of engineers from Lockheed and the US Air Force to manufacture his product.

Making the most of his knowledge, he released his carbon-fiber mountain bike in 1988. It was called the MX-Z and although it represented a step forwards it did not help to dispel the myth that composites were no good for off-roading.

More and more mountain bikes were manufactured using carbon-fiber, even though most producers never made the jump into monocoque technology production, preferring instead the simpler and more inexpensive option of joined tubes with light alloy links. Models such as Trek's 8900 and Yeti's C-26 – used by John Tomac and Julien Furtado at Durango – as well as Raleigh's Tomac Signature drew on the same technology as Peugeot's PY-10 FC. GT stands out above the rest and was based on a system of joints but replaced epoxy resin with thermoplastic resin to join the parts that made the tube.

Difficulties with assembly and joints typical of road bikes also appeared on mountain bikes, to the point that manufacturers were content to supply only professional cyclists and never entered large-scale production.

But the ball was now rolling, and carbon fiber would soon become the focus of attention for all bike manufacturers.

176 TOP DESPITE HIS HEIGHT (6 FEET) AND WEIGHT (80KG), INDURAIN WAS AN EXCELLENT CLIMBER, PERSISTING EVEN WHEN THE ROAD ESCALATED, AND WHEN MORE AGILE AND LIGHTER *GRIMPEUR* (CLIMBERS) MOVED IN FOR THEIR ATTACKS.

176 BOTTOM INDURAIN, A THOROUGHBRED TIME TRIAL SPECIALIST, WAS ABLE TO DEVELOP A 550-WATT MAXIMUM POWER. THANKS TO THIS SKILL HE WAS ABLE TO BEAT HIS WORST ADVERSARIES.

177 INDURAIN, WITH THE PINK JERSEY, TACKLES A TIME-TRIAL STAGE DURING THE 1993 GIRO D'ITALIA. THE "NAVARRO," SO CALLED BECAUSE OF THE SPANISH REGION OF HIS BIRTH, WON HIS MOST IMPORTANT VICTORIES WITH "PINARELLO" MODELS.

178 TOP THE SWISS CYCLIST TONY ROMINGER OPENS THE WAY FOR THE 1995 WORLD CHAMPION ABRAHAM OLANO. THE TEAM CAPTAINS OF THE MAPEI-GB TEAM COMPETED ON COLNAGO BICYLCES EQUIPPED WITH SHIMANO'S DURA-ACE GEAR.

178 BOTTOM LEFT THE YOUNG GERMAN JAN ULLRICH LEADS A GROUP AT THE 1997 TOUR DE FRANCE, WHERE HE TRIUMPHED OVER THE CLIMBERS RICHARD VIRENQUE AND MARCO PANTANI.

178 BOTTOM RIGHT GIANNI BUGNO, WHO WON IN 1991 AND 1992, IS SEEN HERE IN ACTION WITH HIS TOUR DE FRANCE TEAMMATE LAURENT FIGNON. BOTH THE ITALIAN AND THE FRENCHMAN OF UTILIZED BIANCHI BIKES AND SHIMANO GEAR GROUPS WHILE ON THE CHATEAUX D'AX GATORADE TEAM.

179 "KAISER JAN" LEADS HIS T-MOBILE TEAMMATES TO THE FINISH LINE OF A STAGE DURING THE 1997 TOUR DE FRANCE. BESIDES HIS VICTORY IN THE FRENCH RACE, ULLRICH BOASTS TWO RAINBOW TIME-TRIAL TITLES AND AN OLYMPIC GOLD MEDAL ACQUIRED AT SYDNEY IN 2000.

180 LEGS—THE MOST VITAL ASSET AND WEAPON OF A CYCLIST. ALFREDO BINDA USED TO SAY THAT TO BE GREAT, BRAINS WERE
GOOD—BUT ONE ALSO NEEDED LEGS.

181 TOP A GROUP AT HIGH SPEED RESULTS IN A PRISM OF COLORS, A SPECTACLE OF RARE BEAUTY. THE SOUND OF SO MANY WHEELS
TURNING SIMULTANEOUSLY IS NOT UNLIKE THAT OF THE MOUNTAIN STREAMS CROSSED IN SO MANY CLASSIC EUROPEAN RACES.

181 BOTTOM THE LEGS OF THE CYCLISTS IN THE GROUP SEEM LIKE ORGAN PIPES PLAYING IN UNISON, AND THERE IS NO DEARER MUSIC
TO THE ADORING THRONGS THAT GATHER TO APPLAUD THEM ALONG THE RACE COURSE.

182 CIPOLLINI, THE "LION KING," SET OFF A NEW TREND IN CYCLING FASHIONS BY APPEARING AT THE STARTING LINES OF VARIOUS EVENTS WITH JAZZY CUSTOM-MADE SUITS.

183 MARCO PANTANI, THE "PIRATE," WHO TRAGICALLY DIED IN 2004. ONE OF ITALY'S MOST BELOVED CYCLISTS, HE LITERALLY WENT MAD ON ENTERING SPRINTS AND ACCELERATION POINTS.

THE HOUR RECORD AND TIME TRIAL: TESTING GROUNDS FOR THE BEST

The hour record is the most famous record in cycling. From Henri Desgrange's first attempt in 1893 to the twenty-first century, all the great professional cycling champions have tried not only to succeed on the road but also to beat the hour record. In the 1980s and 1990s, the hour record was an excellent testing ground for prototypes made using innovative solutions which would go on to revolutionize road competitions.

Francesco Moser beat the record in 1984 and was the first to surpass the fifth kilometer/hour barrier. He repeated his success in the same field in 1988, this time indoors. He used unique bikes to achieve both records.

Both models comprised a tightly fitted front fork and had carbon-made lenticular wheels, as well as a horn-shaped handlebar introduced in 1980 by the East German Olympic squad. The diameter of the rear wheel was particularly unusual on the 1988 model: it measured 1.03 meters.

In 1987, the American manufacturer Scott unveiled aerodynamic accessories for time trial bikes, also known as "triathlon handlebars". They were designed to allow the cyclist maximum comfort and drive; indeed, the goal was to ensure aerodynamic excellence without affecting the versatility of the position.

It was thanks to Scott's accessories that Greg Lemond won his second Tour de France in 1989, taking the yellow jersey from Laurent Fignon in only eight seconds in the final stage in heart-stopping fashion.

184 BOTTOM IN 1988, FRANCESCO MOSER ESTABLISHED THE IN-
DOOR HOUR RECORD AT STUTTGART ON A FUTURISTIC BIKE WITH A
1.03 M DIAMETER REAR WHEEL; IT UTILIZED A GEAR RATIO WHICH
GENERATED 8.20 METERS EACH PEDALING STROKE.

184-185 ON OCTOBER 3, 1986, MOSER ESTABLISHED THE HOUR
RECORD AT SEA LEVEL, COVERING 49.802 KM ON THE PARQUET
TRACK OF THE VIGORELLI VELODROME, THE SAME DISTANCE WITH
WHICH HE HAD ESTABLISHED THE RECORD IN THE OPEN AIR, IN
MEXICO.

185 TOP FRANCESCO MOSER IN 1984, AT MEXICO CITY'S
VELODROME, DURING HIS ATTEMPT FOR THE HOUR RECORD IN
THE OPEN. THE CYCLIST FROM TRENTO WAS THE FIRST TO USE A
SPECIAL BIKE IN HIS ATTEMPT TO ESTABLISH A NEW RECORD.

185 BOTTOM FRANCESCO MOSER CELEBRATES HIS VICTORY FOR
THE HOUR RECORD. USING A SPECIAL BIKE WITH A GEAR RATIO
OF 57 X 15 FROM 8,27 METERS OF DEVELOPMENT, THE TRENTINO
WAS THE FIRST TO SURPASS THE 50KM-PER-HOUR BARRIER.

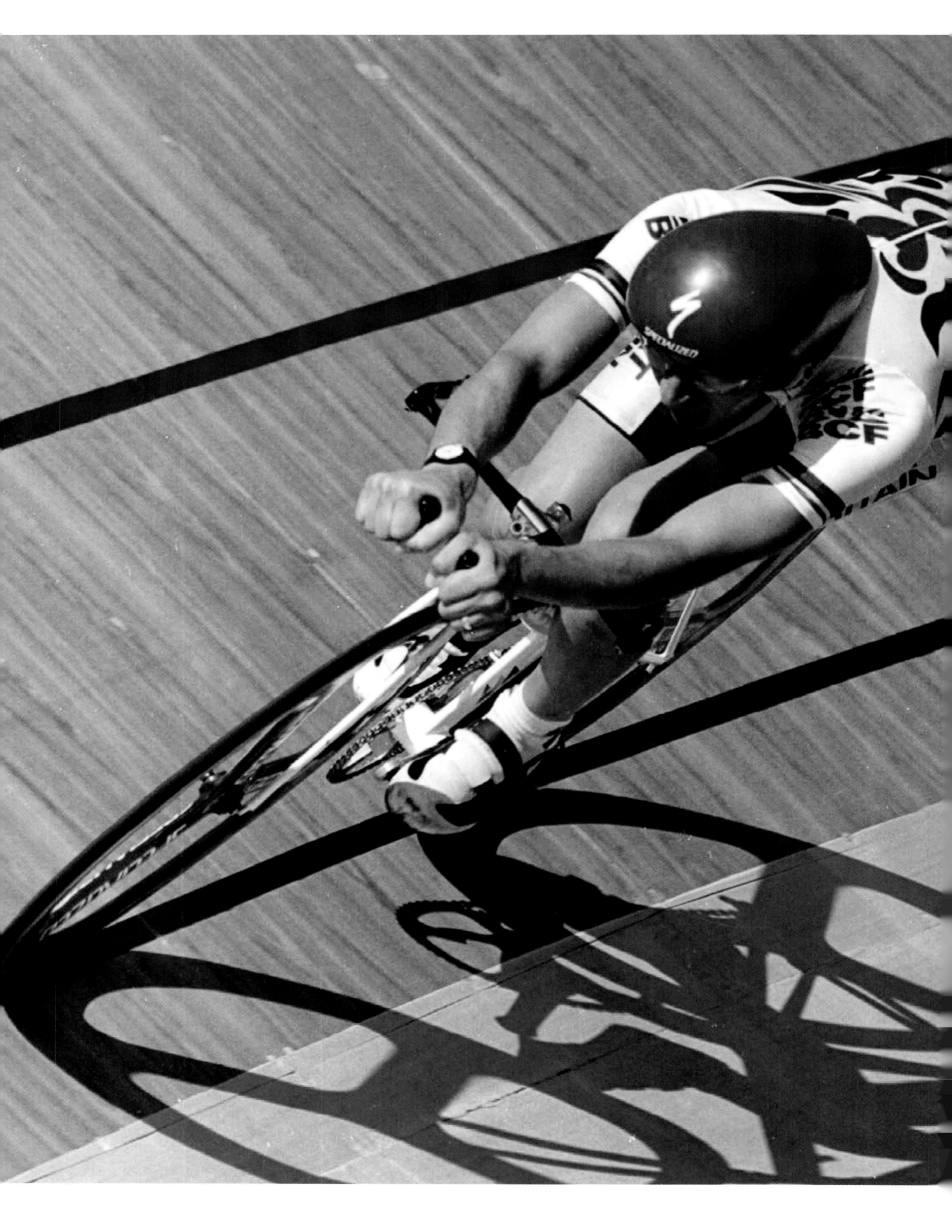

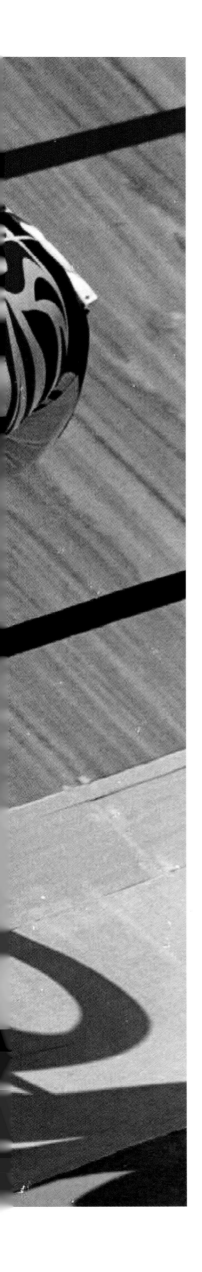

Moser's hour record remained unbeaten for nine years until it was taken by Graeme Obree, a cyclist who at that time was largely unknown outside Great Britain. Even more impressive than his performance was the self-made bicycle itself, which even comprised some old washing machine parts. It meant that the cyclist had to adopt a strange aerodynamic position, which was actually deliberate – the fruit of research aimed at improving power and consequently increasing average speeds. Obree reached 51.596 kilometers and improved on the previous record by almost 500 meters.

The British cyclist had made his mark. But Obree's joy only lasted a week, when another British athlete, Chris Boardman, who had won the Olympic cycling track record the previous year, broke his record. Boardman was the first man to beat 52 kilometers using a standard bike with four-type carbon wheels manufactured by the French company Corima. The model only weighed seven kilograms and signaled the arrival of composite fiber into the hour record race.

Following a series of materials tests, Obree returned to the track in 1994, using a bicycle that was almost identical to the one he had used the previous year. He won back his record in a race against Boardman by another 500 meters. During the race, there was worry he might not pull it off because he chose a set of wheels which did not run smoothly over an indoor track: lenticular wheels were much smoother and faster.

186-187 GRAEME OBREE, THE "FLYING SCOTSMAN," WAS A HIGH-LEVEL TRACK CYCLIST WHO WON A RAINBOW TITLE IN THE 4000-METER INDIVIDUAL PURSUIT EVENT IN HAMAR, IN 1993, AND BOGOTA, IN 1994.

187 TOP OBREE IN HAMAR, WHERE, IN 1993, HE ESTABLISHED THE HOUR RECORD. THE CYCLIST APPEARED AT THE START ON A STRANGELY SHAPED BIKE THAT REQUIRED ASSUMING AN UNORTHODOX POSITION.

187 BOTTOM IN ADDITION TO HIS CRAMPED POSITION, WITH WHICH HE BROKE MOSER'S HOUR RECORD, OBREE TESTED THE SO-CALLED SUPERMAN POSTURE, WHICH WAS LATER COPIED BY THE BRITISH CYCLIST CHRIS BOARDMAN—AND LED TO HIS SETTING A NEW HOUR RECORD IN 1996.

188 TOP AND 188-189 THE CORIMA BICYCLE PROVIDED TO BOARDMAN MARKED THE ENTRANCE OF COMPOSITE FIBER IN HOUR-RECORD ATTEMPTS. INSTEAD OF LENTICULAR WHEELS, THE BRITISH CYCLIST CHOSE A 4-SPOKE MODEL BY THE SAME TRANSALPINE BRAND. BESIDES THE AERODYNAMIC HANDLEBAR, BOARDMAN USED HANDLEBAR GRIPS, A SOLUTION INTRODUCED BY THE AMERICAN RIDER SCOTT IN 1987, AND USED FOR THE FIRST TIME BY GREG LEMOND AT THE TOUR DE FRANCE.

189 TOP IN MANCHESTER, IN 1996, BOARDMAN CONQUERED A NEW HOUR RECORD WITH A COMPOSITE-FIBER MERCKX BICYCLE, SURPASSING THE OLD 56 KMH ONE. HE SET ANOTHER NEW RECORD IN 2000, BUT WITHOUT USING THIS SPECIALIZED BIKE, WHICH UCI HAD IN THE MEANTIME FORBIDDEN.

In late 1994, Miguel Indurain, a rising star of cycling who had won the Tour de France that year for the fourth consecutive time, announced that he wanted to challenge Obree for the hour record. The specialized press began to hypothesize on the possible outcome. Newspapers and fans believed that the Spaniard, who had won the Giro d'Italia and the Tour de France easily over his rivals, would total no less than 55/56 kilometers.

The most cynical technicians noted that although he might win the new record, his saddle position was not the most efficient because he kept his head high rather than down between his shoulders, and that a miracle was unlikely. Not surprisingly, Indurain turned to Pinarello, his trusted manufacturer of many years, who supplied him with his bike named "Espada."

With this project Cicli Pinarello produced its first carbon bike, using advanced monocoque technology tried and tested in computer simulations.

Aesthetically, it resembled the hilt of a sword. In September 1994 the Spaniard remained at 55 kilometers, but he also took the hour record surpassing the 53 kilometer/hour mark. Miguel Indurain also used Pinarello's Espada model for his fourth victory at the Grande Boucle, at the world championship time trial in 1995, and at the 1996 Olympics in Atlanta.

190-191 Pinarello's 'Espada' model accompanied Miguel Indurain in his conquest of the hour record in 1994, a time-trial championship in 1995, and at his conquest of the Olympic gold medal in 1996.

191 top The Espada, which weighed 6.5 kg in total, was made of carbonium using the monocoque technique. The bicycle was mounted with 190cm cranks and a 59x14 gear ratio, and was pedaled by the Navarro at 100 strokes per minute.

192 top Swiss cyclist Tony Rominger broke the hour record on the Bordeaux velodrome by pulverizing the previous record, which belonged to Miguel Indurain. In the course of 15 days he scored twice, covering a total distance of 55.291 km.

192-193 The bike used by Rominger in his attempts to break records was fitted for the occasion by Ernesto Colnago.

His hour record did not last more than two months, however, because Tony Rominger of Switzerland made two winning attempts using a steel Colnago bike – specially manufactured for the occasion – over fifteen days, cycling first 53.832 kilometers and 55 kilometers/hour. Incredibly, his record was not beaten for some time. Two years later the Chris Boardman returned to the throne by breaking the 56 kilometer/hour barrier. He adopted an aerodynamic posture, invented by Obree in 1995, which was achieved by stretching the handlebar and fitting additional aerodynamic devices. The cyclist was fixed to his bike to the point where it looked like he might take flight; it was no coincidence that the posture nicknamed "Superman". On 9 September 2000, the UCI made a decision that set back biking

more than thirty years. It annulled all records for specialist bikes, which were structurally different from traditional racing bikes. Eddy Merckx once again became the record holder and the starting point was again 49.431 kilometers, reached in 1972. In 2000, Boardman reached Merckx's record in Manchester, in conformity with the new regulations. In 2005, Ondrej Sosenka from the Czech Republic reached a distance of 49.700 kilometers, taking the record.

Following the UCI's action, the average record after thirty years had increased by only 300 meters compared with an improvement of seven kilometers during the period when specialized bikes were allowed. The importance of assessing materials and forms can only be proven by these data.

194-195 Arnaud Tournant, one of the most successful Transalpine track cyclists of the late 20th century. He boasts victories at the Olympic games, at the World Championships, and the World Cup.

194 bottom Marco Villa and Silvio Martinello set off in the "American Race" during a six-day event held at Milan's Vigorelli Velodrome in 1996. This specialty, also called the "Madison," is a recognized Olympic event.

195 TOP A TRACK CYCLIST
MUST NURTURE BOTH GENIUS
AND RECKLESSNESS, AS
WELL AS THE ABILITY TO
"READ" A RACE COURSE FAR
ENOUGH IN ADVANCE TO
FIGURE OUT THE POSSIBLE
DEVELOPMENTS OF A
PARTICULAR RACE, AND THE
TACTIC WHICH WILL ALLOW
HIM TO WIN IT.

195 BOTTOM LEFT THE
FRENCHMAN FLORIAN
ROUSSEAU COUNTS AMONG
TRACK CYCLISTS OF THE
MODERN ERA WHO CAN
BOAST THE MOST

REMARKABLE COLLECTION OF
HONORS, INCLUDING FOUR
OLYMPIC MEDALS (THREE OF
THEM GOLD, AND ONE
SILVER), AND AT LEAST TEN
RAINBOW AND FIFTEEN
NATIONAL TITLES.

195 BOTTOM RIGHT THE
GERMAN JENS FIEDLER
OVERTAKES THE AMERICAN
MARTIN NOTHSTEIN IN THE
FINAL 200-METER SPRINT OF
THE 1996 ATLANTA OLYMPICS.
THE TEUTONIC ACE HAS
CLAIMED FIVE OLYMPIC MEDALS
(THREE OF THEM GOLD) AND
FOUR WORLD TITLES.

196-197 WITH THE IMPROVEMENT OF CONSTRUCTION TECHNIQUES, COMPOSITE FRAMES HAVE BECOME THE NORM EVEN IN TRACK DISCIPLINES.

197 INITIALLY USED FOR ON-ROAD TIME TRIAL CHALLENGES AND HOUR-RECORD EVENTS, THE AERODYNAMIC PROSTHESIS COMMONLY
APPLIED TO HANDLEBARS IS NOW SEEN IN TEAM TRACK PURSUITS AS WELL.

THE NEW MILLENNIUM

INTELLIGENT FIBER
PAGE 200

GUARDIANS OF THE FLAME
PAGE 274

A MODEL FOR EVERY SPECIALTY
PAGE 278

INTELLIGENT FIBER

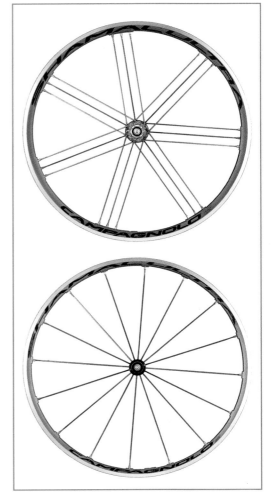

Until the late 1990s, aluminum was the most commonly used material to manufacture bicycles, even for professional cyclists. The spread of TIG soldering had resolved the reliability issues that gluing tubes and nodes could not. After an initial spurt, carbon use had diminished due to high manufacturing costs, with the result that the profit margins were not as high as those from aluminum, which had remained the common material in the Far East. As for TIG, the material and manpower involved were inexpensive, meaning that more bikes could be produced for the same cost. Having put their models to the test in the world of bike racing, a few global manufacturers began a production process dedicated to enthusiasts. Until the twenty-first century, carbon frames for road and mountain bikes were the prerogative of those manufacturers – from Europe and elsewhere – who had put their faith in this new material in the mid-1980s and who had gained the necessary expertise over the last twenty years to put it to use. The C40 model, produced in Italy by Ernest Colnago and presented to the Mapei team, was the first frame to be made entirely from carbon; it was raced first in 1994 and then adopted in 1995 during a race that is stressful for cyclists and bicycles alike: the Paris-Roubaix.

While carbon frames struggled to find their place on the market, other manufacturing parts made of the same material (but with a higher level of safety and reliability) began to be utilized. Lenticular wheels made from composite fiber exploiting aeronautical technology were released in 1981 in Italy (even though similar prototypes had appeared an entire century earlier, in 1896). They soon became well known for racing and for record braking, thanks to reduced aerodynamic resistance.

Francesco Moser was the first to win the hour record in 1984 riding a bike with lenticular wheels. However, they were never widely used and remained a product for very specialized cyclists. A similar mechanism known as the Disc Drive was used by John Tomac in 1990 on the rear wheel of his mountain bike. It was manufactured by Tiogra and consisted of two polyethylene shells filled with kevlar threads.

These zigzagged to form a spiderweb pattern, the outer edges joining at the center in the aluminum circle replacing the spokes. As well as being aerodynamic, this discovery provided sturdiness without extra weight during cross-country races.

Before the frame, the road bike fork was the fiber element that was best known throughout the cycling world. Kestrel was the first manufacturer to produce one when in 1989 it launched the EMS model designed by John Mouritsen. Its design incorporated a steel stem and head to which the composite stays were attached. To ensure aesthetic consistency, the head was fiber-covered. When the new material was introduced, the product became even sturdier and lighter, radically altering the cycling experience: on bends and downhill stretches the bike handled with precision while maintaining a fluid, linear movement compared with steel versions. A new market niche targeting high-end manufacturers was thus born – and led to the further development of the material. Over time, technologies (especially monocoque technology) were perfected, and various manufacturers such as Look, Time and Mizuno began manufacturing a full-carbon fork in various shapes and designs. The product became a standard for almost all racing models, and was later featured in the catalog of several off-road manufacturers, who tended to favor aluminum and light alloys.

Once the manufacturing process had been consolidated and production costs reduced, more and more parts made wholly or partially of carbon appeared. After the fork, fiber was also used to produce the stays in the rear frame triangle. This solution provided improved comfort, given that the composite stays had been carefully molded to withstand the unevenness of the ground better than hard metals such as aluminum, all without compromising the torsional rigidity of the entire frame.

Carbon fiber became increasingly common in bike manufacture and eventually a reliable frame was produced that was affordable to the average cyclist. American manufacturers played their part in this phenomenon by applying the experience gained in the field of aluminum and investing substantially in the market, with the ability to sustain their products by using publicity campaigns and a multi-layered production process achieved by moving production to the Far East. The situation was soon to change, though, as increasingly high technical levels were reached, even with the help of several European manufacturers who began opening production plants in Asia to fight off competition, thus bringing their expertise to the place where production was taking place. Over time the companies that had relocated acquired enough know-how to free themselves from constrictive production procedures and make it possible to reach the leading market positions that had been previously occupied by certain American producers who had relocated to the Far East to contain costs.

The two companies which soon established themselves as market leaders were Giant and Merida, based in Taiwan; they reached the top by producing five million parts each a year across all sectors, from daily use to competitive races.

American and Eastern bicycles became increasingly popular among professional cyclists. In the late twentieth and early twenty-first centuries, most large competitions were won – and indeed sometimes the entire podium was dominated – by cyclists using non-European brands. Lance Armstrong, "Le Roi Américain", won the Tour de France on a Trek bike seven times in a row, from 1999 to 2006, breaking the record for the highest number of victories.

Most manufacturers slowly began to put their faith in carbon, beginning production of almost every accessory and developing increasingly complex parts. The aluminum rims of high-profile wheels were soon replaced with carbon rims, which was just as sturdy but decidedly lighter. Fiber handlebars and clasps were launched onto the market and before long the two parts were integrated into one, using monocoque technology.

As technologies became more advanced, new accessories appeared: pedal cranks made from carbon, saddles, pedals and even fragile parts such as brake housing. The Italian manufacturer Campagnolo, which had launched a ten-speed shifter in 2000, began producing gear levers and certain other components in carbon, as well as a derailleur made from composite fiber. We are talking, of course, about high-end products dedicated to professionals and competitions, because the cheaper products were still made using aluminum –though in some cases these were carbon-coated, even if for aesthetic purposes.

Composite frames rely on various technologies refined over the years. Fiber-tube structures linked to nodes with aluminum were surpassed in efficiency and reliability by those made entirely from carbon, monocoque frames, and mixed technology products. The significant advantage of composite material is that it frees the frame-maker from the ties of ferrous materials: wiredrawing of tubes and soldering are no longer required, for example. In time every manufacturer won the freedom to make tailored structures with a specific use, and so bikes which were sturdy and light (as was the case with aluminum), comfortable (as was the case with steel) and long-lasting (as was the case with titanium) could be produced. Carbon soon became fashionable and a must first and foremost for racing bikes but then for mountain bikes, where fiber was used along with Kevlar and other materials whose purpose was to strengthen the frame against off-road wear and tear.

Magnesium loomed in the distance, a material which along with other structural metals was considered the lightest. Magnesium alloys began to play their part in bike parts while for frames the situation was still in its infancy. In 2003 only Pinarello (with its Dogma) and Merida (with its Elite frame for mountain bikes) manufactured frames made using this material.

The problem with magnesium is its low melting point, which requires meticulous handiwork and adjustments that inevitably increase the cost. As this material becomes established we will probably see its cost fall and a simultaneous rise in its specialties, as has been the case with other materials.

199 The Texan Lance Armstrong, the most famous of all modern cycling champions. His victories are the result of talent and stamina, but also of the most highly evolved training techniques and cycling technologies.

200 and 201 right Campagnolo, the first to introduce ten speeds for the gears, also tested new solutions in the wheel sector by proposing systems of different spokes for rear and front wheels.

201 left The Dogma model presented by Cicli Pinarello in 2003 was one of the first attempts to introduce magnesium to the field of bicycle manufacturing. It may well prove a worthy successor of composite fiber some day.

TOUR DE FRANCE
FRANCE

The Tour de France is the world's most famous and prestigious stage cycling race, and its fame attracts so many competitors and watchers that overall participation is numerically inferior only to the Olympic Games and soccer's World Cup.

The *Grande Boucle*, as the transalpine race is nicknamed, was born in 1903 as a brainchild of the journalist Geo Lefevre, and developed by Henri Desgrange, editor-in-chief of the sports daily *l'Auto*. He promoted it as *the* race for the best cyclists in the field, or, as the French call them, *les géants de la route* ("the giants of the road"). The earliest versions of the race were comprised of little more than six stages about 400 km each, which the cyclists tackled by practically spending the whole day on saddle. The Tour entered into the popular imagination in 1905, when, with the Ballon d'Alsace ascent, mountains were included in the route. In 1907 it was the Alps that crowned the Tour; in 1910, with the first ascent to Col d'Aubisque, the race route entered the Pyrenees as well. Cyclists now had to face new, exhausting obstacles and surpass impressive height differences—and all this before the streets were asphalted. During bad weather, the rough surfaces became dangerous traps. The symbol that identifies the Tour winner is the yellow jersey, worn for the first time by Eugéne Christophe, and subsequently donned, in the next hundred-plus years of the race, by all the greats, from Louison Bobet and Fausto Coppi to Gino Bartali and Eddie Merckx. The champions made world famous by this race – and according to conventional belief, it is winning the Tour that makes a cyclist great – are many, but atop the list there is no one whose aura shines as brightly as that of Lance Armstrong, the cyclist who, with his seven consecutive victories (1999-2005), incarnates the American dream. Armstrong in fact returned to compete after having survived a malignant tumor diagnosed in 1996. The American can therefore feel honored of having displaced, in the hall of fame, other real-enough cycling legends, including the likes of Jacques Anquetil, Bernard Hinault, Eddy Merckx, and Miguel Indurain, each of whom won five editions of the Grande Boucle. The Tour de France is unfortunately not just connected to victories, but also death; to wit, the death on July 13, 1967, of the Briton Tommy Simpson, who succumbed to heat on Mount Ventoux during the "gigantic" climb of Provence; and that of Italian Fabio Casartelli, who died on July 18, 1995, after a fall on the descent of the Col Portet d'Aspet.

sport

202 AMONG ARMSTRONG'S FEW REAL DIFFICULTIES DURING HIS TOUR CAREER WERE THE ASCENT OF COURCHEVEL IN 2000, WHERE HE WAS SURPASSED BY PANTANI, AND TWO STAGES OF THE 2003 TOUR DURING WHICH ULLRICH OVERTOOK HIM.

202-203 AFTER SOME 3400 KM OF UNCERTAINTY, THE TOUR DE FRANCE ENDS, IN PARIS.

203 TOP LEFT THE LEADING PELOTON PASSES A FIELD OF SUNFLOWERS IN FRANCE.

203 TOP RIGHT PROTECTED BY HIS ENTIRE TEAM, LANCE ARMSTRONG (IN YELLOW JERSEY) PASSES A LAVENDER FIELD IN PROVENCE.

204 THOMAS VOECKLER (WEARING THE YELLOW JERSEY) CY-
CLES AT THE CENTER OF A GROUP DURING THE 2004 TOUR.
THOUGH IT WAS HIS FIRST TOUR, THE FRENCHMAN LED THE GEN-
ERAL CLASSIFICATION FOR TEN DAYS, QUICKLY BECOMING AN IDOL
FOR FANS ACROSS EUROPE.

204-205 THE IBANESTO FORMATION DURING THE TEAM TIME-TRIAL
IN THE 2001 TOUR DE FRANCE. THIS EVENT, WHICH DOES NOT SET
INDIVIDUAL ATHLETES AGAINST EACH OTHER, BUT WHOLE TEAMS, IS
ONE OF THE GRANDE BOUCLE'S MOST IMPORTANT TRADITIONS.

206 LANCE ARMSTRONG HAS ALWAYS SURPRISED FANS WITH HIS DIVERSITY OF SKILLS: ALMOST UNBEATABLE IN MOUNTAIN STAGES, HE IS JUST AS GIFTED AT COMPETING IN TIME TRIALS.

207 LANCE ARMSTRONG HAS BEEN THE CYCLING'S FIRST TRULY GLOBAL SUPERSTAR, THANKS TO HIS TOUR VICTORIES, BUT MOST OF ALL THANKS TO THE BATTLE HE FOUGHT—AND WON—AGAINST CANCER.

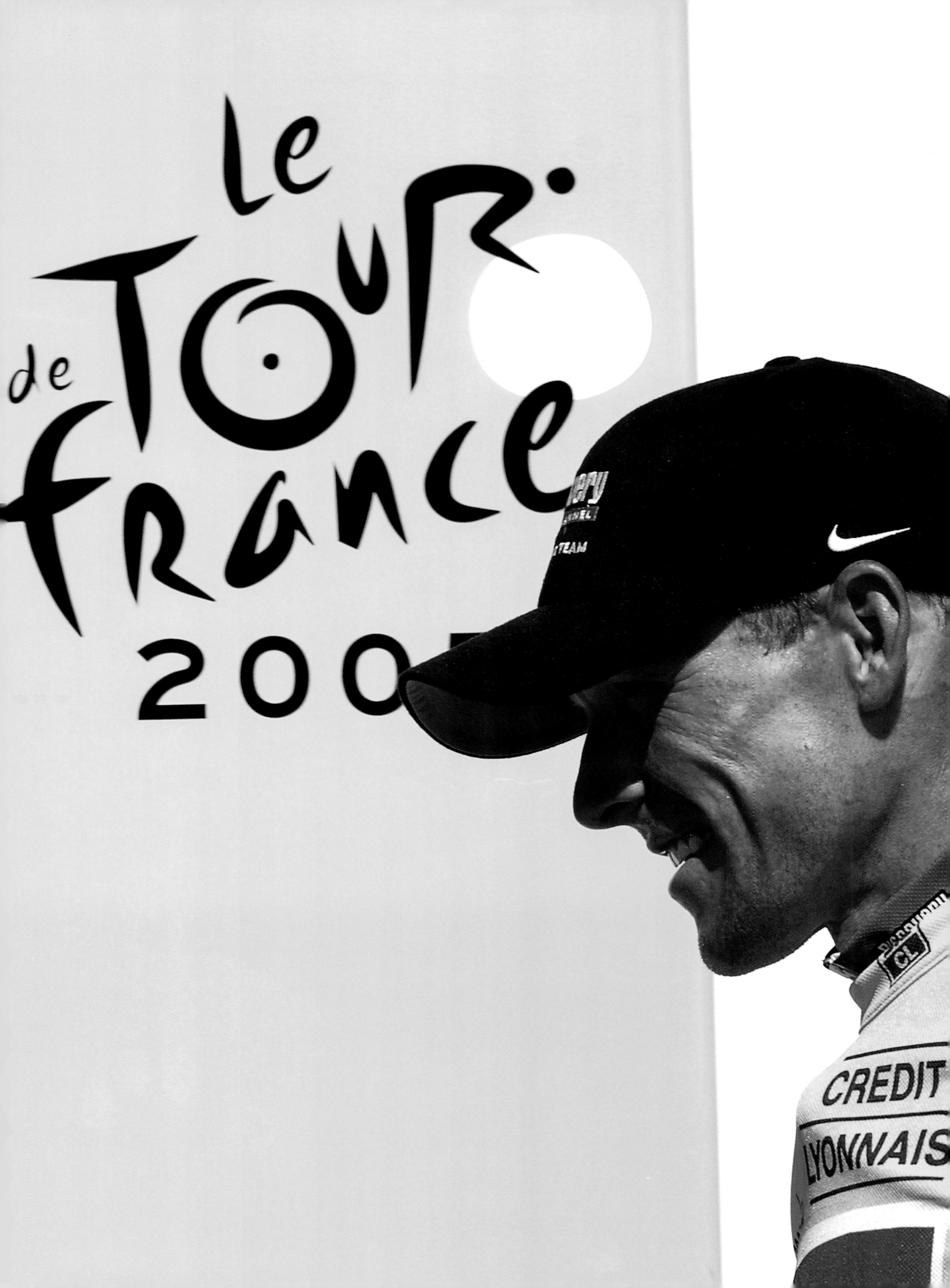
le TOUR de france
200
CREDIT
LYONNAIS

208-209 ALEJANDRO VALVERDE CHECKS LANCE ARMSTRONG'S POSITION DURING THE FINAL SPRINT TO THE FINISH LINE AT COURCHEVEL, IN THE TENTH STAGE OF THE 2005 TOUR. IT WAS ON THIS OCCASION THAT THE SPANIARD WON HIS FIRST STAGE IN THE FRENCH RACE.

209 TOP LANCE ARMSTRONG SEVENTH—AND LAST—TOUR DE FRANCE WIN WAS ALSO HIS MOST IMPRESSIVE. NO ADVERSARY MANAGED TO REALLY WORRY HIM DURING THE 3600 KM RACE; AND HE WORE THE YELLOW JERSEY FOR 17 (OF A TOTAL 21) RACE DAYS.

209 BOTTOM LANE ARMSTRONG CONGRATULATES ALEJANDRO VALVERDE AFTER HIS 2005 VICTORY IN COURCHEVEL.

> *In the new millennium, cycling has transcended the confines of the traditional European arena to assume a globalized dimension on race courses across other continents.*

Today's cycling world is marked by the juxtaposition of a majority that follows the rapid development of technology imposed by the market and a minority for whom style and tradition are still the main points of reference.

210 top ONE FACTOR WHICH CAN SWING THE RESULTS OF A TOUR DE FRANCE STAGE IS HEAT EXHAUSTION. TAKING PLACE IN JULY, THE RACE ALWAYS ASSUMES TEMPERATURES OF 30+ DEGREES CELSIUS.

210-211 A GROUP TACKLES A HAIRPIN DESCENT IN SINGLE FILE DURING THE NINTH STAGE OF THE 2007 TOUR DE FRANCE, A DAUNTING STRETCH THAT INCLUDES THE ASCENT UP THE ISERAN, THE COL DU TELEGRAPHE AND THE LEGENDARY PEAK GALIBIER.

211 top BEFORE ENDING UP IN PARIS, THE TOUR ALWAYS MAKES A LARGE ARC THROUGH THE ALPS AND THE PYRENEES, BUT THE PRECISE COURSE AND THE ORDER IN WHICH TRADITIONAL TOUR PEAKS ARE TACKLED CHANGES YEARLY.

211 bottom AS A GROUP LEAVES A TUNNEL DURING THE MONTPELLIER-CASTRES STAGE IN THE 2007 GRANDE BOUCLE, CYCLISTS EMERGING INTO SUNLIGHT REACH FOR THEIR SUNGLASSES.

212-213 THE DANISH CYCLIST MICHAEL RASMUSSEN, IN YELLOW JERSEY, IN ACTION DURING THE 2007 TOUR. AFTER WINNING TWO STAGES, THE DANE WAS EJECTED FROM HIS TEAM, RABOBANK, FOR HAVING LIED ABOUT HIS WHEREABOUTS DURING AN ANTI-DOPING TEST.

GIRO D'ITALIA
ITALY

The Giro d'Italia is the second most followed stage race in the world. As with the older Milano-Sanremo race, the original idea for an event of this sort was born with the adaptation of a car stage race conceived by the Corriere dell Sera.

The first edition of the Giro dates back to 1909. On March 13, 127 competitors started out from Milan, though only 49 managed to return after eight stages – a total length of 2,448 km. The win-

ner of the first pink jersey, symbolizing mastery, was Atala's standard bearer, Luigi Ganna.

The ascents and descents – downright raceways – were noted for their difficulty from the first; and that grew in 1937, when the Giro was rerouted to include not only the Italian Alps, but also the Dolomites, namely the Rolle Pass and the Costalunga. Since then, increasingly important names joined the roster associated with

the mythical "pink race" – as did the names of peaks like the Pordoi, the Falzarego, the Graden and the Fedaia, which will now be forever tied to cycling prowess.

The Giro acquired its reason for lasting success not only with the addition of the "pale mounts" Dolomites) but also with peaks like the Stelvio, the Gavia, and the Mortirolo.

The Stelvio was introduced in 1953, and right away gained prominence when Coppi managed to distance himself on it from Hugo Koblet, obtaining his fifth final success.

The Gavia was inserted in 1960 by Vincenzo Torrioni, the patron of the event at that time; the first to conquer it was Imerio Massignan. The Mortirolo gained renown in the 1990 Giro d'Italia, and from that year onward it has been widely perceived as the inflexible judge of race outcomes. In 1994 it demonstrated, to great acclaim, the young Marco Pantani's great climbing skills.

Five-time winners of the Giro include Alfredo Binda 1925, '27, '28, '29 and '33), Fausto Coppi 1940, '47, '49, '52 and '53) and Eddy Merckx 1968, '70, '72, '73 and '74); three-time winners include Gino Bartali 1936, '37 and '46), Fiorenzo Magni 1948, '51 and '55), Felice Gimondi 1967, '69 and '76), and Bernard Hinault 1980, '82 and '85).

The 1924 edition of the race made history by virtue of the fact that Emilio Colombo, then director of the *Gazzetta dello Sport*, admitted Alfonsina Strada to the Giro d'Italia: it was the one and only time that a woman raced in the team otherwise composed of male cyclists only.

214-215 THE DOLOMITES, A PART OF THE GIRO D'ITALIA SINCE 1937, HAVE BEEN THE SETTING FOR INNUMERABLE MEMORABLE CYCLING FEATS.

215 TOP A TEAM DESCENDING FROM THE FOSCAGNO PASS IN THE 14TH STAGE OF THE 2005 GIRO D'ITALIA. WHENEVER THE TOUR ROUTE EXCEEDS AN ALTITUDE OF 2000 METERS, THERE IS THE RISK OF SNOW – EVEN THOUGH THE TOUR IS ALWAYS HELD IN SUMMER.

215 BOTTOM A GIRO D'ITALIA GROUP FACING THE 17TH STAGE OF THE 2007 EDITION. THE *DOMESTIQUES*, IN PINK JERSEYS, LEAD THE FLEET AND ARE CHARGED WITH MONITORING THE RACE AND DEFENDING THEIR CAPTAIN.

216-217 The Italian Gilberto Simoni and the Dane Michael Blaudzun, both in the Saunier-Duval formation, lead their elongated group through the 19th stage of the 2006 Giro d'Italia, which runs from Pordenone to the San Pellegrino Pass.

217 top Decked out in pink from head to foot, the Italian Ivan Basso darts through the Piazza dei Miracoli in Pisa during the individual time-trial of Pontedera in the 2006 Giro d'Italia. He took second place, behind Jan Ullrich.

217 bottom left Alessandro Petacchi won the final sprint at Pinerolo in the 11th stage of the 2007 Giro d'Italia. Behind him, the Russian Nikolai Trussov has lost his balance and is falling to the ground.

217 bottom right Alessandro Petacchi, a cyclist from La Spezia and a worthy heir of the "Lion King" Mario Cipollini, has proved his prowess as a sprinter not only at the Giro, but also at the Tour and the Vuelta a España.

218-219 In 2007, the first stage of the 2007 Giro was rerouted, and ran from Caprera to Maddalena, in Sardinia.

219 TOP ALESSANDRO PETACCHI WON 9 OUT OF 20 STAGES IN THE 2004 GIRO, AND DEMONSTRAT-ED IN EACH HIS SUPERIORITY AS A FINISH-LINE SPRINTER.

219 BOTTOM CYCLISTS PASSING THE CASTLE OF MARINA DI ROSETO DURING THE THIRD STAGE (POLIPORI-TERMI LUIGIANE) OF THE 2003 GIRO.

VUELTA A ESPAÑA
SPAIN

The Vuelta a España is the world's third largest cycling stage race. Despite a course that includes several challenging sections across the Meseta Plateau, the Pyrenees, and the Sierra Nevada, and a controversial reputation in a nation of avid cyclists, the race nonetheless plays an important role as the "little sister" of the Tour de France and the Giro d'Italia.

As with the other two great races, the Vuelta was organized by a newspaper executive, in this case Juan Pujol of the newspaper *Informaciones*, who was convinced that tying the newspaper to a sports event would increase its circulation.

The first version of the race, comprised of 14 stages (totaling 3,411 km), was won by the Belgian Gustaaf Deloor, who took the golden jersey of the third stage, and repeating his victory in the following edition, which made history as the longest disputed race: 22 stages (totaling 4407 km). The race came to a temporary standstill in 1937, when the Spanish Civil War broke out, making a sporting event of that size impractical.

The Vuelta resumed its course in 1941, only to be shelved again soon after, firstly because of World War II, and then because of other impediments in the Fifties. In 1955 the race, whose sponsorship had meanwhile been handed off to the newspaper *El Correo Espanol*, and then to *El Diario Vasco*, finally resumed. The Vuelta's prestige grew after this thanks mainly to the increase of important participants, including established champions and winners of other great classics such as the Tour and the Giro.

From the 1960s on, all of cycling's legendary names appeared at this race with the intention of leaving their mark. Jacques Anquetil won the 1963 race and became the first cyclist to triumph in all three major stage races.

220-221 CYCLISTS IN CLOSE-KNIT FORMATION DURING THE 2003 VUELTA A ESPAÑA. LEADING THE PELOTON IS THE FORMATION ONCE-EROSKI, WHICH DEFENDED THE YELLOW JERSEY OF ISIDRO NOZAL AGAINST SUCH ADVERSARIES AS ROBERTO HERAS.

221 TOP THE SIXTEENTH STAGE OF THE 2006 VUELTA PASSED THROUGH ALMERIA, AN ANDALUSIAN CITY FAMOUS IN ITALY BECAUSE OF THE FILM DIRECTOR SERGIO LEONE, WHO USED IT IN HIS SPAGHETTI WESTERNS.

The transalpine *Maitre* was next followed in this special class of victors by Felice Gimondi, and then by Bernard Hinault and Eddy Merckx as well—the latter winning the 1973 edition by racing in his usual cannibalistic manner. (His opponent was Luis Ocana, and besides taking the golden jersey, Merckx beat him in six stages, leaving to his adversary only the "best climber" classification.)

In the hall of fame, firmly lead by native cyclists, three consecutive wins by the Swiss Tony Rominger stand out (1992, 93 and 94). Together with Roberto Heras, who also had 3 wins, he is one of the best performers of this race. Scrolling the list of winners one finds the names of bicycle aces like the climber José Manuel Fuente, Pedro Delgado, Alex Zulle, Sean Kelly and Jan Ullrich.

222 TOP THE CITY OF AVILA, WITH ITS ANCIENT TOWERS AND WALLS, PROVIDES A FITTING FRAME FOR THE TRADITIONAL FINISH LINE OF THE VUELTA.

222 BOTTOM A GROUP PASSING BETWEEN THE CROWDS GATHERED IN A REGIONAL TOWN CENTER DURING THE 2003 VUELTA.

222-223 FLYING THROUGH THE STREETS OF SPAIN WITH AN AMERICAN FAN IN PURSUIT. THE ANTICS OF CERTAIN SPECTATORS ARE AS VITAL AS THE ACHIEVEMENTS OF COMPETITORS IN CREATING THE FOLKLORIC AURA OF EUROPE'S GREAT CLASSICS.

223 BOTTOM ROBERTO HERAS AND HIS TEAM MAKE AN ASCENT DURING THE 2004 VUELTA. TOGETHER WITH THE SWISS CYCLIST TONY ROMINGER, THE SPANIARD WON THIS RACE THREE TIMES.

224 Cyclists on the Meseta plateau during the 18th stage, Bejar-Avila, of the 2004 Vuelta. The peloton, led by Liberty Seguros, is defending Roberto Heras' yellow jersey.

225 top Pedaling across the vast central Spanish plateau during the 2002 Vuelta.

225 bottom The Pelotone proceeds in single file (always an indication of high velocity) during the 2002 Vuelta.

PARIS-NICE
FRANCE

Paris-Nice, a short stage race which runs across France, was first organized in 1933 by the manager of the newspaper *Le Petit Nicois*, Albert Lejeune. With time and successive alterations, the length was standardized at around 1,200 km, divided into seven stages.

The race was held (with the interruption of the Second World War) until 1951, and then recast as the Paris-Côte-d'Azur, a name kept for only two years; in 1953, under the direction of the journalist Jean Leulliot, it took back its original name.

The race was held in the beginning of March, usually at the same time as the Tirenno-Adriatico, resulting an optimal event at which to test one's conditions after the long winter training season. The direction of the race passed to Leulliot's daughter Josette in 1982, a position she held until 2000, when it passed to the two-time Tour and one-time Giro winner Lauren Fignon.

Since 2002, the Paris-Nice has been run by Amaury Sports Organization, a company which holds several of cycling's most important events, including the Tour de France, the Roubaix, and the Liegi.

The race route changes practically every year, though it maintains certain traditional stage venues like Mont Faron, in Toulon, the Turbie, and the Col d'Eze, which is usually chosen as the penultimate stage. From 1973 to 1995, the race was decided on an uphill time trial on the Col d'Eze; in 1996 and 1997, it was decided with a time trial between Antibes and Nice. Since 1998, the finish line has been positioned on Nice's famous seafront, the *Promenade des Anglais*.

The legend of this race, the Irishman Sean Kelly, obtained seven consecutive wins from 1982 to 1988. He is followed by the "Maitre Jacques" Anquetil, with five wins, and by other notables of cycling's crème-de-la-crème, including Eddy Merckx (1969, 1970, and 1971), Joop Zoetemelk (1974, 1975, and 1979), and Laurent Jalabert (1995, 1996, and 1997).

226 SINCE 1998, THE FINISH LINE OF THE PARIS-NICE RACE HAS BEEN SET IN THE MOST IMPORTANT STREET OF THIS MEDITERRANEAN CITY: THE PROMENADE DES ANGLAIS.

226-227 FLOYD LANDIS AND TEAM PROCEEDING THROUGH THE VINEYARDS SOUTH OF SAINT-ETIENNE, IN THE RODANO-ALPS REGION.

227 TOP IN THE 2005 PARIS-NICE RACE (THE EVENT IS HELD EVERY MARCH), A GROUP SOUTH OF THE FRENCH CAPITAL WAS CONFRONTED BY SNOW COVERED FIELDS AND FREEZING TEMPERATURES.

TOUR OF GERMANY
GERMANY

228 ALONG THE 1200 KM ROUTE THAT MAKES UP THE TOUR OF GERMANY, CYCLISTS LEAVE THE HEIGHTS OF SÖLDEN AND DESCEND TOWARD FRIEDRICHSHAFEN, A CITY ON LAKE CONSTANCE.

228-229 THE TOUR OF GERMANY DATES TO 1911, BUT IT WASN'T UNTIL 1999 THAT IT GAINED A FIRM PLACE ON THE INTERNATIONAL RACING CALENDAR.

229 TOP JENS VOIGT, IN YELLOW JERSEY, PURSUING THE SPANIARD DAVID LOPEZ IN THE ASCENT TO SÖLDEN, DURING THE 2007 TOUR OF GERMANY. HE ARRIVED SECOND.

The Tour of Germany is one of the oldest stage races in the international cycling panorama, having been held for the first time in 1911. Even though its longevity puts it on a par with other classics, it has never been included on the calendar's most noted competitions; a result of Germany's tormented history during the first half of the 20th century.

As with all cycling events of the Old World, external circumstances have shaped the development of the race; in this case, there were the continuous interruptions from 1911 to 1922, when the second edition was finally held, and a total of only eight editions up to the outbreak of the Second World War.

After 1946, the competition resumed, but only irregularly, and with the continual alternation of routes and lengths—and long periods of absence from international racing calendars.

Rising from the ashes in 1999, when it finally stabilized in its resent form, the Tour of Germany has since exploited the rising popularity of cycling in Germany triggered by the victories of Jan Ullrich and Erik Zabel, and is now fast becoming a classic appointment for European athletes and fans. Like the Paris-Nice and the Critérium du Dauphiné Libéré, both of which are little more than a week long, the length of the Tour of Germany is about 1,200 km, divided into eight stages of equal length.

Browsing the hall of fame, it is difficult to find a racer who was not born in the hosting nation. In fact, alongside the home idol Jens Voigt, winner of two consecutive editions (2006-2007), practically only German names appear, interspersed (especially in the 21st century) by champions like the Australian Michael Rogers (2003), the Kazakhstani Alexandre Vinokourov (2001) and the American Levi Leipheimer (2005).

230 TOP LED BY HIS DOMESTIQUES, JENS VOIGT, WHO TOOK FIRST PLACE IN THE GENERAL CLASSIFICATION, AND AMONG THE SPRINTERS, PROCEEDS DURING THE 6TH STAGE OF THE 2007 TOUR OF GERMANY, WHICH RAN FROM LANGENFELD TO KUFSTEIN, ENTIRELY IN AUSTRIAN TERRITORY.

230 BOTTOM OLIVIER ZAUG DURING THE PROLOGUE TIME-TRIAL OF THE 2006 TOUR OF GERMANY, IN DUESSELDORF. THE CYCLIST RIDES ON THE TIP OF HIS SADDLE IN ORDER TO MAXIMIZE HIS PEDAL-PUSHING POWER.

230-231 WITZENHAUSEN-SCHWEINFURT, THE THIRD STAGE OF THE 2006 TOUR OF GERMANY.

TOUR DE SUISSE
SWITZERLAND

The Tour de Suisse is a stage cycling event that boasts an important position immediately behind cycling's three most sacred cows: the Tour, the Giro, and the Vuelta. Given the Helvetian Confederation's terrain, the competition has always been considered a natural for climbers. The first edition dates back to 1933 and was won by the Austrian Max Bulla, while the first native racer to w n the general classification was Karl Litschi in 1937. Unlike from Züri-Metzgete, which was not stopped even by the Second World War, the Tour de Suisse was not held in 1940, nor from 1943 to 1945.

As in the day-long classic held in the canton of Zurich, the hall of fame is dominated (up to the 1950s) by native racers, with three editions each for the archrivals Ferdi Kubler (1942, '48 and '51) and Hugo Koblet (1950, '53 anc '55), and only a few editions left to champions like Gino Bartali, who won twice, in 1946 and 1947. From the end of the 1950's and especially in the following decade and since, the top of the podium has mostly been taken by other nations, namely Italy, whose Pasquale Fornara won in 1952, '54, '58 and '59. Along Gianni Motta and Vittorio Adorni, this athlete proved best at meeting the Tour de Suisse's unique challenges.

The 1970s, on the other hand, were the domain of the Belgians who dominated the decade generally: Eddy Merckx, Roger De Vlaeminck and Michel Pollentier.

In recent years the participant field has been further enriched, given the timing of the competition in mid-June, which renders it the perfect event to precede the Tour de France. Among the champions who have tied their name to this prestigious race are Giuseppe Saronni (1982), Sean Kelly (1983 and '90), Andy Hampsten (1986 and '87), Oskar Camenzind (2000), Lance Armstrong (2001), Alex Zülle (2002), and Jan Ullrich (2004 and 2006).

CRITÉRIUM DU DAUPHINÉ LIBÉRÉ
FRANCE

The Critérium du Dauphiné Libéré is a short stage race which takes place in the Dauphiné region, an ancient French region, and crossing the departments of Isère, Drômea and Hautes-Alpes. This transalpine zone between the Mediterranean and the Alps includes some of the same peaks which have gained legendary status because of their inclusion in various editions of the Tour de France; for instance, the Col du Galibier, the Col d'Izoard, the Col de la Chartreuse, and Mont Ventoux, the giant of Provence. Upon its birth, the Criterium immediately earned a certain importance thanks to the later participation of its contenders in the Tour; in fact, the streets of the Dauphiné are widely regarded as *the* place to hone one's weapons in preparation for the Grande Boucle and the donning of the yellow jersey.

Organized by the local newspaper *Le Dauphiné Libéré*, the race was first held in 1947. That opening edition was won by the Pole Edouard Kablinski, one of the few foreigners to triumph in it. Until 1982, in fact, 24 out of 34 editions (the race was not held in 1967 and 1968) were won by a transalpine athlete. The multi-time winners of this race are, of course, all Frenchmen: Nello Lauredi (1950, '51 and '54), Bernard Hinault (1977, '79 and '81), and Charly Mottet (1987, '89 and '92). Also worthy of mention is the Spaniard Luis Ocaňa (1970, '72 and '73). Aside from these, Louison Bobet, Jacques Anquetil, Eddy Merckx, Bernard Thevenet, Greg Lemond, Miguel Indurian and Lance Armstrong all appear in the roster of winners.

234 top The American Levi Leipheimer in action during the 6th stage of the 2006 Dauphiné Libéré, which ran past the Savoie skiing station of La Toussuire.

234 bottom The Frenchman Christophe Moreau at Mont Ventoux during the 2007 Dauphiné Libéré. The so-called Giant of Provence, a legendary climb, is often included in the Tour de France as well.

234-235 Defending their captain, Levi Leipheimer, the Gerolsteiner team tackles the fifth stage of the 2006 Critérium du Dauphiné Libéré.

235 top The Lithuanian cyclist Tomas Vaitkus, captain of the Discovery Channel team, in action (and pouring rain) at the Grenoble time trial prologue, during the 2007 Dauphiné Libéré. It was won by the Englishman Bradley Wiggins.

VUELTA AL PAIS BASCO

SPAIN

The Vuelta al Pais Vasco ("Tour of the Basque Country") is a stage race held in the autonomous region of the Basques, in northern Spain. The first edition, which was won by the Frenchman Francis Pelissier, dates to 1924 and entered history as the "Circuit of the North." After seven consecutive editions the race was interrupted; it resumed in 1935, with Gino Bartali as winner.

After this, the Spanish Civil War—and longstanding financial problems—led to the race's demise; only in 1969 was it reinserted in the international racing calendar.

The local newspaper *El Pais Vasc* has always played the role of event organizer, setting the total length at over 800 km, and dividing it into eight stages, each of which is carefully chosen to correspond with the characteristics of a well-rounded cyclist; of course, climbing skills are vital, as the terrain, though it includes several short reliefs, is mainly characterized by accentuated slopes. Moreover, the wind that often sweeps the maritime edges of this Atlantic-leaning province, and the mercurial climate, render this an exceptionally difficult competition.

The winner of the first "modern" edition (1969) was Jacques Anquetil, but the true ruler of this race is the native racer, José Antonio Gonzalez Linares, who was able to win four editions (1972, '75, '77 and '78). Other illustrious names whose thirst for victory was fulfilled by competing in this event include Gonzalez Linares, Sean Kelly (1984, '86 and '87), Tony Rominger (1992, '93 and '94), Alex Zülle (1995 and '97), and Danilo Di Luca, who, in 2005, starting from the laurel crown won on the Basque streets, started to build his victory in the overall classification of the ProTour's first edition.

TIRRENO-ADRIATICO
ITALY

The Tirreno-Adriatico is a short stage race held in Central Italy's Apennine Mountains. The competition is thus named because the race route starts above the Tyrrhenian Sea and ends on the Adriatic Sea. The newspaper *La Gazzetta dello Sport* introduced this event to the national racing calendar in 1966, further enriching the pink catalogue that already included the Giro d'Italia, the Sanremo, the Giro di Lombardia, the Milano-Torino (the oldest Italian race, whose first edition was held in 1897), and the Giro del Lazio (1933).

The starting point and the race route vary yearly, but remain basically contained in the regions of Central Italy, from Lazio to the Marche, while the historic finish line is San Benedetto del Tronto. As with the route, the length and number of stages has varied over the years, in conformity with the dictates of the International Cycling Union.

Until the 1980s, the race was usually divided into five stages totaling 850 km; from 1984 on, the stages grew, with the total length reaching circa 1,000 km. Given the timing of the race at the beginnings of March, it is considered by many athletes as the ideal appointment to refine their preparations for Milano-Sanremo, which is usually held less than a week after the arrival at San Benedetto del Tronto.

The "gypsy" Roger De Vlaeminck won this race six consecutive times (1972-1977), and was followed by Francesco Moser, Giuseppe Saronni, Rolf Sörensen, and Tony Rominger—each with two victories. In the hall of fame champions of the caliber of Dino Zandegu, who won the first edition, and world champions like Maurizio Fondriest, Abraham Olano, Paolo Bettini, and Oscar Freire also appear.

TOUR OF QATAR
QATAR

The Tour of Qatar is a recently introduced race which has nonetheless acquired, in a very short time, moderate success—perhaps due to the large prizes given by the sponsoring organization. It was first held in the Emirate (which only became independent in 1971) in 2002 and is the result of a global cycling phenomenon that seems to know no bounds, especially given the increased visibility of corporate sponsors, and the procuring of new competitors who in turn attract investors to finance (and profit from) their careers.

The event is favored as well by its timing in January and February, when harsh winter temperatures in Europe do not permit high-level competitions. The Tour of Qatar is thus the ideal way to keep on top of one's sport in milder temperatures.

Divided into five stages over a distance of almost 800 km, the route unwinds on almost the whole road network of the country (the total number of asphalted roads in Qatar is slightly superior to 1,000 km), between sandy dunes and bare rock. Starting (and ending) in the capital city, Doha, fon the Persian Gulf, it passes through all ten of the Emirate's municipalities.

Not characterized by large altimetric variations, the competition favors sprinters; in fact, reviewing the winners' list, one finds all the stage winners to be legends of speed: Mario Cipollini and Robbie McEwen; the German Thorsten Wilhems, the Italian Alberto Loddo (2003), the South African Robert Hunter (2004) and the 2005 world champion Tom Boonen who, in 2006, took the rainbow jersey (though in 2007, he arrived second behind his teammate Wilfried Cretskens).

240-241 The Tour of Qatar follows almost the entire road network of this Middle-Eastern state, touching ts ten major municipalities and also several important historical sites, like Fort Al Zubarah, which is visible in this photograph.

240 bottom left Cyclists in the Tour of Qatar pass an oil refinery in the vicinity of Doha.

240 bottom right The wearer of the yellow jersey at the 2006 Tour of Qatar, Tom Boonen.

242 Lacking large height variations, the Tour of Qatar is eminently suited to sprinters like the Austrian Bernhard Eisel, who won the fourth stage of the 2006 edition.

243 Held while Europe is still in the grip of winter, the Tour of Qatar offers cyclists a chance to keep fit before the summer months—and the onset of such classics as the Tour de France.

TOUR DE LANGKAWI
MALAYSIA

The existence of this race is a reflection of the way cycling has, along with sports like soccer and Formula One, become a global phenomenon—and one whose advocates are tirelessly promoting in their search for greater visibility and additional corporate sponsors. That is, it reflects the need to organize events in territories that do not form part of the centenary tradition of the competitions, which is basically Europe. Taking its name from an archipelago in the Andaman Sea, the Langkawi has been held since 1996, though recent economic afflictions have placed its future in doubt.

Usually the Tour is held at the end of January, when European weather is unfavorable for cyclists; it thus provides a useful training ground for the acquisition of new skills, and the honing of old ones. The most representative stages include the climb to the Genting Highlands (Tanah Tinggi Genting, in Malaysian), a distance of some 30 km long which levels off at around 1,700 meters, and the conclusive one, which is generally held in downtown Kuala Lampur, at the shadow of the Petronas Towers.

In the short history of race, the first edition, dated 1996, was won

by the Australian Damian McDonald, while the only one to have repeated his success is the Italian Paolo Lanfranchi, who won the 1999 and 2001 editions. The Tour de Langkawi has favored Italians, both as regards their stage wins and for their final victories. After Italy on the roster comes Columbia (with the victories of Hernan Dario Munoz and Freddy Gonzalez) and South Africa, thanks to Ryan Cox and David George.

244 LEFT PASSING A MIDDLE-EASTERN MOSQUE, SYMBOL OF NEW TERRITORIES AND CULTURAL WORLDS THAT HAVE BEEN WON OVER TO THE SPORT OF CYCLING IN RECENT YEARS.

244 TOP RIGHT A PELOTON PASSES KUALA LUMPUR'S SULTAN ABDUL SAMAD BUILDING. THE RACE WAS ESTABLISHED IN 1996 BY FORMER PRIME MINISTER TUN MAHATIR MOHAMAD.

244 BOTTOM RIGHT THOUGH MOSTLY COVERED BY DENSE EQUATORIAL FOREST, MALAYSIA ALSO BOASTS THE GENTING HIGHLANDS, WHICH PROVIDE A BACKDROP FOR THE MOST SIGNIFICANT ASCENT OF THE TOUR DE LANGKAWI.

245 THE TOUR OF MALAYSIA IS CHARACTERIZED BY AN URBAN STAGE HELD IN THE SHADOW OF THE PETRONAS TOWERS.

TOUR
DOWN UNDER
AUSTRALIA

The Tour Down Under, was first held in 1999 in Adelaide, South Australia. Organized under the initiative of the Tourism Commision, the Tour is, for Australia, a useful showcase to demonstrate to the world its natural beauties, but it has also become the nation's passport of entry into the world community of nations that host premier international cycling competitions.

The significance this race has managed to garner in a short time originates from its timing during the northern winter, when European temperatures are unfavorable for cycling; the fact that it is meanwhile midsummer in the land Down Under allows athletes from other climes to keep fit year-round and prepare them for arrival at Europe's spring cycling events in tip-top shape.

The Tour Down Under is, however, only a part of the "Festival of Cycling," a week-long event entirely dedicated to bicycles which involves the whole of Southern Australia in a number of events aimed to expand the pedaling vehicle's target group.

Supremacy in the hall of fame belongs to natives, especially Stuart O'Grady, whose 1991 and 2001 victories stand out. Sometimes all three steps of the podium have been occupied by Aussies (for example in 2001, 2002, when Michael Rogers won, and in 2006, when Simon Gerrans did). It is a race where fast wheels are favored foremost because there are no exhausting climbs. Sprinters have thus climbed the final podium often, most notably Aussie idol Robbie McEwens.

246 TOP A PELOTON ON THE ESPLANADE OF ALDINA BEACH, ON THE OUTSKIRTS OF ADELAIDE, AUSTRALIA.

246-247 LEAVING ADELAIDE DURING THE FOURTH STAGE OF THE 2003 TOUR DOWN UNDER, WHICH WAS WON BY THE SPANIARD MIKEL ASTARLOZA.

247 TOP AND BOTTOM FOR AUSTRALIA, THE TOUR DOWN UNDER IS LARGELY A PLATFORM TO SHOW OFF THE BEAUTY OF ITS NATURE, WHICH WAS IT WAS FIRST CONCEIVED BY THE TOURISM COMMISSION.

TOUR OF CALIFORNIA
UNITED STATES OF AMERICA

The Tour of California is a very young race which, together with a similar stage race held in the State of Georgia, is rapidly inserting itself into the collective mind of the international cyclist. The first edition took place in 2006 and was won by the American Floyd Landis; the 2007 edition was won by Levi Leipheimer. One week long, and set over about 1,110 km, it runs from San Francisco Bay through several Californian tourist destinations, including the vineyards of Sonoma Valley, the farming region of the Central Valley, Silicon Valley, San Jose, Santa Clara, and Greater Los Angeles.

It seems it was only a matter of time that the Tour of California should come into being, given the longstanding prominence of San Francisco Bay as a reference point for the American cycling community. Phenomena like the BMX, born in Los Angeles, and the mountain bike, which was invented near San Francisco, in Marin Country, in the 1970s, all gained popularity through Californians like Joe Breeze, Gary Fisher, and Tom Ritchey. In short, the Pacific Coast has assumed a fundamental role in the history of the bicycle and of cycling in general.

Here one cannot but note as well the vitality of the Californian cycling movement, which in 1992, thanks to San Franciscan Chris Carlsson, spawned Critical Mass, one of the liveliest sociopolitical movements of our times.

American cycling generally reflects the same vitality: from Greg Lemond's multiple Tour de France victories in the 1980s to Lance Armstrong's in the late 1990s and early 2000s, the sport has been gaining visibility and appeal across the entire country.

248-249 AN ELONGATED PELOTON ABOVE THE PACIFIC OCEAN DURING THE MONTEREY-SAN LUIS OBISPO STAGE IN THE 2006 TOUR. THE RACE'S LONGEST STAGE, IT WAS WON BY THE ARGENTINEAN JUAN JOSE HAEDO.

249 TOP DURING THE FOURTH STAGE OF THE 2007 TOUR OF CALIFORNIA, THE GROUP CROSSES THE BIXBY BRIDGE, A PANORAMIC POINT SYNONYMOUS WITH THE BIG SUR.

249 BOTTOM CYCLISTS TACKLE A SERIES OF MURDEROUS CURVES IN SINGLE FILE DURING THE PENULTIMATE STAGE (SANTA BARBARA TO SANTA CLARITA) OF THE 2007 TOUR OF CALIFORNIA. THE STAGE WAS TAKEN BY THE ARGENTINIAN JUAN JOSE HAEDO.

250 top Utilizing a skillful *finisseur* move, the German cyclist of the CSC Team, Jens Voigt, sprints to the finish line in San Jose—and takes first place.

250-251 Cyclists during the last stage of the 2007 Tour of California, in Long Beach.

251 top A GROUP OF
RUNAWAY CYCLISTS IN LONG
BEACH, DURING THE LAST
STAGE OF THE 2007 TOUR
OF CALIFORNIA. (THE
PELOTON CAUGHT UP WITH
THEM ON THE FINAL STRETCH.

251 CENTER THE FINISH
LINE OF THE TOUR OF
CALIFORNIA, IN DOWNTOWN
LOS ANGELES.

251 BOTTOM THE 2006
CYCLING WORLD CHAMPION

PAOLO BETTINI GOES HEAD
TO HEAD WITH THE GERMAN
SPRINTER GERALD CIOLEK AT
THE END OF THE FOURTH
STAGE OF THE 2007 TOUR
OF CALIFORNIA, IN SAN LUIS
OBISPO.

TOUR OF DENMARK
DENMARK

Famous in the cycling field for being the homeland of athletes like Rolf Sorensen, Bjarne Riis and Michael Rasmussen (1999 Mountain Bike World Champion), the Tour of Denmark is the most prominent stage race in Scandinavia.

The race was held for the first time in 1985, with the simultaneous debut of the Italian Moreno Argentin. It was interrupted after 1988 (when the Australian Phil Anderson won it), but resumed in 1995. Peculiarities of the race include the award conferred for Best Dane (1987 and 1988) and Best Amateur (1995).

Sponsored (in recent years) by the Danish national postal agency, the race is about 850 km in length, and divided into six stages. Denmark is almost completely flat, with a few mild reliefs, so the sections are commonly resolved with a flight in compact ranks, or else with a

finisseur action in the final kilometers. The separations remain contained even after the sole chronometrical stage, usually set at mid race.

The sole two-time winner of this race is the Norwegian Kurt Asle Arvesen (2004, 2007), but Bjarne Riis (1995), Tyler Hamilton (1999), Rolf Sorensen (2000), and Fabian Cancellara (2006) have left their mark on this tour as well.

The Italian Ivan Basso dominated in 2005 after winning four of six stages. In two editions, the time that separated the first cyclist at the finish line from the second was only two seconds: in 2003, when the German Sebastian Lang beat the Belgian Jurgen van Goolen; and in 2004, when Kurt Asle Arvesen beat his CSC teammate, Jens Voigt by the same difference.

252 TOP LEFT BECAUSE OF ITS ALMOST COMPLETELY FLAT TERRAIN, STAGES IN THE TOUR OF DENMARK ALMOST ALWAYS END WITH A SPRINT, INCREASING THE POSSIBILITY OF FALLS LIKE THIS THE ONE, DURING THE FIRST STAGE OF THE 2007 EDITION, IN WHICH ALEX RASMUSSEN WAS THROWN TO THE GROUND.

252 TOP RIGHT THE ITALIAN SPRINTER FRANCESCO CHICCHI RAISES HIS ARMS IN VICTORY AT THE END OF THE FOURTH STAGE OF THE 2007 TOUR OF DENMARK, AFTER A SPRINT IN WHICH HE OVERTOOK MARK CAVENDISH AND MATTI BRESCHEL.

252 BOTTOM THE URBAN CIRCUIT OF FREDERIKSBERG, ARRIVAL POINT OF THE TOUR OF DENMARK 2007. THE CSC TEAM ATHLETES LEADING THE RACE HAVE LINED UP AT THE GROUP'S HEAD IN ORDER TO PROTECT GENERAL CLASSIFICATION LEADER KURT ASLE ARVESEN.

253 SURROUNDED BY A CHEERING CROWD, CYCLISTS PASS THROUGH THE STREETS OF HILLEROD DURING THE FOURTH STAGE OF THE 2006 TOUR OF DENMARK. HILLEROD IS FAMOUS FOR ITS RENAISSANCE CASTLE, FREDERIKSBORG, VISIBLE IN THE BACKGROUND.

WORLD ROAD RACE CHAMPIONSHIP

The World Cycling Championship is one of the most prestigious one-day races in the international panorama. As regards the route, it cannot boast the technical relevance or difficulties offered by monuments like the Paris-Roubaix or the Liège-Bastogne-Liège, but it still allows the competitor to establish himself as a global champion – and bestows on him the right to wear the rainbow jersey – *l'arc en ciel* ("symbol of victory") – until the next year's victor displaces him.

The World Championship takes place annually, but the venue is changed every time; depending on the host country. The route may be flat (and favor speed demons), as it was in Madrid in 2005,when it was won by the Belgian Tom Boonen, who beat the Spaniard Alejandro Valverde and the Frenchman Anthony Geslin. Or it may favor climbers, as did the Columbian race in Duitama, in 1995, when Abraham Olano beat countrymen Miguel Indurian and Marco Pantani.

The first edition was held in 1927 in the autodrome of the Nürnberg Ring, in Germany, where the Italian Alfredo Binda made his mark as the first world champion. Binda would later attain (along with other giants of the sport such a Rik Van Steenenbergen, Eddy Merckx, and Oscar Freire) the magical number of three rainbow jerseys. In 1931 the title was held by the "Human Locomotive" Learco Guerra at the end of a most unique chronometer competition. Reviewing the Hall of Fame, one will also find such high-caliber athletes as Georges Ronsee (1928 and '29), Rik Van Steenbergen (1956 and '57), Rik Van Looy (1960 and '61) and Gianni Bugno (1991 and '92), the only competitors to have won two consecutive editions.

The cycling championship is a strange race – an event whose outcome is always difficult to predict and before which even the best cyclist is apt to stand feeling inadequately prepared; it is therefore easy to find, among its representative participants, the names of illustrious strangers

who, with the race of their life, have given the carrier of the rainbow jersey the sense that he is the bearer of a an almost mythic legacy. On the other side of the coin are those cyclists who have rightfully found a permanent place among the world's sports elite, but have never managed to win laurels here – to wit, Gino Bartali, Jacques Anquetil, and Miguel Indurain.

254 THE SPANIARD OSCAR FREIRE IN HIS RAINBOW JERSEY, THE TROPHY GIVEN TO WORLD CHAMPION ROAD RACERS. THOSE HONORED WITH THE JERSEY WEAR IT FOR THE ENTIRE FOLLOWING SEASON.

254-255 A GROUP CLIMBS TORRICELLE DURING THE 2004 WORLD CHAMPIONSHIPS HELD IN VERONA. ASIDE FROM BEING A SPORTS EVENT, THE RACE IS A CELEBRATION FOR FANS OF ALL NATIONS TO COME TOGETHER, CHEER THEIR FAVORITES, AND SHARE IN A GENERAL SHOW OF GOOD WILL.

255 TOP A GROUP PASSES A WINDMILL DURING THE 1998 WORLD CHAMPIONSHIPS, WHICH WERE HELD IN VALKENBURG. THE SWISS CYCLIST OSKAR CAMENZIND WON THE RAINBOW JERSEY THAT YEAR AFTER DEFEATING PETER VAN PETEGEM AND MICHELE BARTOLI.

255 BOTTOM THE RACING COURSE USED AT WORLD CHAMPIONSHIP EVENTS VARIES EACH YEAR, ACCORDING TO THE HOST NATION. THE 2005 EDITION, WHICH WAS HELD IN MADRID, PLAYED TO SPRINTERS' STRENGTHS.

256 TOP A CLOSE-KNIT GROUP PROCEEDS ALONG THE STREETS OF PLOAUY AT THE 2000 WORLD CHAMPIONSHIPS. IN THIS RACE, WHICH IS HARDLY CONTROLLABLE BY THIS OR THAT TEAMS, THE OUTCOME IS LARGELY DEPENDANT ON THE PROWESS OF A PARTICULAR INDIVIDUAL OVER HIS ADVERSARIES.

256-257 THE DUTCHMAN MICHAEL BOOGERD SPRINTS TOWARD THE PEAK OF TORRICELLE DURING THE LAST ROUND OF THE 2004 CHAMPIONSHIPS IN VERONA, WITH THE SPANIARD OSCAR FREIRE AND THE ITALIANS DAMIANO CUNEGO AND IVAN BASSO IN HOT PURSUIT.

257 TOP THE BELGIAN TOM BOONEN DARTS TO THE FINISH LINE AT THE 2005 WORLD CHAMPIONSHIPS, WHICH WERE HELD IN MADRID. COMING AT THE CLOSE OF AN ALREADY MEMORABLE SEASON, BOONEN'S VICTORY GAVE HIM HIS FIRST WORLD CHAMPIONSHIP TITLE.

257 CENTER ALEJANDRO VALVERDE ON THE FINISH LINE IN HAMILTON, CANADA, IN 2003. HE CAME IN SECOND, AFTER IGOR ASTARCLA.

257 BOTTOM THE 2001 CHAMPIONSHIPS, HELD IN LISBON, WERE WON WITH A SPRINT BY OSCAR FREIRE, WHO OVERTOOK PAOLO BETTINI AND ANDREJ HAUPTMAN. THE DUTCH ERIK DEKKER AND ERIK ZABEL ALSO COMPETED IN THE RACE.

LIÈGE-BASTOGNE-LIÈGE
BELGIUM

258-259 Flat stretches are few and far between in the Liège-Bastogne-Liège, which is characterized by short but steep climbs and a total height difference of some 4,000 meters.

259 top The Liège-Bastogne-Liège is one of the international cycling calendar's oldest events. Held in Belgium since 1892, its nickname is *la Doyenne* — the "old lady" of the races.

Organized for the first time in 1892, the Liège-Bastogne-Liège is the oldest cycling classic—hence its nickname, *la Doyenne* ("eldest woman"). The first eight editions, which were held non-consecutively from 1892 to 1913, started and finished in the town of Spa, which was at that time famous for its thermal springs.

After the end of the First World War, from 1919 on, it gradually assumed its current form, with starting and finish lines set in the city of Liège. The track unwinds over the Houffalize Plateau, near the border with Luxembourg; from these it turns backs towards Liège, along a different route, and bringing the total distance to about 260 km. Especially characteristic of this race, which professionals call the hardest classic on the calendar, is the presence of the *côtes*, the hills of the Ardennes, which are concentrated on the second part of the race, and which render the route similar to that of a track built for a roller coaster. In fact, the road alternates up and down not only continuously, but to an unbelievable extreme, the altitude difference between the peaks and troughs being totaling about 4000 m.

The most famous ascent is the Côte de la Redoute, 293 meters high and ascending at an average slope of 8.3 % which, after 220 km, almost always breaks down more than a few worthy competitors. It is along this tortuous legendary stretch that several champions have added immortal pages to the annals of great cycling, especially as they flew to victory at the finish. Not surprisingly, on the occasion of the centennial anniversary of the race, a stele was placed at the foot of the climb to celebrate the deeds of "the heroes of the Ardennes." The inscription reads thus: "*1892-1992 Ici, les plus grands champions cyclistes forgèrent leurs victoires dans Liège-Bastogne-Liège.*"

Champions who won *La Doyenne* include Eddy Merckx who raced it eleven times, obtaining five victories, one second place, and a third place and the Venetian Moreno Argentin, with four victories. These two great performers of the Ardennes share their record of three consecutive victories with the Belgian Léon Houa, who took the first three editions (1892, '93, and '94).

The historic 1980 race bears mentioning here: it was won by Bernard Hinault in heavy winds and in a snow storm that beset the racers for over 80 km, though it was already the 20th of April. Only 21 of the 174 racers who started arrived at the finish line. First among them, of course, was the Badger—Hinault—who bolted at 60 km from the start and incurred such a great ead time that his next-closest adversary, Hennie Kuiper, came in second a full *9 minutes* after him.

PARIS-ROUBAIX
FRANCE

The Paris-Roubaix is probably the most famous one-day classic in the international cycling sphere. Nicknamed the "Hell of the North" or "Cycling's Last Folly," it distinguishes itself from other races by the presence of some 26 stretches of cobblestone road that together make up almost 50 km of the route—stretches so dangerous that cyclists curse their every meter and which, if traversed during bad weather, become deadly slicks that send the best drivers spinning out of control. The race was born in 1896, the same year as the modern-day Olympics resumed. At first, the race started from Paris and, after 279 km, ended in Roubaix, a town in the coal mining region of France on the Belgian border. Later, with the improvement of the local transportation network through the introduction of asphalt surfaces, the organizers rerouted the race to include several cobblestone-covered secondary streets, and thus preserve the reputed challenges of the race. The starting point was thus moved twice, first to Chantilly and then (in 1977) to Compiègne. (In doing so, the route was shortened to 261 km.) The most famous cobblestone sectors are the forest of Arenberg, introduced in 1968, the Carrefour de l'Arbre, used for the first time in 1980, and the road through Mons-en-Pévèle,

inserted in 1955. These fear-inducing sectors are often the places where the race both ignites and is decided. The last stretch takes the name of "Espace Charles Crupelandt," in honor of a cyclist born in the French town that holds the finish line. To win the Roubaix, one needs strength, an impeccable technique, courage, and a good dose of luck. The cyclist who best models these characteristics is Roger De Vlaeminck—*Monsieur Roubaix* ("the gypsy")—a nickname he earned after winning the "Hell of the North" four times (1972, 1974, 1975 and 1977). Many other champions have confronted each other on this exhaustive race as well, of course,

and leaving their names in the hall of fame. Among them one must at least mention Josef Fisher, the first one to win it; Octave Lapize (1909, '10 and '11); Rik Van Looy (1961, '62 and '65); Eddy Merckx (1968, '70 and '73; Francesco Moser (1978, '79 and '80); Johan Musseuw (1996, 2000 and 2002); Rik van Steenbergen (1948 and '52); and Gilbert Duclos-Lasalle (1992 and '93), to whom a sector of cobblestone has even been dedicated.

The Frenchman Bernard Hinault hated this race, but won it anyway in 1981, overtaking two cobblestone specialists right at the finish line: the Belgian De Vlaeminck and the Italian Moser.

260-261 The Paris-Roubaix does not offer respite even during dry weather, when the sand covering the cobblestone stretches causes innumerable bicycle problems – and annoying itches for the cyclists riding them.

261 top Johan Museew, one of the best performers of the Paris-Roubaix. His three victories place him second only to his fellow countryman, Roger De Vlaeminck, the only cyclist who boasts four victories in the Hell of the North.

261 center In bad weather the Roubaix shows its infamous hellish side: cobblestone stretches covered with mud become traps, and riders wishing to avoid holes hidden by puddles are forced to confine their course to the middle of the lane.

261 bottom A handful of runaways in action on one of the 26 cobblestone stretches which characterize the Paris-Roubaix, the queen of the classic cycling calendar. Keeping one's balance on such surfaces is a skill for tight-rope walkers.

MILANO-SANREMO
ITALY

262 TOP A GROUP PROCEEDS IN CLOSE-KNIT FORMATION DURING THE 2007 MILANO-SANREMO, WHICH WAS THE CENTENARY EDITION.

262-263 THE PELOTON FLIES DOWN AURELIA STREET DURING THE MILANO-SANREMO.

263 TOP LEFT A GROUP PROCEEDS, ELONGATED BUT AT REDUCED SPEED, ACROSS A TOWN IN THE LOMBARD FLATLANDS DURING THE 2007 MILANO-SANREMO.

263 TOP RIGHT OSCAR FRIERE BASKS IN THE GLOW OF VICTORY (HIS SECOND) AT THE 2007 MILANO-SANREMO, HAVING DEFEATED THE SPRINTERS ALLAN DAVIS, TOM BOONEN, AND ROBBIE McEWEN.

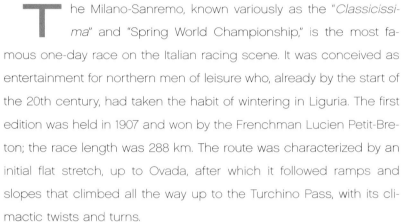

T he Milano-Sanremo, known variously as the "*Classicissima*" and "Spring World Championship," is the most famous one-day race on the Italian racing scene. It was conceived as entertainment for northern men of leisure who, already by the start of the 20th century, had taken the habit of wintering in Liguria. The first edition was held in 1907 and won by the Frenchman Lucien Petit-Breton; the race length was 288 km. The route was characterized by an initial flat stretch, up to Ovada, after which it followed ramps and slopes that climbed all the way up to the Turchino Pass, with its climactic twists and turns.

After crossing the pass the route descended to Gevona Voltri and followed the Aurelia road to the finish line in Sanremo, "city of flowers." The road, even though following the coast, was not flat but interspersed by hills, the most famous being the Mele, the Berta and the Cervo, short, steep hills which, if approached without due preparation, exhaust even the best climber.

To make the competition even harder, and making an even greater spectacle of this race, which was often concluded with a final rush in past years, two new climbs were added behind the finishing point: Costarainera (better known as Cipressa), set at the 272 km point and inserted in 1982, and Poggio, introduced at the 288 km point in 1960: a grating extra challenge that made cyclists deviate from the Aurelia when they were already in Sanremo, and thus extended the length of the race to 294 km.

The cyclist who, more than any other, has tied his name to this race is Eddy Merckx, who in his series of records can boast seven Milano-Sanremo wins: 1966, 1967, 1969, 1971, 1972, 1975 and 76. Immediately after him comes the "Cannibal," Costante Girardengo, with six victories (1918, 1921, 1923, 1925, 1926 and 1928); then Gino Bartali (1939, 1940, 1947 and 1950), and Erik Zabel (1997, 1998, 2000 and 2001), in whose Palmarès four victories appear, followed by Roger de Vlaeminck (1973, 1978, and 1979) and Fausto Coppi (1946, 1948 and 1949) who attained victory three times. The *Campionissimo* was the protagonist of one of the most beautiful happenings associated with this race: in 1946 he attacked at Binasco and, on the Turchino, left all his companions behind, racing the remaining 147 km to the finish line completely alone.

TOUR OF FLANDERS (RONDE VAN VLAANDEREN)
BELGIUM

The Tour of Flanders is for Belgians, and particularly the Flemish, *the* sports event of the year. For a Belgian, citizen of a country where cycling is a sort of religion, winning this race is thus akin to winning a world championship, and means definite consecration on the Olympus of cyclists.

The characteristic elements of this race are the "walls," steep hills that rear like a bucking bronco and, as if this were not enough, are often paved with cobblestones. Naturally, the race route has been modified since the first edition of 1913 and, almost every year, new more-or-less insidious cobbled hills are introduced; in any case the race length has by now been settled at 257 km, and the number of hills stabilized at 18, of which only 10 are asphalted.

The most famous and difficult, however, are those made of cobblestone, like the Oude Kwaremont (old Kwaremont), the Koppeberg and the Grammont (known in Flemish as the Muur-Kapelmuur or Muur). The latter is a sort of symbol of the race, like the Huy, for the Flèche Wallonne, or the Redoute for Liège, and it is the penultimate difficulty of the race (and site of numerous decisive attacks)

The first winner of this classic race was the Belgian Paul Demani in 1913, and ever since, the majority of victories has been taken by the host country. Among the pedaling champions which have tied a large part of their fortunes to this race is the Flemish Johan Museew, who can boast three victories (1993, 1995 and 1998), besides numerous second and third place results, standings which have earned him the nickname "Lion of the Flanders" (a name he shares with the Italian Fiorenzo Magni, who won three consecutive victories from 1949 to 1951).

Multi-time winners of this race also include the Belgians Achiel Busse (1940, 1941 and 1943) and Eric Leman (1970, 1972 and 1973), Eddy Merckx (1969 and 1975), the Dutch Jan Raas (1979 and 1983), and the Belgian Tom Boonen (2005 and 2006).

264 THE TOUR OF FLANDERS IS CHARACTERIZED BY A SERIES OF SO-CALLED WALLS: STEEP, NARROW CLIMBS OFTEN COVERED BY COBBLESTONES, AND SO DIFFICULT THAT THEY DRAIN EVEN THE BEST CYCLISTS OF THEIR ENERGY.

264-265 THE KOPPERBERG WALL IS CHARACTERIZED BY SLOPES THAT REACH 22%. IN 2006, BAD WEATHER BEFORE THE RACE RENDERED THE COBBLESTONES SO SLIPPERY THAT THEY BECAME A VIRTUALLY INSURMOUNTABLE OBSTACLE.

265 TOP IN BELGIUM CYCLING IS NOT ONLY THE NATIONAL SPORT BUT SOMETHING OF A RELIGION. FROM THIS VIEWPOINT, THE TOUR OF FLANDERS IS A YEARLY RITE WHOSE CELEBRATORY FUNCTION IS REFLECTED BY THE EAGERNESS OF THE CROWDS GATHERED ALONG EVERY ROADSIDE.

AMSTEL GOLD RACE
HOLLAND

The Amstel Gold Race, the classic Dutch race, is among one of the most recent races, having been launched only in 1966. The race owes its name to the renowned Netherlands brewery which has sponsored it since its birth. This is a race that celebrates the passion for cycling which a country like Holland exhibits on a par with only other three European nations (Belgium, France and Italy) – a land in which pedaling has been a centuries-long tradition.

The course is similar to Belgian races, having an infinite number of short and very hard climbs (fortunately without cobblestones). As with older competitions, the course has undergone numerous adaptations and improvements.

The first version, which set out from Amsterdam, arrived, after 280 km, in Maastricht, where the starting point was later moved (but where the finish line nevertheless remained).

Over the years, the race has grown in length to total about 250 km, and the number of hills has stabilized to around thirty. The hardest of these is the Keutenberg, with a maximum slope of 22%; it rises, in less than a kilometer and a half, 141 meters.

In 2003 the route was further modified to render it even more spectacular. The new arrival point had been set not in the Dutch city famous for the signature of the European Union's treaty – the Hague – but in Valkenburg, which is reached after covering a route composed by three concentric rings. Starting with this edition, the finish line was set at the end of the Cauberg, a hill about a kilometer and a half with a maximum slope of 12%, which is run three times and which, in view of the arrival point, more or less at the 250th kilometer, wears out the best pair of cycling legs.

Jean Stablinski, a Frenchman with Polish origins, was the first winner, but the Dutch brewery race is doubly tied to the home idol Jan Raas who triumphed on these roads five times (from 1977 to 1980, and in 1983) and to whom the race organizers have since dedicated a commemorative stele set on Cauberg.

266 TOP THE AMSTEL GOLD RACE IS A COMPETITION WHICH THE DUTCH, A POPULATION WITH A DEEP LOVE FOR CYCLING, FOLLOW WITH PASSION — AND THE OCCASIONAL PARTICIPATORY SURGE RIGHT ONTO THE RACE COURSE, WHERE THEY CHEER ON THEIR FAVORITE PROSPECTS.

266 CENTER THE STREETS FOLLOWED BY THE AMSTEL GOLD RACE TEND TO BE QUITE NARROW, AND IN CASE OF GROUP FALLS OR SLOW-DOWNS, IT IS NOT RARE TO SEE CYCLISTS MAKE A DETOUR THROUGH A NEARBY FIELD, SO AS NOT TO FIND THEMSELVES IN A BOTTLENECK.

266 BOTTOM THE AMSTEL GOLD RACE IS HELD ALMOST ENTIRELY INSIDE THE PROVINCE OF LIMBURG. STARTING FROM MAASTRICHT, IT ENDS, AFTER 250 KM, IN VALKENBURG, AT THE TOP OF THE CAUBERG — A FINAL CLIMB WHICH GENERALLY DECIDES THE WINNER.

267 BEFORE ARRIVING AT THE FINISH LINE IN VALKENBURG, THE AMSTEL TAKES COMPETITORS THROUGH A SERIES OF EXTREMELY DIFFICULT SHORT BUT STEEP CLIMBS.

HAMBURG VATTENFALL CYCLASSICS
GERMANY

268 TOP AND BOTTOM THE HAMBURG VATTENFALL CYCLASSIC MEASURES 250 KM IN LENGTH AND WINDS THROUGH THE BOTH GERMANY'S SECOND LARGEST CITY AND THROUGH THE SURROUNDING HILLS BEFORE RETURNING BACK TO THE URBAN CENTER.

268-269 LED BY THE GEROLSTEINER TEAM, A GROUP OF ATHLETES AT THE 2006 HAMBURG VATTENFALL CYCLASSIC CROSSES THE RIVER ELBE ON THE MAJESTIC KOHLBRAND BRIDGE, THE CITY'S NEWEST LANDMARK.

269 TOP OSCAR FREIRE OVERTAKES ERIK ZABEL AND FILIPPO POZZATO TO WIN A SPRINT IN THE 2006 VATTENFALL CYCLASSICS. GROUP ARRIVALS ARE NORMAL IN THIS RACE, WHICH DOES NOT PRESENT THE SORT OF OBSTACLES THAT NECESSITATE SELECTION.

Today, cycling is the result of a union between bicycles built with specific geometries and materials, and champions who can avail themselves of all the advances gained by athletic preparation.

Of all famous one-day races, the Vattenfall Cyclassics is the youngest, having been launched in 1996. The race takes its name from the city which serves both as its starting and finishing point, and from the electrical plant, Vattenfall Europe Hamburg, that sponsors it. This event gained attention first nationally and then as a world championship event thanks to the rapid growth, at the end of the 1990s, of the German cycling movement—a phenomenon attributed largely to German enthusiasm over the respective 1997 and 2001 victories of Jan Ulrich and Erik Zabel, two athletes who have become synonymous with Nordic cycling.

The 250 km race track is formed by a first broad ring around the city center, and then by a route through the hilly outskirts of Hamburg (Germany's second largest city); it then returns back toward the city via a route that follows the Elbe River—a stretch that is covered three times.

The race's main difficulty is the Waseberg: a 400-m hill with a maximum slope of 18% that must be climbed three times.

The last passage is set less than 20 km from the finish line, thus becoming the race's decisive point. This is, in fact, an attacker's last chance to take off with a small peloton, or at least distance himself from contending sprinters, who tend to overcome earlier adversities along the route without trouble. Generally, however, the Waseberg is not a harsh judge of race outcomes—unlike, for example, the Cauberg or the Huy Wall. In fact, the ultimate victory has been decided several times by a sprint in closed ranks.

The Vattenfall Cyclassics has so far favored Italian cyclists, who can boast victories in the first twelve editions, starting with Rossano Brasi 1996) and more recently, Alessandro Ballan (2007). In the short but prestigious hall of fame (aside from Ullrich and Zabel) such pedaling champions as Johan Museew and Oscar Freire also appear.

THE CHAMPIONSHIP OF ZURICH
SWITZERLAND

The Championship of Zurich is one of the richest classics in the history of the international cycling calendar, but it has never managed to attract the same public following as other races. The first edition was organized in 1914 and, since then, the race was held without interruption (with the exception of 1915-16, during World War I) until 2006. In 2007, unfortunately, the absence of adequate sponsors to support the costs of the race did what even the Second World War could not: force a cancellation.

The race route, which is particularly demanding in bad weather, was altered several times over the years, but the starting point was always the Zurich lakefront. The finish line, however, moved: at first it was set at the Oerlikon Velodrome, but from 1993 to 1999, when the race was renamed the Grand Prix of Switzerland, it wound through Basel, and then returned to Zurich. In the final editions the race course unwound across the hills surrounding the city, bringing the total length to almost 250 km.

After having traversed a transitional stretch, cyclists were convoyed in a 41-km ring, which they repeated several times. The most famous passes on this race were the Forch and the Pfannenstiel, inclines of 2 km at 5% and 3 km at 10% respectively. The Pfannenstiel is, as the last pass, about 20 km from the finish line, ideal for executing an attack, and the able timer can assure certainty of winning without his pursuers being able to narrow the margin of difference. The Swiss Heinrich Suter and his compatriot athletes in general were the rulers of this race at least until the 1950s. Suter took first place six times (1919, '20, '22, '24, '28, and '29), followed by Paul Egli with three victories (1934, '35, and '42). Non-Helvetic cyclists who won more than once include the Italians Gino Bartali, Franco Bitossi and Paolo Bettini, and the Belgains Walter Godefroot and Johan Museeuw. Among the names that appear in the hall of fame of this class, however, the prestigious one of Eddy Merckx is missing.

270 TOP LEFT THE CHAMPIONSHIP OF ZURICH IS CHARACTERIZED BY A DEMANDING RACE COURSE WHICH EXCEEDS A HEIGHT DIFFERENCE OF 3000 METERS OVER ITS TOTAL LENGTH OF SOME 240 KM. BAD WEATHER MAKES THE RACE EVEN MORE DAUNTING.

270 TOP RIGHT THE CHAMPIONSHIP OF ZURICH TAKES RIDERS OVER THE MOUNTAINS THAT SURROUND THE CITY, ALONG THE LAKE THAT BEARS THE SAME NAME, AND THROUGH THE LUSH FORESTS THAT COVER A GOOD THIRD OF THE CANTON.

270 BOTTOM A CLOSE-KNIT GROUP PROCEEDS IN SINGLE FILE DURING THE 2006 CHAMPIONSHIP OF ZURICH.

271 CYCLISTS RIDE THROUGH THE STREETS AT THE 2004 CHAMPIONSHIP OF ZURICH. THAT YEAR, THE RACE WAS WON BY THE SPANIARD JUAN ANTONIO FLECHA, WHO OVERTOOK A GROUP OF THIRTY ATHLETES.

FLÈCHE WALLONNE
BELGIUM

The Flèche Wallonne is a northern classic held in Vallonia, the Francophone region of Belgium, on the insidious undulations of the Ardennes. It is a relatively young competition, having been conceived by two sports journalists in Brussels and held for the first time in 1936. In that year the Belgian Philippe Demeersman won, but soon after him, almost èvery hero of cycling would leave his signature on the event. In the course of its history the Flèche Wallonne route underwent different variations, though it has always kept its primary characteristic intact: the frenetic undulations along the *côtes* of Vallonia— insidious ramps that

must be climbed more than once. For this reason, and because of its geographic proximity to *La Doyenne*, the race is regarded as the younger sister of that classic, the Liège-Bastogn-Liège. The trademark stretch of this event is the Wall of Huy, a steep uphill slope of 12 to 20%, which ascends 128 meters in little more than a kilometer. The Wall of Huy is tackled three times during the race, the last upward slope taking one to the finish line and almost always, serving as impartial judge of the final result. Only he who is able to preserve his strength in the face of this obstacle can win in the Flèche Wallonne. In the hall of fame of nations, the laurels for this race

belong first and foremost to Belgium, which boasts 50% of all victories, followed by Italy and France. The Belgians Marcel Kint and Eddy Merckx and the
Italian Moreno Argentin are champions who, in winning three victories, have
forever tied their name to that classic race. The "Cannibal" and the cyclist of
San Dona di Piave, together with the Belgian Claude Criquelion, make up a
secondary group: the athletes who have climbed the race podium the most
times. Scrolling down the list of winners, one might also note such cyling legends as Fausto Coppi, the Swiss Ferdi Kubler, Raymond Poulidor, the Dutchman Joop Zoetemelk, Bernard Hinault, and the American Lance Armstrong.

GUARDIANS
OF THE FLAME

The introduction of methods that industrialized bicycle manufacture inevitably led to a reduction in hand-crafted production, especially for competition models with proven success. Industrialization and the increase in the number of bikes produced forced many famous global manufacturers to scale back the care with which each bicycle was created in favor of line production. Of course, there remained a small core of builders who preferred to continue their hand-crafted processes and refused to give in to the demands of the modern market. Naturally they remained outside the reach of the market leaders, who were trying to maximize profits while paying no attention to declining quality. Richard Sachs was a leader of this counter-revolutionary movement, along with Dario

Pegoretti and Yoshiaki Nagasawa. They demonstrated why it was still worth buying a well-produced, hand-made product. Sachs, who came from Connecticut, argued that cyclists chose hand-made products because they believed that technology was no substitute for experience. Of course, industrially-manufactured frames had improved in terms of quality and reliability over the years, but machine soldering and mass production could never compete with the care and passion invested by those who truly cared about their work.

This movement obviously represents a small part of the bicycle world, but it would be wrong to believe that this niche is insignificant. In fact, more and more people are turning tc hand-crafted products, because more and more people want to see the face behind the product they have bought. In cycling as in any other market segment, we are faced with a contrast between the fast and the slow, where two ways of thinking are pitted against each other. And yet even those who prefer handcrafted machines are often dismayed at price differences, even when the gap is not that large, and especially by the substantial amount of time required to make a personalized frame. Then there are those enthusiasts for whom bikes are worth more than just sport. For them, it's an object to be treasured, not just for its qualities but also for its uniqueness.

274 TOP CLEANLINESS OF SHAPE AND TRADITIONAL GEOMETRY CHARACTERIZE THE PRODUCTIONS OF RICHARD SACHS, A CONNECTICUT BUILDER WHO INVESTS EVERYTHING IN CREATING AUTHENTIC JEWELS OF STYLE.

274-275 RICHARD SACHS BUILDS HIS FRAMES WITH TRADITIONAL METHODS, SPURNING THE USE OF TIG WELDING, THOUGH NOT BRAZED MICROFUSED LUGS, COMPONENTS HE PERSONALLY POLISHES BEFORE THE ASSEMBLAGE.

275 RICHARD SACHS IS OF THE MIND THAT THE EXPERIENCE AND PASSION UTILIZED BY TRADITIONAL CRAFTSMEN RESULTS IN FRAMES THAT ARE SUPERIOR TO THOSE MANUFACTURED WITH MORE MODERN TECHNIQUES.

Craftsmen generally work alone or in very small teams, choose their own designs, prepare the tubes, and do their own soldering. Those who still follow traditional methods, such as Richard Sachs and the Australian Darrell McCulloch, do not use TIG soldering but prepare joints that are first melted together and then filed down. Using their own hands, such artisans draw on a variety of skills to produce the entire frame. It is very difficult for frame makers to also manufacture the series of tubes used in their work, but some do, such as the Italian Dario Pegoretti who, thanks to his experience in the field of metallurgy, worked with partners such as Excel, Dedacciai and Columbus to develop tubes that were later put into line production. Pegoretti also developed two patented tubes known as the Radius and Dyna Lite as part of his twenty-year partnership with Cicli Pinarello.

The principle material used was steel, which, due to consolidated manufacturing processes (in contrast to carbon), guaranteed quality and balance between components, thus ensuring comfort, performance, and longevity. The manufacture of these unique models was not only based on this element, however, and actually drew on previously acquired experience, without offering the possibility of new technologies and new materials. Kent Eriksen and Seven, for example, based their production on titanium models, while Craig Calfee preferred to stick with carbon. In 1991, the Californian manufactured eighteen composite frames which the Z team, for which Greg Lemond raced, used during the Tour de France. In the face of these facts, it would be hard to believe that the models this created were merely intended as prototypes or exercises in style to be exposed at exhibitions and shows. If the frames were designed and refined with extra care, it was so as to ensure peak performance. To wit, there are the racing models which Japanese champions Yoshiaki Nagasawa and Yoshi Konno – whose bike was marked 3Rensho – supplied to the ten-times world champion Koichi Nakano,

277 TOP KENT ERIKSEN WORKS WITH HIS HANDS TO PRODUCE NOT MORE THAN 200 FRAMES PER YEAR. ALONE, AND ONLY WITH THE HELP OF FEW ASSISTANTS HE CUTS, SGOLA AND WELDS THE TUBING WHICH ALLOWSHIM TO PRODUCE HIS CREATIONS.

276 TOP KENT ERIKSEN USES TITANIUM TO BUILD HIS FRAMES—A MATERIAL THAT REQUIRES SPECIAL WELDING PRECAUTIONS.

276-277 CRAIG CALFEE PROPOSES, BESIDES BICYCLES BUILT IN CARBONIUM, MODELS BUILT WITH BAMBOO. BESIDES BEING LIGHTER THAN METAL THIS MATERIAL, ACCORDING TO THE AMERICAN BUILDER, IS ABLE TO GUARANTEE A HIGH DEGREE OF COMFORT.

the king of speed and the keirin who became established long before the UCI officially recognized it.

Since this is a particularly specialized niche, it has been sheltered from the crises and normal rules of the market, for example the aggressive competition between the large manufacturers and, at times, the supply-side concerns that affect a product's smooth development. Industry is always having to maximize its profits and follow fashions, as well as increase production in the face of reduced costs. This leads to shortcuts, such as a reliance on underpaid manual labor compared with standards in the Western world, or a reduction in the care taken to produce each individual part. Ron Cooper firmly believes that quality must be maintained just as religiously as appearance and aesthetics.

The cycling culture is one where the product is not made for profit. It is for this reason too that models in craftsmen's catalog do not change frequently, because once the correct set of tubes and

sections have been selected, they are always made available to clients.

One aspect overlooked by the industrial process and a continual search for profits is a good bicycle frame's longevity, which in the twenty-first century economy can not have long life, because it must (it is assumed) soon yield for newer "updates."

Craftsmen such as Darrell McCulloch of Llewellyn Bikes stress this point, and deliberately finalize a large part of their design choices themselves to ensure control over them, and to make sure that the construction material will be maintained for many years to come.

These "guardians of the flame," as one might call them – the flame being that of a welding torch – are cycling's nobility. It consists of that small, close-knit group of artists whose work still means something more than sport or recreation, and in attempting to preserve the best traditions of cycling and bicycle-making, it stands the best chance of carrying them into the future.

277 BOTTOM CRAIG CALFEE PERSONALLY PREPARES ALL THE COMPOSITE FIBER FRAMES BEFORE PUTTING THEM IN THE FURNACE. THE CALIFORNIAN BUILDER PRODUCED IN 1991 THE FRAMES USED BY THE TEAM Z, WITH WHOM GREG LEMOND RAN, DURING THE TOUR DE FRANCE.

A MODEL FOR EVERY SPECIALTY

The evolution of the bicycle has led to maximum specialization in every field, with dedicated models boasting special features for every individual user. What follows is a list of the most important types of bike.

The Racing Bike

The racing bike is the competition bike *par excellence*. For more than a century, this sector has guided the bike's evolution. From the birth of the first races in the 1800s, frame makers and manufacturers of accessories have always placed great importance of testing new solutions in road racing competitions, with the firm goal of making the bike perform better and more efficiently. When the mountain bike entered the market, the racing bike had to step aside. It has even required inspiration to renew itself and keep up with the times. Nevertheless it has kept its place as the first image in the enthusiast's imagination – enthusiasts who still fill the streets of Europe and beyond when a mountain bike competition takes place.

THE RACING BIKE

The Time-trial or Triathlon Bike

This is similar to the racing bike, but over the years it has radically forged its own identity thanks to its more vertical structure and an obsessive study of form and materials (often the result of experiments in a wind tunnel) which allow full transmission of the power to pass to the wheel with minimum air resistance, thus saving energy and shaving off seconds. It is equipped with longer gears, a handlebar in the shape of a horn (to which aerodynamic accessories are attached), and high-profile carbon or lenticular wheels. Development of this model was spurred by in the 1980s and 1990s by various champions' attempts to break the hour record. They fitted their bikes with special discoveries which today are traditionally seen in time trials.

THE TIME-TRIAL OR TRIATHLON BIKE

The Track Racing Bike

Track competitions established themselves long before road races, but they soon slipped into second place because people were fascinated with larger competitions and staged races. At first glance the track bicycle looks identical to road bikes, but when you look closely you'll notice the absence of brakes and only one fixed gear ratio. This makes pedaling more efficient but requires a lot of skill because the cyclist can never take his feet off the pedals. The gear ratio must be correctly calibrated to ensure a smooth departure and it must be done on site. At the same time, it prevents the bike from coming undone in races at up to sixty kilometers per hour. Given the particular requirements, the frames have special angles and the bicycle's parts are specially designed for use in a cycling stadium. For example, the pedal crank is smaller to ensure that the cyclist can continue pedaling on corners without his feet touching the ground.

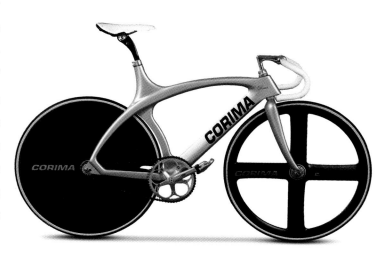

THE TRACK RACING BIKE

THE CYCLO-CROSS BIKE

The Cyclo-cross Bike

Like the track bike, this model is very similar to its more famous sister, the racing bike. Various traditions govern competitions in this field too, and we have seen a rise in indexed components aimed uniquely for use in cyclo-cross cycling. The wheels, for example, at a diameter of 28 inches, use wider-section tires, measuring only 34 millimeters, fitted appropriately and dependent on the type of terrain to be covered. Over time the cyclo-cross frame has adopted aspects of the mountain bike and racing bike frame, with one a few variations: the central movement unit is higher, the rear triangle is wider and tighter, and it uses cantilever brakes to avoid mud from sticking to the wheels.

The Cross-country and Marathon Mountain Bike

The cross-country mountain is the most commonly used bike worldwide. Its origins date to the mid 1970s, when the first competition to be officially recognized was held by the UCI. In 1996 it became recognized at the Olympics. Thanks to its unique design, the cross-country mountain bike can be used for simple outings as well as serious competitions. From the first models put forward by pioneers in the field, cross-country mountain bikes and marathon mountain bikes have evolved and radically adapted their appearance, so much so that some of today's models bear little or no resemblance to their predecessors. The most commonly sold version on the market consists of a sturdy frame and stabilized fork, even though full suspension models are appearing, thus making the saddle even more comfortable. Marathons have become increasingly specialized, meaning that endurance competitions can even last between six and eight hours. The desire for improved comfort has sometimes resulted in the customization of stabilized rear frames, where cyclists carefully assess the demands of the terrain and structure their bikes accordingly in a bid to retain the energy built up by pedaling.

THE CROSS-COUNTRY MOUNTAIN BIKE

The Trail Mountain Bike

This type of mountain bike is designed for those who want to embark on particularly long excursions, perhaps lasting an entire day. The trail bike provides stability and can be easily handled on down-hill stretches, such as free-ride bikes, and is good for up-hill stretches as well, like the cross-country bike. It is not particularly well suited to competitions but can be used for 12-24 hour races, where comfort and smoothness are preferred to rigidity and bursts of speed.

The Endurance Mountain Bike

The endurance mountain bike is for off-road us; like motorized models, it is light and agile. It is particularly well suited for mountains and other high-pressure areas. Fast climbs, steep descents, and medium-sized jumps can all be executed using the endurance bike, which (like the trail bike) needs to be comfortable and quick. Like free riders, an endurance cyclist must be well trained and able to control the bike perfectly in all situations.

THE CROSS-COUNTRY MOUNTAIN BIKE

The Downhill Mountain Bike

This is used exclusively in downhill mountain bike competitions. Along with the cross-country version, it became famous at Durango. The downhill bike is the off-road model which has undergone the greatest change. When one looks back on the clunkers with which Breeze and company raced the first Repack, and the models used by Fabien Barel and colleagues, for example, there has been substantial alteration: for instance, the frame is now fully suspended and completely rigid. Powerful, precise hydraulic systems have replaced the counter-pedal brakes, which in turn have been correctly sized so that they can be fitted to other mountain bike models. Given their flexibility (the result of a dual-plate front fork, self-ventilating disk brakes, and oversized frame) some downhill bikes resemble motocross bikes more than bicycles.

The Freeride Mountain Bike

The freeride mountain bike falls into the "heavy" category, the adjective not only referring to the bike itself, but also to its use, which entails relatively high jumps and difficult obstacles such as rocks and other debris. The freeride bike is both robust and easy to handle. The frame is fully suspended with a fork and shock-absorber suitable for long journeys. In North America it is possible to practice the sport in national parks, the most famous of which is the Whistler Blackcomb Mountain Bike Park in British Columbia, Canada, which offers a large number of paths with varying degrees of technical difficulty and height.

THE FREERIDE MOUNTAIN BIKE

Other Types of Mountain Bike

There are more and more types of mountain bike on the market. Some are called street bikes, but they are in fact a hybrid of a BMX and a mountain bike, though smaller and lacking a gear shifter. They are used especially on flatland by prestigious riders such as Bob Haro. The dirt jump model comprises a closed frame and is mainly used for races in equipped areas where obstacles are jumped in breathtaking fashion. Four-cross bikes are a mix between dirt jump and freeride bikes. They are unique in that they provide table tennis-like races in which four competitors compete on a half-motocross (with jumps and obstacles) and freeride-tracks.

THE STREET OR DIRT-JUMP BIKE

The BMX

Like the mountain bike, the BMX injected the world of cycling with an air pf juvenile recklessness – and thus helped to drive the entire industry forward into the popular culture. From the first Sting-Ray in 1963 to today's models, this type of bike has evolved substantially while staying true to its principles, such as a single gear ratio and twenty-inch wheels. Given the record levels of technological development reached, the BMX is generally seen in ramp competitions with skateboards and roller-skates rather than in pure cycling competitions. In 2008, however, the Olympic Committee will recognize its original use – akin to that of the cross race bike – as a sport which might one day be approved for appearance in the Olympic games.

THE BMX

THE CITY BIKE

The City Bike

Over the years the most significant changes made to competition bikes have also been transferred to city bikes. Once the mountain bike made its debut and manufacturers began production with aluminum, the city bike enjoyed a second youth and has become a vehicle seen in daily use. It can be fitted with gear shifters and V-brakes. Mud guards are often fitted to city bikes to avoid spray from the roads, and lights to ensure safe cycling in the dark. City bikes are usually fitted with a stand, a bell, and a protective casing covering the crank and a large section of the chain. City bikes use wider-section covers compared with racing models; and recently, plugged rubber versions have made an appearance. These are known as country bikes and are also fitted with a shock-absorber fork to ensure smooth off-road cycling.

The Folding Bike

A folding bike has small wheels, normally between sixteen and seventeen inches. It is usually fitted with clips and equipment which enables it to be quickly and easily dismantled. The folding bike first appeared in France in 1939 and was known as *le petit-bi* (the small bike). It evolved in particular under Alex Moulton and Teodoro Carnielli in the 1960s, through Bickeron and Dahon's versions from the 1970s and 1980s are once again enjoying a certain renaissance in the twenty-first century as a quick way to get around congested cities.

THE FOLDING BIKE

THE RECLINING BIKE

The Reclining Bike

The reclining bike also made its first appearance in France. In 1932 Charles Mochet designed a vehicle known as Velocar on which the cyclist took up an entirely different position on the bike from that used nowadays. The components of this model have remained largely unchanged right into the twenty-first century. The cyclist settles onto the bike using not only his posterior, but also his back, and to make the bicycle move, he has to push pedals which are at almost the same height as the seat. The handlebar stretches along the fork to the point where the rider is seated. Although this bike offers reduced balance and is harder to handle, this position also enables to the cyclist to reach extremely high speeds. Indeed, the hour record for the reclining bike is almost twice that achieved using a racing bike.

The Tandem Bike

This is a bike for two people. It is an excellent way of traveling in a pair and also an excellent option for blind and disabled travelers. Riding a tandem requires both cyclists to pedal in a coordinated manner, indeed; they must trust each other in order to synchronize their movements to capitalize on their doubled power. Even though the tandem is popularly associated with lazy holidays and gentle outings, it has had its fair share of success in competitions too. It was an Olympic sport between 1906 and 1972. From 1966 until 1994 it was worthy of the rainbow-striped jersey.

THE TANDEM BIKE

VISIONS OF
THE FUTURE

BETWEEN DESIGN
AND MOBILITY
PAGE 284

BETWEEN DESIGN AND MOBILITY

The bicycle has evolved tremendously in the last two-hundred-plus years; and aside from the fact that bicycles still have two wheels, it isn't easy to find a common point linking the earliest models – the 1790 *celerifere* and the *draisine*, which appeared some 25 years later – with those of our time. Even if one takes the last 120 years, during which the basic shape of the bicycle remained relatively stable, the design has been continuously modified and become increasingly sophisticated.

The diamond frame, for example, arrived at the end of the 17th Century, but is similar to current models only insofar as the shape; beyond that, the use of new materials, first and foremost composite fibers, take the product into a completely different sphere form earlier versions.

Add to that the different techniques used for the building frames - TIG welding and the development of epoxy joints – and the revolution set off by the introduction of gear shifting mechanisms – and one cannot but stand in awe of the radical changes the bicycle has undergone. And these alterations which not only improved the vehicle but also expanded the boundaries of human performance on it.

The bicycle's history, however, does not rest; despite the most impressive developments, its evolution will surely never end, thanks to those companies that believe in research and development and continue to invest in real improvements – and not just the perceived enhancement of their own product line. As in any other field, no matter how venerated, the pioneering impulse remains fundamental.

Without ongoing research, new roads will never be taken, nor will anyone stumble on those innovative solutions which, once to the next generation of the same. The bicycle still have incredible untapped potentials. Fortunately, the major brands are becoming increasingly open tote sort of collaboration that yields progress; to wit, the collaboration of Giant with Michael Young on his Citystorm model; and the rise of public competitions at universities and design schools to find new shapes for new vehicles, rediscover systems that have fallen by the wayside, rationalize older techniques, or replace them with new ones.

One accessory that still begs for giant steps forward is the gear. Its new "El Dorado" is the electronic gear, unveiled (as a prototype) already 1974, by Browning Research. Throughout the 1990s, the models of the French firm Mavic gained visibility, as did the electronic gear tested by Campagnolo in 2005, but updates of this accessory are now appearing almost regularly during racing competitions, on this or that professional's bicycle. Until now, however, no one has been able to guarantee a standard of performance that could render this device's input on the general market worthwhile. It is, however, probable that with time, the system will be made trustworthy enough for any type of condition and will establishes itself alongside or in place of the mechanic version.

Utilitarian bicycles for everyday use are also improving with the standardization of inventions unveiled first on the racing bike and later with the mountain bike. This group of models, having lived for over a century in the shadow of competition models, is gaining new life at last and acquiring a sort of emancipation from its "elder sisters," as the Italians say, thanks to urban congestion and the resulting popularity of the bicycle as the fastest vehicle for getting around the world's largest cities. More specifically, innovative forms expressly dedicated to city use are being studied, besides different materials ranging from aluminum to carbonium. The idea of a transmission system to replace the bike chain is also being developed in certain quarters, with tests geared towards solutions that utilize cogwheels, straps, cardan joints and even hydraulic systems.

In the R and D offices of the major brands, as in design studios, it is increasingly easy to find designs or prototypes that reflect the development of an even newer

zaira perry

284 The first versions of the folding bike appeared at the end of the 1970s. Their acceptance by the public at large, however, remains a question of the future. Up till now they have been embraced only by a niche.

285 The A-Bike takes its name from the shape of the frame. Designed by Sir Clive Sinclair, it represents the ideal model for urban transport, being foldable and extremely lightweight, due to the use of aluminum and glass fiber.

283 Like other vehicles, the bicycle keeps moving toward the future as the discovery of new materials and the development of new building techniques result in the evolution of new working models, or at least prototypes that anticipate them.

idea: an "intelligent" bicycle, suitable for the exigencies of different users, and effective not only for leisure but also for getting around the city on work assignments.

Design basics for such vehicles revolve, of course, around dynamism and efficiency, since the end product must be adaptable both to situations typical of daily life, like getting to work, and longer weekend trips. They are characterized by efficient suspensions to deaden the shocks caused by the bumps in the terrain, by precise and safe braking systems and innovative dismantling systems or clasps to render them foldable – and indispensable solution that eases cyclists' ability to carry them on public transport (trains, subways, etc.) or in the trunk of a car.

Model and component variations aside, the task of bringing the bicycle into to the future is a bet which must inevitably take into account the long traditions honored by this democratic and popular vehicle – a vehicle which, on just two wheels, has carried many of us through our own personal own histories. This chapter, then, presents a series of concept bikes realized in recent years by famous designers: visions of the future that demonstrate how the simplest vehicle can also star as an example of the best avant-garde techniques.

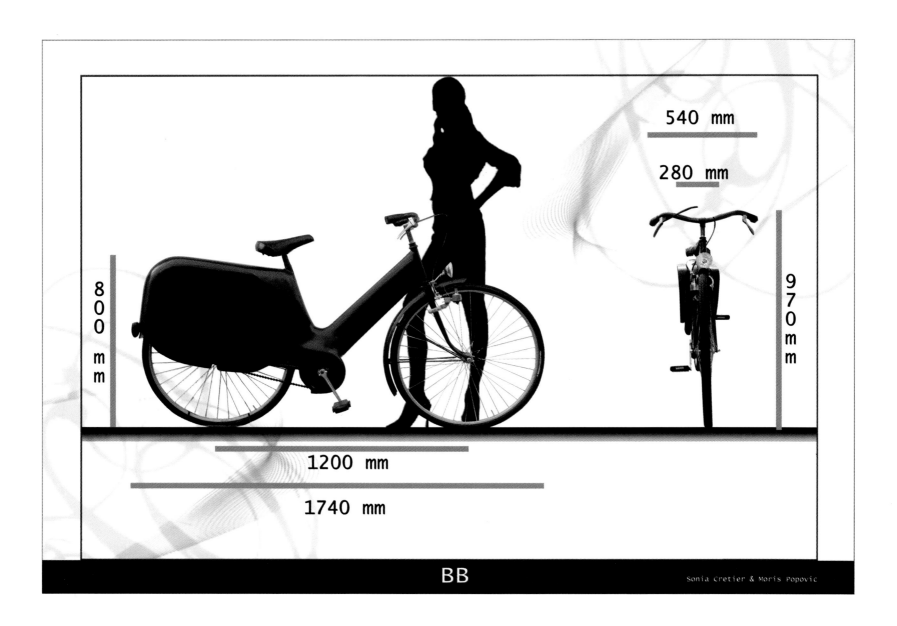

540 mm

280 mm

800 mm

970 mm

1200 mm

1740 mm

BB

Sonia Cretier & Moris Popovic

286 top and 287 top Inspired by the actress and feminine icon Brigitte Bardot, the BB Bike was designed by Sonia Cretier and Moris Popovic as part of a project commissioned by Applied Art and Design of Turin. It reflects special attention to the ergonomics of the saddle, pedals, and handlebar, and is notable for a posterior keel which holds two elegant lateral accordion bags.

286 bottom The Egg-Bike is a prototype of the folding bicycle made especially for young children. It is characterized by two shells which cover the bicycle when folded, so as to make carrying it easier.

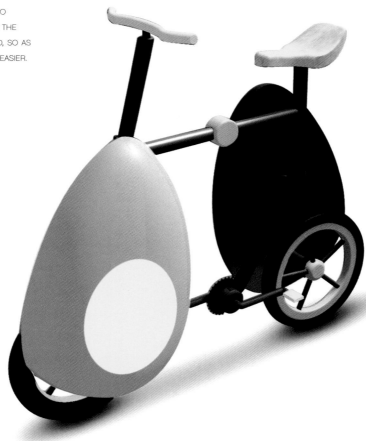

BB

Sonia Cretier & Moris Popovic

287 BOTTOM THE BIOLOVE BICYCLE IS THE RESULT OF CONCERTED EFFORTS BY ROSSE LOVEGROVE, BIOMEGA, AND FLAVIO DESLANDES. BUILT WITH BAMBOO, IT BLENDS GOOD DESIGN SENSE WITH ENVIRONMENTAL AWARENESS AND SUSTAINABILITY.

288 TOP THE MN MODEL DESIGNED BY MARK NEWSON FOR BIOMEGA IS REALIZED WITH AN ALUMINUM ALLOY AL5038. RESISTANT TO CORROSION, THIS MATERIAL REFLECTS THE DANISH BRAND'S PHILOSOPHY OF MERGING TECHNIQUE WITH ETHICS AND AESTHETICS.

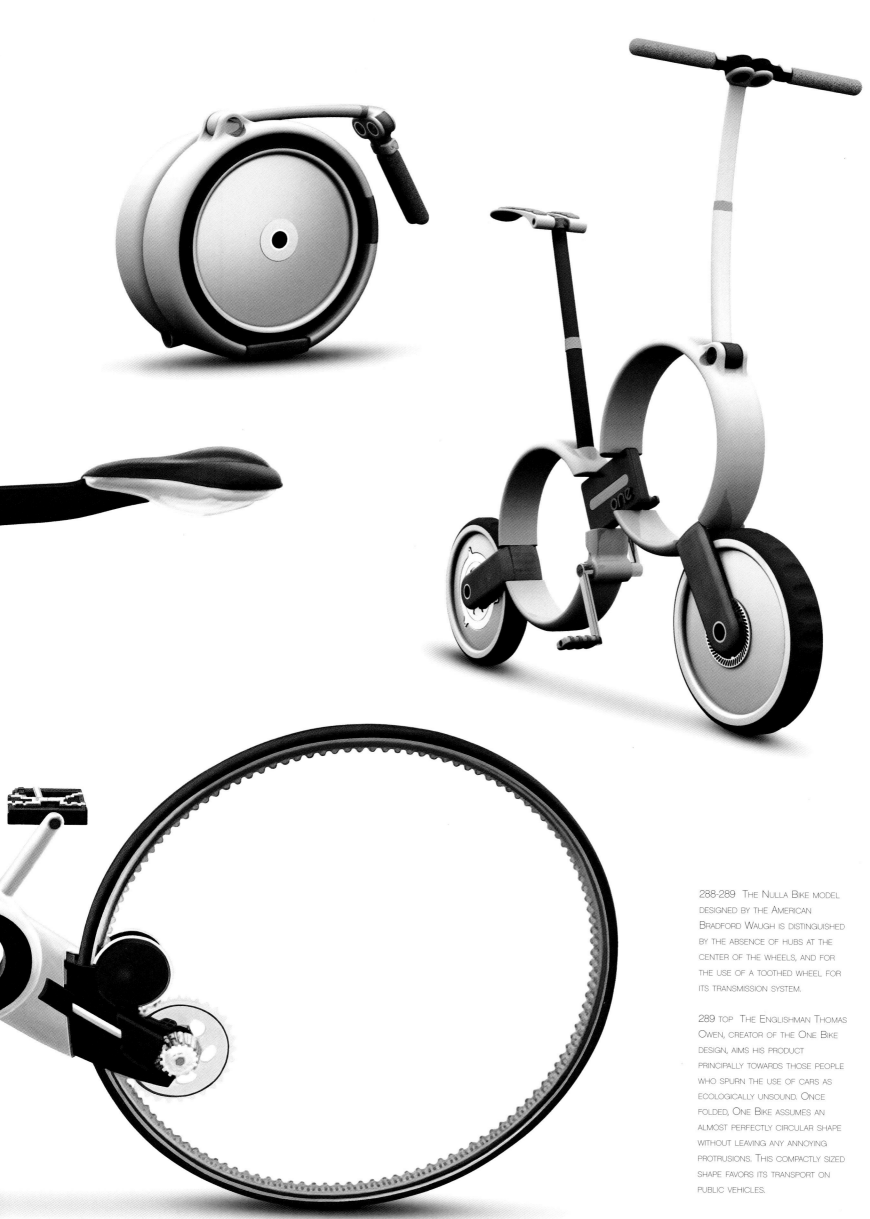

288-289 The Nulla Bike model designed by the American Bradford Waugh is distinguished by the absence of hubs at the center of the wheels, and for the use of a toothed wheel for its transmission system.

289 top The Englishman Thomas Owen, creator of the One Bike design, aims his product principally towards those people who spurn the use of cars as ecologically unsound. Once folded, One Bike assumes an almost perfectly circular shape without leaving any annoying protrusions. This compactly sized shape favors its transport on public vehicles.

290 TOP THE RECENT DESIGN EVOLUTION HAS LEFT ITS MARK NOT ONLY ON URBAN MODELS BUT ALSO ON COMPETITIVE ONES. THE 3W CONCEPT OFFERS A MOUNTAIN BIKE WITH THE SINGLE-SIDED FORK AND A REAR SUSPENSION INTEGRATED IN THE SEATPOST.

290 BOTTOM THE URBAN WAS REALIZED BY CRISTIAN CIURANETA IN A PROJECT DEVELOPED BY THE HIGH SCHOOL ELISAVA OF BARCELONA. IT WAS SPONSORED BY THE AMERICAN BICYCLE FIRM CANNONDALE.

291 THE CREATION OF A PROTOTYPE REQUIRES AN IMMENSE AMOUNT OF DESIGN WORK AND THE UTILIZATION OF HIGH-TECH 3D DESIGNS AND COMPUTER MODELS. EVERY VARIABLE, EVERY COMPONENT, AND EVERY MATERIAL MUST BE CONSIDERED.

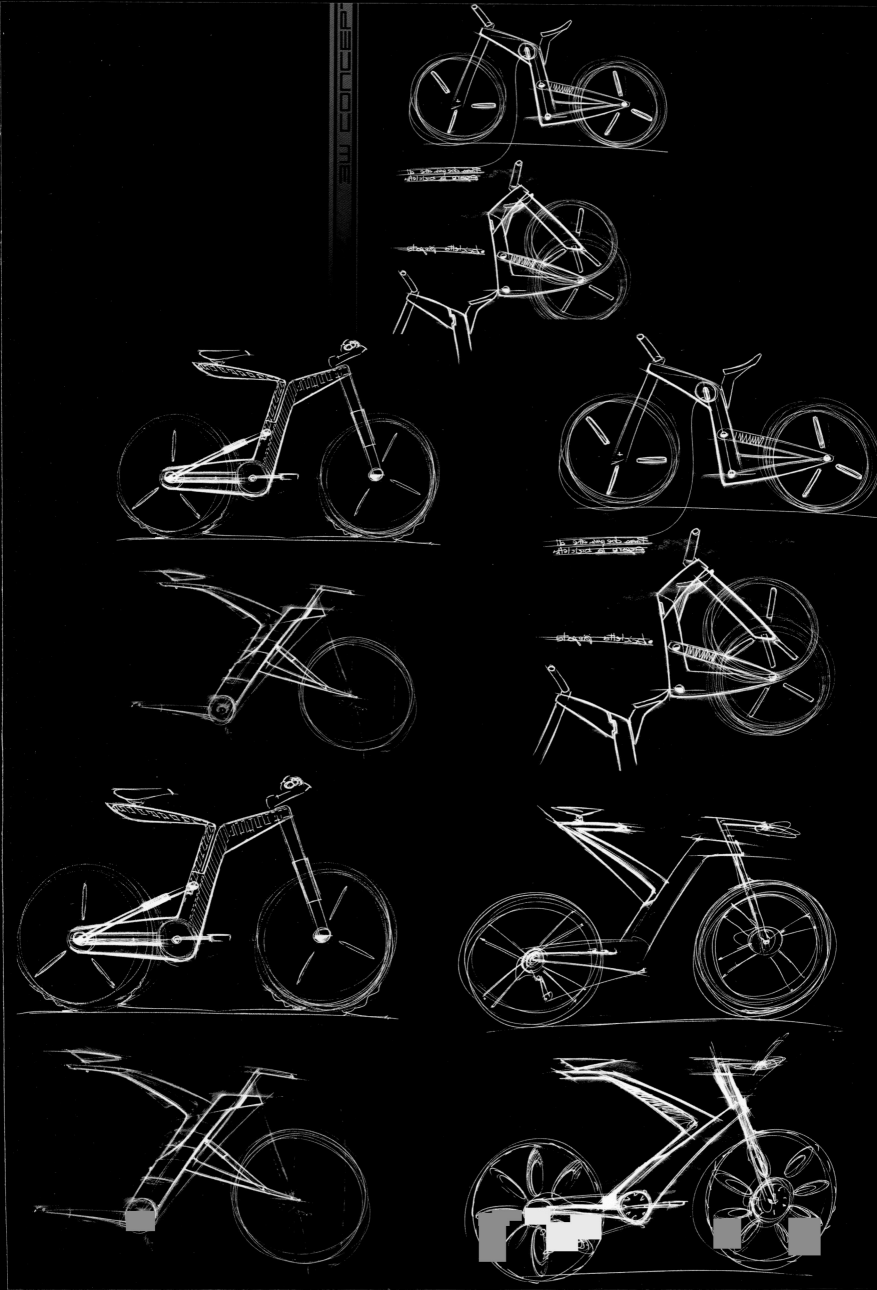

Pör Blanking

Svepa

Pör Blanking
Pierre Franco

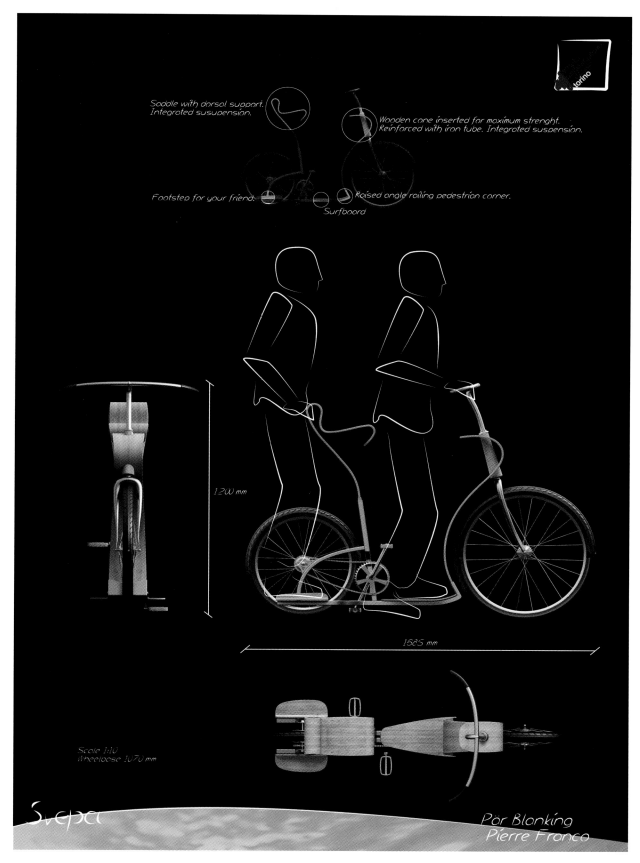

Saddle with dorsal support.
Integrated suspension.

Wooden cone inserted for maximum strenght.
Reinforced with iron tube. Integrated suspension.

Footstep for your friend.

Raised angle railing pedestrian corner.

Surfboard

1200 mm

1525 mm

Scale 1:10
Wheelbase 1070 mm

Svepa

Par Blanking
Pierre Franco

292-293 Pierre Franco's Svepa prototype is comprised of a unique curved wooden body which joins the handlebar, the fork, and the rear metal case. The shape of the wooden component allows a sort of integrated suspension.

292 bottom Svepa is an anagram of the "Vespa," which inspired it: the world-famous scooter whose name still evokes the 1960s and *La Dolce Vita* – the good life.

293 Svepa was ergonomically realized in order to best adapt to the specific morphologies of the human body.

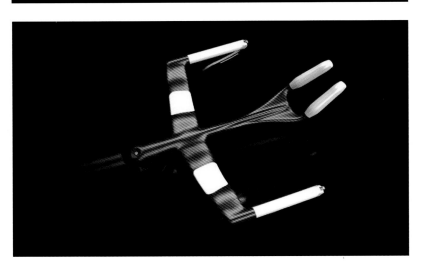

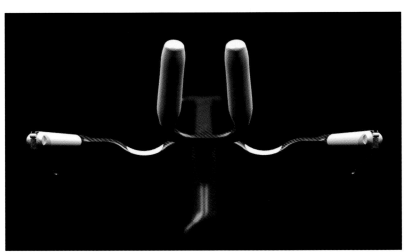

294 TOP THE ORYX, A MODEL ESPECIALLY MADE FOR TIME TRIALS OR TRIATHLONS, IS EQUIPPED WITH SUCH USEFUL COMPONENTS AS AN OX-HORN-SHAPED HANDLEBAR AND AN APPENDIX THAT GUARANTEE SUPERIOR AERODYNAMIC FLOW.

294 CENTER TOP DESIGNED BY HARALD CRAMER, THIS ORYX HAS BEEN REALIZED TO THE FINEST DETAIL, TAKING INTO ACCOUNT THE IDEAL POSITION AN ATHLETE MUST ASSUME TO MEET THE CHALLENGES OF A TIME TRIAL.

294 CENTER BOTTOM THE AERODYNAMIC APPENDIX AND THE OX-HORN-SHAPED HANDLEBAR ARE MADE OF COMPOSITE FIBER, RESULTING IN LIGHT BUT RESISTANT COMPONENTS.

294 BOTTOM THE ORYX BIKE IS CHARACTERIZED BY ITS ALMOST INEXISTENT FRONTAL SECTION, A SOLUTION CHOSEN TO MINIMIZE FRICTION.

294-295 THE ACCESSORIES OF HARALD CRAMER'S PROTOTYPE ARE REALIZED IN MAGNESIUM, IN THE SHAPE OF A RING SUBMERGED WITHIN THE FRAME. IN ORDER TO SPIN, IT EXPLOITS THE WORK OF TWO SEALED BUFFERS.

295 BOTTOM THE ORYX IS COMPOSED OF TWO PRINCIPAL BLOCKS REALIZED IN CARBONIUM: THE SINGLE-SIDED FORK, THE HANDLEBAR, AND THE ATTACHMENT ARE ALL COMBINED. THE FRAME IS BASICALLY Y-SHAPED, AND INTEGRATES THE SEAT POST AND THE SADDLE.

296 AND **296-297** THE LOCUST FOLDS ON ITSELF THANKS TO A
SYSTEM OF LOCKS AND JUNCTIONS REALIZED BY THE PRAGUE
DESIGNER JOSEF CADEK. THE SIZE OF THE COMPLETELY FOLDED
VEHICLE IS THAT OF A SINGLE WHEEL.

297 THE LOCUST DOES NOT MAKE USE OF A CHAIN
TRANSMISSION, BUT OF A TOOTHED STRAP THAT ACTS ON THE
MECHANISM INSTALLED ON THE WHEEL. THE REAR HUB INTEGRATES
THE SPEED GEAR, WHICH IS ACTIVATED BY HANDLEBAR CONTROLS.

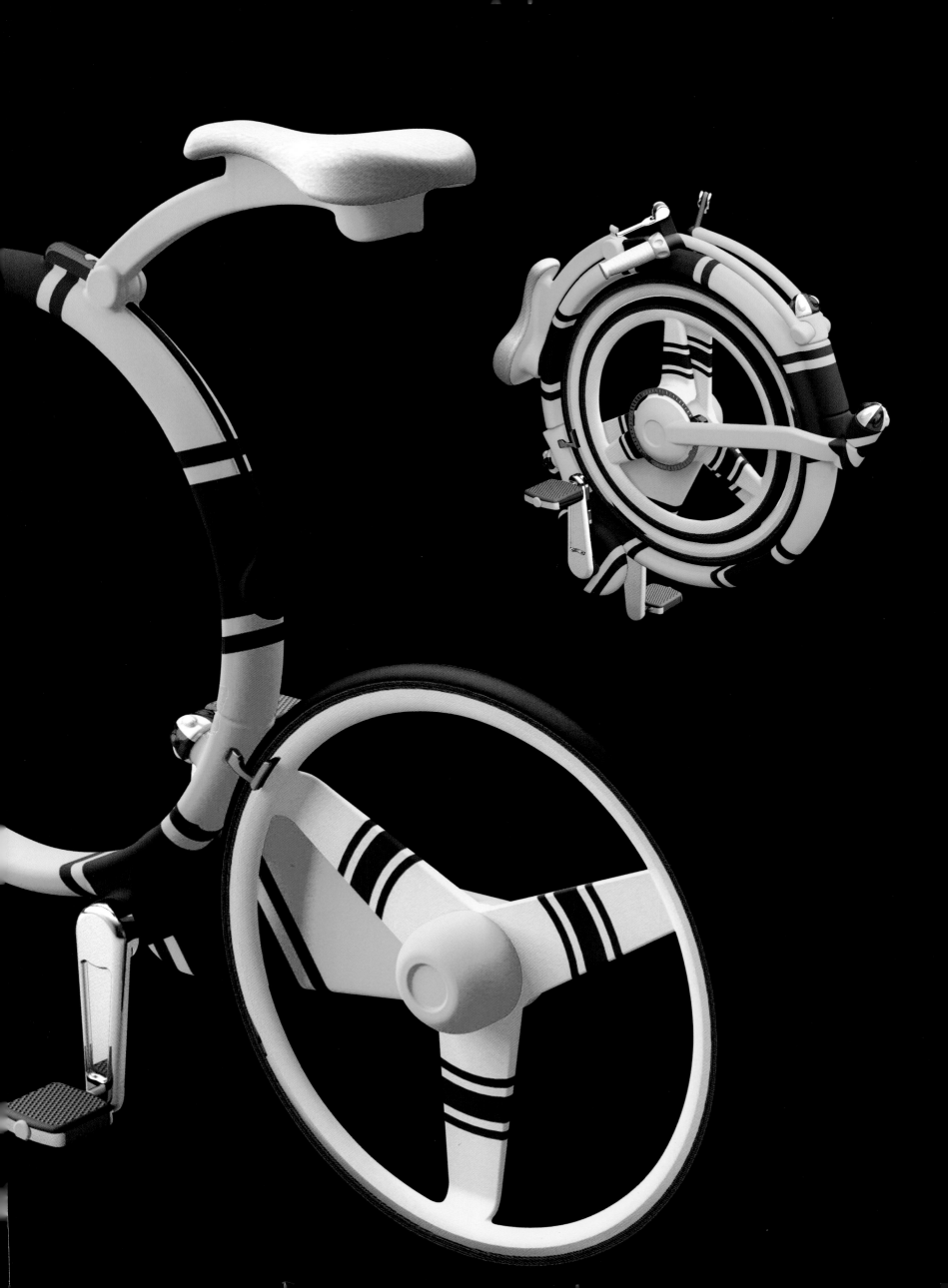

BIBLIOGRAPHY

Andric Dragoslav, Ormezzano Gian Paolo, Bozzini Giuseppe, *Storia della bicicletta: dalle origini alla mountain bike*, Milan, Italian Touring Club 1991

Ariosi Vittorio, *La bicicletta: uso e manutenzione, ciclismo amatoriale e agonismo*, Milano, U. Hoepli, 1987

Berto Frank J., *The dancing chain. History and development of the derailleur bicycle*, San Francisco, Cycle Publishing, 2000

Boninsegna Franco, *La bicicletta: evoluzione, meccanica, accessori, manutenzione, modelli*, Milan, Hoepli, 1990

Castelnuovi Giuseppe, *100 anni di corsa*, Cassina de Pecchi (Mi), Sep Editrice, 2003

Castelnuovi Giuseppe, *Ghisallo. Cuore del ciclismo*, Cassina de Pecchi (Mi), Sep Editrice, 2006

Cipollato Pietro, La balla di Leonardo, Empoli (Fi), Geo Editions, 2005

Gardellin Angelo, *Storia del velocipede e dello sport ciclistico*, Padova, Tipografia Libreria Antoniana, 1946

Gentile Antonio, *Edoardo Bianchi*, Milan, Giorgio Nada Editore, 2003

Heine Jan and Pradères Jean-Pierre, *The Golden Age of Handbuilt Bicycles*, Seattle, Vintage Bicycle Press, 2005

L'Equipe, *Paris Roubaix. Une journée en enfer*, Paris, L'Equipe, 2006

Lloyd-Jones Roger and Lewis M.J., *Raleigh and the British Bicycle Industry. An economic and business history, 1870-1960*, Ashgate, 2000

Marchesini Daniele, *L'Italia del Giro d'Italia*, Bologna, Il Mulino, 1996

Marchesini Daniele, *Coppi e Bartali*, Bologna, Il Mulino, 1998

Martin Theresa and Simon Brian, *Mountain biking Marin*, San Anselmo, Martin Press, 1998

Negri Rino, *Quando la bici è arte*, Legnano (Mi), Centro Stampa Olgiati, 1998

Picchi Sandro (by), *La storia illustrata del ciclismo*, Firenze, La Casa Dello Sport, 1987

Regazzoni Guido, *La bicicletta*, Milan, Arnoldo Mondadori Editore, 1993

Sidwells Chris, *Complete bike book*, Milan, Mondadori, 2004

Spada Romano and Costa Carlo, *La bici e i sogni della nuova Italia. Storia di un paese che pedala e rinasce (1945-1960)*, Stresa (Vb), Andrea Lazzarini Editore, 2004

Specialized, *Stumpjumper. 25 years of mountain biking*, Halcottsville, Breakaway Books, 2005

Turrini Leo, *Bartali. L'uomo che salvo l'Italia pedalando*, Milan, Arnoldo Mondadori Editore, 2004

INDEX

ACKNOWLEDGMENTS

The author wishes to thank the following:
Director Massimo Vallini and the editorial staff;
his family,
Emmeuno,
Dario Pegoretti;
Massimo Gilardoni;
Domenico Gioffrè;
the Bike Carpiano Sports Association.

PHOTO CREDITS

Page 146 Archivio Shimano, Giappone

Pages 146-147 Archivio Shimano, Giappone

Page 147 left and right Archivio Shimano, Giappone

Page 148 top Roberto Bettini/Olympia/Olycom

Page 148 bottom Jean-Yves Ruszniewski/TempSport/Corbis

Pages 148-149 Jean-Yves Ruszniewski/TempSport/Corbis

Page 149 top and bottom Roberto Bettini/Olympia/Olycom

Page 150 DiMaggio/Kalish/Corbis

Pages 150-151 Ken Redding/Corbis

Pages 152-153 David Stocklein/Corbis

Pages 154-155 Franck Siteman/Agefotostock/Marka

Page 156 Goodshoot/Corbis

Page 157 top Roman Dial/Getty Images

Page 157 bottom Kate Thompson/Getty Images

Page 158 Archivio Cannondale

Pages 158-159 DK Limited/Corbis

Page 159 top e center Archivio Cannondale

Pages 160-161 Annie Griffiths Belt/Corbis

Page 161 top e bottom Annie Griffiths Belt/Corbis

Page 162 top e bottom Karl Weatherly/Corbis

Pages 162-163 Annie Griffiths Belt/Corbis

Page 164 top and bottom Phil Walter/Getty Images

Page 165 Phil Walter/Getty Images

Pages 166-167 Francois Lenoir/Reuters/Contrasto

Page 167 Francois Lenoir/Reuters/Contrasto

Pages 168-169 Duomo/Corbis

Page 169 top and bottom Alexander Hassenstein/Getty Images

Page 170 Barry Harcourt/Reuters/Contrasto

Page 170-171 Laurent Gillieron/epa/Corbis

Page 172 Archivio Giant

Page 173 Angelo Colombo/Archivio White Star

Page 174, 174-175 Archivio Colnago

Page 176 top Jean-Yves Ruszniewski/TempSport/Corbis

Page 176 bottom Farabola Foto

Page 177 Farabola Foto

Page 178 top Franck Seguin/TempSport/Corbis

Page 178 bottom left Olivier Labalette/TempSport/Corbis

Page 178 bottom right Jerome Prevost/TempSport/Corbis

Page 179 Olivier Labalette/TempSport/Corbis

Page 180 Olivier Prevosto/TempSport/Corbis

Page 181 top Owen Franken/Corbis

Page 181 bottom Jean-Yves Ruszniewski/TempSport/Corbis

Page 182 Jean-Yves Ruszniewski/TempSport/Corbis

Page 183 Farabola Foto

Page 184 Roberto Bettini/Olympia/Olycom

Pages 184-185 Farabola Foto

Page 185 top and bottom Omega Fotocronache

Page 186 Ross Kinnaird/Getty Images

Page 187 top Phil O'Connor

Page 187 bottom Mike Powell/Getty Images

Page 188 Claude Fougeirol/Corima

Pages 188-189 Claude Fougeirol/Corima

Page 189 Jerome Prevost/TempSport/Corbis

Pages 190-191, 191 Yuzuru Sunada/Archivio Pinarello

Page 192 Roberto Bettini/Olympia/Olycom

Pages 192-193 Roberto Bettini/Olympia/Olycom

Page 194 Roberto Bettini/Olympia/Olycom

Pages 194-195 Dimitri Iundt/TempSport/Corbis

Page 195 center Duomo/Corbis

Page 195 bottom left Dimitri Iundt/TempSport/Corbis

Page 195 bottom right Jean-Yves Ruszniewski/TempSport/Corbis

Pages 196-197 Franck Seguin/TempSport/Corbis

Page 197 Ross Kinnaird/Getty Images

Page 199 Alexandre Marchi/Gamma/Contrasto

Page 200 Courtesy of Campagnolo S.r.l. – Vicenza

Page 201 left and right Courtesy of Campagnolo S.r.l. – Vicenza

Page 202 Jimmy Bolcina/Gamma/Contrasto

Pages 202-203 Tim de Waele/Corbis

Page 203 left Tim de Waele/Corbis

Page 203 right Jean-Paul Pelissier/Reuters/Corbis

Page 204 Tim de Waele/Corbis

Page 205 Laurent Baheux/TempSport/Corbis

Page 206 and 207 Tim de Waele/Corbis

Pages 208-209 Tim de Waele/Corbis

Page 209 top Alexandre Marchi/Gamma/Contrasto

Page 209 bottom Tim de Waele/Corbis

Page 210 Roberto Bettini/Olympia/Olycom

Pages 210-211 Eric Lalmand/epa/Corbis

Page 211 top Eric Lalmand/epa/Corbis

Page 211 bottom Olivier Wieken/epa/Corbis

Pages 212-213 Olivier Wieken/epa/Corbis

Pages 214-215 Tim de Waele/TDWsport.com/Corbis

Page 215 top Tim de Waele/TDWsport.com/Corbis

Page 215 bottom Remo Monsa/eoa/Corbis

Pages 216-217 Tim de Waele/Corbis

Page 217 right Debernardi/epa/Corbis

Page 217 bottom left Maurizio Brambatti/epa/Corbis

Page 217 bottom right Tim de Waele/TDWsport.com/Corbis

Pages 218-219 Roberto Bettini/Olympia/Olycom

Page 219 top Fabrizio Zani/Olympia/Olycom

Page 219 bottom Chiodi/ANSA/epa/Corbis

Pages 220-221 Tim de Waele/Corbis

Page 221 Luis Tejido/epa/Corbis

Page 222 top and bottom Tim de Waele/Corbis

Pages 222-223 Tim de Waele/Corbis

Page 223 Tim de Waele/Corbis

Page 224 Tim de Waele/Corbis

Page 225 top and bottom Tim de Waele/Corbis

Page 226 AP/LaPresse

Pages 226-227 Olivier Wieken/epa/Corbis

Page 227 AP/LaPresse

Page 228 Tim de Waele/Corbis

Pages 228-229 Gero Breloer/epa/Corbis

Page 229 Tim de Waele/Corbis

Page 230 top Wessel van Keuk/Cor Vos

Page 230 bottom Tim de Waele/Corbis

Pages 230-231 Tim de Waele/Corbis

Page 232 AP/LaPresse

Pages 232-233 AP/LaPresse

Page 233 Tim de Waele/Corbis

Page 234 top and bottom AP/LaPresse

Pages 234-235 AP/LaPresse

Page 235 AP/LaPresse

Pages 236-237 Cor Vos

Page 237 top and bottom Cor Vos

Pages 238-239 Marketa Navratilova/Cor Vos

Page 239 Roberto Bettini/Olympia/Olycom

Page 240 left and right Michel Gouverneur/Reporters/Contrasto

Pages 240-241 Tim de Waele/Corbis

Page 242 and 243 Michel Gouverneur/Reporters/Contrasto

Page 244 top, center and bottom AP/LaPresse

Page 245 AP/LaPresse

Page 246 Tony Lewis/Getty Images

Pages 246-247 Tony Lewis/Getty Images

Page 247 top and bottom Marketa Navratilova/Cor Vos

Pages 248-249 Tim de Waele/Corbis

Page 249 top and bottom Doug Pensinger/Getty Images

Page 250 Elizabeth Kreutz/NewSport/Corbis

Pages 250-251 Christian Petersen/Getty Images

Page 251 top and center Christian Petersen/Getty Images

Page 251 bottom Elizabeth Kreutz/NewSport/Corbis

Page 252 top left and right Cor Vos

Page 252 bottom Cor Vos

Page 253 Cor Vos

Page 254 Tim de Waele/Corbis

Pages 254-255 Tim de Waele/Corbis

Page 255 top Photo News/Gamma/Contrasto

Page 255 bottom Brun Lennon/Getty Images

Page 256 Roberto Bettini/Olympia/Olycom

Pages 256-257 Tim de Waele/Corbis

Page 257 top Tim de Waele/Corbis

Page 257 center Roberto Bettini/Olympia/Olycom

Page 257 bottom Tim de Waele/Corbis

Pages 258-259 and 259 Tim de Waele/TDWsport.com/Corbis

Pages 260-261 Vincent Kalut/Photo News/Gamma/Contrasto

Page 261 top AP/LaPresse

Page 261 center Roberto Bettini/Olympia/Olycom

Page 261 bottom Tim de Waele/Corbis

Page 262 Tim de Waele/Corbis

Pages 262-263 Cor Vos

Page 263 left and right Tim de Waele/Corbis

Page 264 Tim de Waele/Corbis

Pages 264-265 Tim de Waele/Corbis

Page 265 Tim de Waele/Corbis

Page 266 top Tim de Waele/Corbis

Page 266 center Tim de Waele/TDWsport.com/Corbis

Page 266 bottom Marketa Navratilova/Cor Vos

Page 267 Olivier Weiken/epa/Corbis

Page 268 top Carsten Rahder/epa/Corbis

Page 268 bottom Tim de Waele/Corbis

Pages 268-269 Tim de Waele/Corbis

Page 269 Carsten Rahder/epa/Corbis

Page 270 top left and right Marketa Navratilova/Cor Vos

Page 270 bottom Tim de Waele/Corbis

Page 271 AP/LaPresse

Pages 272-273 Wessel van Keuk/Cor Vos

Page 273 top Wessel van Keuk/Cor Vos

Page 273 bottom Tim de Waele/Corbis

Page 274 Richard Sachs

Pages 274-275 Richard Sachs

Page 275 Richard Sachs

Page 276 Kent Eriksen

Pages 276-277 Craig Calfee

Page 277 top Kent Eriksen

Page 277 bottom Craig Calfee

Page 278 top Claude Fougeirol/Corima

Page 278 center per gentile concessione di Guru Bicycles

Page 278 bottom Claude Fougeirol/Corima

Page 279 top and center Archivio Cannondale

Page 279 bottom Merida Industry Co, Ltd

Page 280 top, center and bottom Merida Industry Co, Ltd

Page 281 top BIOMEGA

Page 281 center right www.muji.de

Page 281 center left Challenge

Page 281 bottom Archivio Cannondale

Page 283 BIOMEGA

Page 284 Istituto d'Arte Applicata e Design - Torino

Page 285 Mayhem, UK

Page 286 top and bottom Istituto d'Arte Applicata e Design - Torino

Page 287 top Istituto d'Arte Applicata e Design - Torino

Page 287 bottom BIOMEGA

Page 288 BIOMEGA

Pages 288-289 Bradford Waugh

Page 289 Thomas Owen

Page 290 top Istituto d'Arte Applicata e Design - Torino

Page 290 bottom Elisava Image Archive

Page 291 Istituto d'Arte Applicata e Design - Torino

Page 292 top and bottom Istituto d'Arte Applicata e Design - Torino

Page 293 Istituto d'Arte Applicata e Design - Torino

Pages 294-295 Harald Cramer

Pages 296-297 Josef Cadek